JOURNEY TO THE SOUTH

All Annie Hawes knows of distant Calabria, way down in the toe of Italy and a thousand miles to the south of her hillside home in Liguria, is that it's a wild, unruly place, poverty-stricken and Mafia-ridden. Or so her neighbours in the village of Diano San Pietro would have her believe. But on the other hand, ever since she got together with Ciccio de Gilio, his Calabrian family have spoken of their homeland as an earthly paradise, of wild nights dancing the tarantella, of almond milk sold fresh from roadside stalls, of honey cakes and amaro made from wild liquorice roots . . . Now, at last, Annie and Ciccio are travelling down to see the ancestral home and extended family for themselves, along with a bunch of vocal and lively de Gilios who don't want to miss out on the fun.

Will everything Annie has learnt in her years among the Ligurians stand her in good stead among the Calabresi? Or is she in for another steep learning curve in the intricacies of Italian rural life?

JOURNEY TO THE SOUTH

A Calabrian Homecoming

Annie Hawes

**WINDSOR
PARAGON**

914.578

First published 2005
by
Penguin Books Ltd
This Large Print edition published 2005
by
BBC Audiobooks Ltd by arrangement with
Penguin Books Ltd

ISBN 1 4056 1190 1   (Windsor Hardcover)
ISBN 1 4056 2178 8   (Paragon Softcover)

The extract from *The History of Contemporary Italy*
by Paul Ginsborg is reprinted by permission of
PFD on behalf of Paul Ginsborg, © Paul Ginsborg
1990

The name of the village and the names of some of
the people have been changed

British Library Cataloguing in Publication Data available

Printed and bound in Great Britain by
Antony Rowe Ltd., Chippenham, Wiltshire

To the erstwhile Repulic of Urris
and all who sail in her

Prologue

Jewels! That's what you are! Jewels in the crown of our home town! says the large leather-jacketed man who has just introduced himself as Aldo. Our own lost children come home to us!

Leaning over the bar, Aldo orders another round for us three newcomers, just to celebrate. He turns back to grip Ciccio by the shoulders, and holds him at arm's length to gaze rapturously at him for a long moment. Ciccio gets his glass down on to the bar in the nick of time, as our new friend moves in for the clinch.

Now Aldo turns his attentions to Ciccio's sister Marisa, spreading his arms proprietorially wide, as if to display her charms to the rest of the clientele in this tiny whitewashed bar, before taking her to his bosom.

Perfect. At last, after a tricky start, my two companions are getting the welcome home they've been looking forward to for all these years.

Marisa resurfaces, finally, from Aldo's bear-hug; and now—somewhat surprisingly, since I am certainly not a lost daughter of this tiny town in the heart of Calabria, right down in the toe of the boot of Italy—it is my turn to be engulfed in warm black leather.

Truth to tell it was my own obvious foreignness, the light skin, the freckles and the grey eyes, that were at the root of the small misunderstanding that occurred when we first arrived; a misunderstanding for which Aldo is doing his best to make amends. The trouble began when Marisa and I walked in here out of the darkness, alone and apparently unaccompanied, Ciccio having fallen some way behind us in the narrow cobbled streets, checking out his childhood memories. The dozen or so men in here, drinking and playing cards at rickety tables in the various nooks and alcoves off the neon-lit central area, looked up in surprise at the sight of us. Not hard to guess that down in the backwoods of the Deep South of Italy you don't get a lot of unaccompanied women popping into bars at close on midnight. We made for the barman at the back of the tunnel-like room, greeting the company as we passed with a cheery *buona sera!*—and got no response beyond a few sotto-voce mutterings and sidewise glances.

Not a good start to getting back to your Roots. Ever since I first knew them, my partner Ciccio, his sister Marisa and their family have been billing the South to me as a warm and friendly place, a place that may be a lot poorer than the rich North of Italy, their family's adoptive home—and my own, come to that: but where good-neighbourliness abounds.

Does it just! Even the cold and selfish North would do a lot better than this. You'd at least get a good-mannered chorus of *buona sera*'s in response. Now, as we ordered a drink from a bartender who seemed unable to meet our eyes, Ciccio arrived to join us. *Buona sera*, he said as he entered—and got no more warm and friendly a response than Marisa and I had. Ciccio was so intent on getting that long-awaited beer, though—he'd been in the driving seat for the last 500 miles—that he was in no state to be bothered.

Marisa and I began to sip our beers. Ciccio

waited to order, drumming his fingers on the bar in anticipation. Meanwhile, several of the younger men were rising purposefully from their seats and gathering by the door. One produced a mobile phone and handed it to another, who went outside to use it, while his companions lounged nonchalantly in the doorway, blocking the exit.

Ciccio, leaning on the bar, noticed nothing of the silent commotion going on behind him. As I stood wondering whether to draw his attention to the strangely tense state of affairs in here, the phone-caller came back in, and the phone was passed back to its owner. Meaningful looks were exchanged, eyes flickering between us and the door. Evidently, we were expecting a new arrival.

Marisa and I, following the local lead, exchanged looks too—though you could hardly call ours meaningful, since neither of us could begin to imagine what was going on. Whatever it might be, though, it was unnerving. Here we were, just arrived in the foothills of the wild Aspromonte, renowned Mafia-and-bandit country—however much my nearest and dearest may protest that all that stuff is a mere figment of nervous Northerners' imaginations, a hangover from the distant past—and here was a bar full of men carrying on in a most undeniably Mafia-like way. Were we about to be kidnapped and held to ransom? You may laugh, but a mere decade or two ago, kidnapping-and-ransoming was a major industry in these parts. What if the locals hadn't really given it up after all? Marisa was doing her best to keep her cool—well, she had to, didn't she, after going on so much about all the hearts of gold down here?—but I could tell that she was as perturbed as I was.

Outside the bar, a car banged to a halt; and now a big burly man, iron-grey stubble, slicked-back hair, black leather jacket—a Mafioso from Central Casting—stepped in and stood stock-still in the doorway, taking the measure of the situation. Nodding a silent greeting to the rest of the bar, he fixed the three of us interlopers with a fierce eye and loudly announced, '*Buona sera!*'

Marisa and I meekly *buona-sera*'d back. But Ciccio, busy necking his first beer for over a thousand miles, and with his back to the action, assumed that this was an ordinary, general sort of greeting aimed at everybody present—the sort of *buona sera* to which it's perfectly fine not to respond if you happen to have your nose buried deep in your beer-glass. He went on supping, making no reply.

Bated breath all round. Not good enough. The newcomer, it seemed, wanted to speak to the man in charge. He took a step towards us.

Buona sera! he repeated. I nudged the oblivious Ciccio. All the younger men's eyes were fixed upon the drama about to unfold.

I think you need to say hello, I muttered into his ear.

At last Ciccio turned, looked vaguely around him, not being sure exactly whom he was meant to address, and pronounced the magical words 'Good evening'. The newcomer returned the greeting, eyeball to eyeball. The formalities had been observed in time-honoured manner. Now the interrogation could begin.

Who was he? Where was he from? demanded the gentleman in the leather jacket. Why was he here?

4

We're here for Enzo's commemoration Mass, answered Ciccio. We're staying with my Aunt Annunziata, down in the piazza at the bottom of the hill.

A long pause. Obviously not the answer anybody expected.

Ah, Annunziata's folk! The barman eventually broke the silence, sounding immensely relieved. His bar was safe. Trouble was not about to break out after all . . .

Yes, said Ciccio. I'm Francesca's son.

Francesca? said our leather-jacketed interrogator.

Enzo's sister! Francescella! contributed one of the older men from his card-players' alcove, slapping his knee in happy recognition.

Ah, Francescella! echoed several of the others, breaking into smiles at last.

I've never heard Ciccio's mother called Francescella before, and the name was being pronounced in an oddly Spanish-sounding way, the double 'l' so soft it was almost a 'y': still, hopefully, seeing they seemed to find the notion so soothing, they had the right person in mind. The tense nervous atmosphere was melting rapidly.

Francescella's son! Then you're a nephew of Enzo's, God rest his soul!

Lots more 'Ah!'s from all round the bar . . .

This was the first visit he'd paid in ten years, Ciccio added. That would be why nobody had recognized him . . . He hadn't been here since he was barely out of his teens. And there's no chance they would know his sister Marisa, she only ever came here once, as a tiny tot . . .

Seeing our interlocutor's glance fix on me, a

5

most unlikely-looking Calabrian returnee, Ciccio explains that I am his English fiancée, come down to meet the Family at last, and get to know the Old Country.

The large leather-jacketed man takes Ciccio's hand and introduces himself: I am Aldo, he tells us. Ciccio does the same: I am Antonio, he says.

Just for a second, I think Ciccio has taken leave of his senses: why on earth is he pretending to be called Antonio, for heaven's sake! Aren't things tricky enough as it is? Then I breathe again: of course, that really is Ciccio's baptismal name. It's just that nobody in the world ever calls him by it.

Known as Ciccio, he adds.

Our own children come home! says Aldo, going all misty-eyed. Jewels! he says, spreading his arms wide. That's what you are! Jewels in the crown!

Now, as Aldo finishes his round of hugs, the barman comes out from behind his bar to slap him on the back, shake all our hands with great enthusiasm, welcome us back to the old home town, and roar with laughter at the misunderstanding.

*   *   *

But what *was* the misunderstanding? Who did they think we were? Surely there's no need to be so suspicious of strangers, in a tiny country town like this?

The answer, when it comes, is baffling.

He hopes we won't take offence, says Aldo, but, naturally enough, our fellow customers took Marisa and me for a pair of Polish good-time girls; equally naturally, when Ciccio walked in after us,

6

they concluded that he would be our Bulgarian pimp. That's why Aldo had to be called to come and check us out.

A Bulgarian? I echo, bewildered . . . though truth to tell I am no more bewildered by his being a Bulgarian than by his being a pimp. Or, indeed, by Marisa and me being prostitutes. Wearing jeans and T-shirts? And if we were, why on earth would we be touting for trade in a small scruffy local bar in a tiny citrus-farming town in the middle of the Calabrian countryside? And why, for the Lord's sake, from Poland? We're only a few hundred miles from the coast of North Africa here. An extremely long way from Poland, you'd say.

Of course a Bulgarian! says Aldo expansively, his arm still around Ciccio's shoulders. A man drinking beer at this time of year, you'd hardly think he'd be Italian, would you? An Eastern European, you'd say. But you couldn't be Polish, could you? Much too dark, much too curly, Aldo adds, ruffling as best he can the Astrakhan-fur effect on Ciccio's scalp, all that's left of the curls since he got a Number One at the barber's last week, the better to survive the Calabrian heat. Looks like a local, they said to themselves, but obviously not one, or he would be known in here, wouldn't he? So naturally, logically, he would be a Bulgarian.

Would he, now? I have seldom felt my grasp of logic to be so tenuous. Still, at least we have it firmly established that we're not Eastern European sex traders, but Jewels in the Crown. The first night of the homecoming has been a success. Welcome to Calabria!

1

My first encounter with the huge gulf between North and South, the great rift in the Italian worldview—though whether it was a gulf of mere perception or one of concrete reality, it was hard to tell—came not long after my sister and I had moved here: to the Province of Imperia in the Region of Liguria, right at the top of the boot of Italy, only an hour's drive from the border with the South of France. We were doing our best to settle into life in this olive-farming hinterland of the Italian Riviera, where, three miles up a hill from the nearest village, we had inexplicably bought ourselves an abandoned farmhouse. Inexplicably as far as our new neighbours were concerned, at any rate. The thing seemed pretty sensible to us. We had no hope, as far as we could see, of ever owning a home in our own expensive land, and since this one, encountered by lucky chance, cost almost nothing, it seemed churlish, under the circumstances, not to give Diano San Pietro a try. Still, two foreign females firmly set upon living all alone in an olive grove in the middle of nowhere— the plan seemed seriously deranged to our new neighbours.

It wasn't long, though, till we made our first two friends in the Diano valley. The owners of the next-door olive grove, Domenico and his wife of fifty years, Antonietta, observed us from a distance for some weeks as we did everything wrong; and eventually concluded that our strange behaviour was not caused by clinical insanity, but merely

9

by total ignorance of correct olive-farming procedures. They decided to adopt us, give us a few lessons, and set us on the straight and narrow. And so it came about that, one long hot Easter Sunday afternoon, in the peaceful lull after a very large lunch *al fresco*, they began to tell us the tale of their North–South courtship.

Domenico had met Antonietta, he told us, when she came up from distant Calabria to work on the Ligurian olive harvest. Quite a few Calabrian girls would appear in Liguria at harvest time, looking for work: shocking to local folk, who in those distant days might well expect their daughters to work on the family groves come harvest time, certainly, yes—but how desperate would you have to be to send a young girl away from home, to work for unknown strangers! Terrible!

Down in Calabria at that time, though, people were, it seemed, very desperate indeed. They were also, we gathered as the tale proceeded, very scary indeed.

Domenico had fallen for the exotic stranger: but if he wanted to marry her, he was going to have to go in person to that lawless and unpredictable land, travel down the whole length of Italy, to ask for her father's blessing. Calabria lies well over a thousand miles to the south of Liguria, the last stop before the island of Sicily: about as far away as you could possibly get from here and still be in Italy. And such was its ferocious reputation that Domenico thought it prudent to take the advice of his Ligurian friends and relations and spend his entire month's wages on a shotgun. He would need it, everyone told him, to protect himself from the rampaging brigands he was practically bound to

10

encounter on the way. A week's target practice on the family olive trees, and off he set, quaking in his boots . . .

Still, Domenico himself admitted that the gun had turned out not to be necessary for courting purposes. And Antonietta laughed uproariously all the way through her husband's tale, shaking her head at the foolishness of Northerners. The gun came in handy enough, though, she said, once Domenico got back home; times weren't so easy up here in Liguria either, in those days. Many's the time there would have been no meat in the family pot if it hadn't been for that shotgun! So there you are—there was some benefit, after all, to coming from a land with such a terrifying reputation!

*   *   *

Long after being told Domenico's story, I went on truly believing that Antonietta was the only Calabrian I knew. How wrong can you be? Once my grasp of Italian culture had caught up with my grasp of the mere language, I was to discover that almost everyone I considered a close friend was in fact a Calabrese. Including Ciccio, with whom I now shared a home. How, you may ask, did I manage not to know this? Well, largely because I had no notion that in this part of the world people go on being defined by their geographical origins unto the third and fourth generation. Ciccio was born in Liguria, schooled in Liguria, brought up in Liguria: his parents lived nearby, farming the usual few olive groves and bits of land dotted about these valleys, just like everybody else. To look at the matter from another standpoint: my own family

11

came to London, originally, from the northern highlands of Scotland—almost as far from London as Calabria is from Liguria—but would any of my old neighbours in Shepherd's Bush have taken it into their heads to tell me that I wasn't really a Londoner at all, but a Scots highlander? I think not. Only in Italy . . .

*　　*　　*

Here is my first experience of the phenomenon: I am standing outside the *Comune*, the town hall, in Diano San Pietro, my home village, with my friend Patrizia, who is (as I see it) from Diano Marina, two miles down the road on the seashore. We are waiting for the offices to open, so that we can discuss how much inheritance tax she has to pay on an ancient stone roundhouse her father left her in his will: a building high on a steep hillside that falls under the jurisdiction of San Pietro. It is being taxed as a dwelling: Patrizia wants to convince the *Comune* that it's more in the goat-shed-or-storehouse category.

The heat of the sun being fierce this afternoon, and the town hall late in opening after the siesta (again), we move to the shady side of the piazza and start to chat to a local olive farmer, Umberto, one of my younger neighbours. We discuss the outrageous way the *Comune* is always late opening, not surprising they never get a shred of work done in the place . . . and while we do so, it is impossible not to notice Umberto gazing admiringly at Patrizia's sloe eyes and shining dark curls. Eventually he asks, most formally, to be presented to my friend. Well, as it happens, Patrizia is all

12

alone in life at the moment; and Umberto is known to be looking for a wife . . . Umberto is nice-looking, though maybe a bit too much of a country boy for Patrizia. Still, you never know . . . !

May I present Patrizia, I say.

Patrizia who, may I ask? says Umberto.

Patrizia Zinghini, say I.

Piacere, says he, in Italian, since that is the language we happen to be speaking. But now, shaking her hand and looking her boldly in the eye, he launches straight into the local dialect.

Do we speak the same language? he asks her, in Ligurian.

Afraid not, Patrizia answers, in Italian. My grandparents were not from here, she adds.

And that, amazingly, is the end of that! The delighted gaze is withdrawn: Umberto goes on chatting desultorily to us, but Patrizia has obviously been totally eliminated from his matrimonial-possibility list.

Fast work, and quite mystifying to the foreigner. Naturally, as soon as Patrizia and I are alone, I make enquiries. What on earth went on there? Could Umberto never love a woman who didn't speak Ligurian dialect, then? Is his Italian so ropy that he wouldn't know how to flirt in it, or something?

Patrizia laughs. No, he was just trying to find out if I was a Calabrese, she says.

And are you? I ask incredulously.

Of course, says she. How could you not know that?

But how can Patrizia be a Calabrian? Her mother lives in Diano Marina. Her granny lives up in Diano Castello, another tiny hilltop olive-

13

farming village just up this valley. I know both of them. Her family has vineyards, vegetable gardens and olive groves scattered around these hills just like everybody else.

Yes, says she, but that makes no difference. Her grandparents were from Calabria: she counts as a Calabrese. Why do I think she doesn't speak Ligurian?

Well, why would I notice that? . . . Hardly anybody speaks dialect to me, except for very old people who have never really got to grips with learning Italian: I look too obviously foreign. And anyway, most younger Ligurians save their dialect for home, won't speak it in public at all, for fear it will give them a country-bumpkin *figura*.

Patrizia, realizing the full depths of my ignorance, kindly decodes her recent exchange with Umberto for me.

You can't actually ask somebody if they're from Calabria, it seems. If they are, they might demand to know why you care, and call you a racist. Whereas, if they aren't, they might take offence. Patrizia doesn't look definitely Southern, but then she easily might be. Her skin, as she points out, is pale; but her hair is raven black. Her surname would give Umberto a clue: that's why he asked for it. And Zinghini is certainly not a good old Ligurian name. Worse, names beginning with Z are often Southern names. So, onwards to the dialect test. Can't speak Ligurian? Then her parents, or her grandparents, are from somewhere else. (You learn your dialect at Mamma's knee: and if your family is Calabrian, that is the dialect they will have spoken at home. Where would you have learnt Ligurian? Especially when even Ligurians hardly

14

speak the language in public.) Then again, if your interviewee comes from Somewhere Else, but doesn't name the place, it has to be Calabria. If she was from the Veneto, Bologna, Emilia Romagna, even Sicily, she would have said so. Only Calabria, apparently, is so shameful a place of origin that you don't name it; everyone will guess anyway, by the mere fact of your silence.

(Not long after this strange discovery, I test the theory out on a bus driver with whom I am stuck, due to the vagaries of the Italian bus timetabling system, for twenty long minutes in an empty bus on a hairpin bend way up in the hills. He has said he's not from round here. Where is he from, then? I ask. Farther South, he replies, looking a bit shifty. But where exactly South? Ah, a long, long way away. But what's the place called? Might I not have heard of it? Ah, no, it's a tiny wee place . . . Is it near anywhere I might have heard of, then? And so we went on for a good five minutes, the word 'Calabria' floating between us like a ghostly miasma, unspoken; until we were interrupted by the arrival of another passenger.)

Patrizia now informs me, to my amazement, that almost all my good friends in this part of the world are in fact Calabresi of this notional kind. How can this be? All this time in Liguria, and I've only been making friends with Calabresi?

Obvious, says Patrizia. We may have been born and bred here, but we're still outsiders—so of course we're more open to making acquaintance with other outsiders.

I suppose she could be right. Come to think of it, Domenico and Antonietta were the only neighbours to put themselves out to make friends with us. I now discover, to my utter amazement, that even Ciccio, who has been a favourite friend for some years, and with whom I am, at this time, just getting on to romantic terms, is a Calabrese.

Of course he is! says Patrizia. How could you not have known that?

Well, I growl, because I happen to know he and all his sisters were born here, and he has a restaurant up here just above San Pietro, and an olive farm up in the hills, and his parents live down on the coast in Diano Marina too . . .

Yes! And look at the colour of him! Look at the black hair, the dark eyes! Did you ever hear him speak Ligurian?

He just looks like an Italian to me, I say apologetically. I can't see any difference . . . and moreover, as it happens, Ciccio rather enjoys speaking Ligurian dialect, especially to old men in the hills: he loves picking up new words or expressions, and savours them delightedly for days afterwards. Maybe I should have guessed that this meant Ligurian was not his first language? But dialect changes a lot from one village to the next, and I assumed that it was normal to still have a lot to learn from the older generation.

Thanks to Patrizia I now understand, in a blinding flash, the true significance of a recent strange event. One morning a couple of weeks ago, Ciccio, leaving for work at dawn, bumped into two local olive-farmers heading for their groves, coming along the path outside our door. He greeted them in Ligurian. And after he had driven off, I thought I heard the one say to the other, 'Look at that, *They* have even started speaking dialect these days.' So incomprehensible was this remark—what sort of *They* could Ciccio be?—that I decided I must have misheard. Now I know. He really is one of *Them*.

*   *   *

And what do my Calabrian connections make of their homeland's terrible reputation? Second-generation Calabrians like Ciccio and his sisters, who have grown up here in the North under the weight of it, are—naturally, I suppose—half-proud, half-mortified. Bigoted Northerners may enjoy calling you *'terrone'*—somewhere between 'bogtrotter' and 'peasant' is the closest you'd get to the word in English—and they may be horrified at the thought of having you for a neighbour: you will probably keep pigs in the parlour and coal in the bath. And your mere presence could bring down the value of other properties in the street. But then, as Ciccio points out, all you have to do is give your Northerner a menacing sidewise look, and thoughts of the vengeful *'ndrangheta*, the Calabrian Mafia, will cause him to fall suddenly silent.

So, did Domenico really have anything to fear? Was Calabria really so different from Liguria? Or was it all in the imagination? No idea. An academic question, in any case—or so I thought. Until, that is, I found myself intimately connected, like it or not, with the place: and honour bound, for reasons not dissimilar to Domenico's, to pay the place a visit. Ciccio's parents would never rest happy until we had made the trip down to the Old Country to present ourselves officially for The Family's blessing. The Family has waited five years so far. But we're off to Calabria, at long last, next week.

Should I be saving up for a shotgun?

Certainly the very thought of this journey has struck terror into the hearts of my respectable Ligurian neighbours, several of whom have warned me to remove my watch every time I step outside the house. And never to step outside it at all after dark, except under armed escort. I have a strong suspicion, though, that this is just a general Italian technique for dealing with the unknown—stick to the hours of daylight and never wear a watch. Ciccio's mother Francesca, fearful for my life when I was off for a week's visit to Rome last year, gave me the exact same warning. And I survived that trip all right, in spite of spending rather a lot of time out of doors after dark, with my timepiece in its usual place on my wrist.

It may sound pretty cosmopolitan, the Englishwoman living in Italy, but truth to tell, the opposite is the case. I've gone thoroughly native: which is to say that, like my neighbours, I am about as provincial as you can get. What I think of as Italian normality is this tiny corner of thrifty olive-farming folk, the Italian equivalent of one of the more prosperous parts of Scotland—though with a lot more sunshine and palm trees, naturally: whatever I know of the rest of my adoptive country, I have picked up from my neighbours and see through their eyes. The people of our Diano valley, here in the Province of Imperia, talk of the next-door Province of Savona—also in Liguria—as though it were utterly alien. And yes, going to Savona, I too have found the food strange, the local language hilariously hard to decipher, and the customs and habits entertainingly eccentric. Foreign, not to put too fine a point on it. Hard to imagine how much of a culture shock Calabria might be. A wild, unruly, poverty-stricken place Calabria still looks, viewed through the North Italian lens: strangely similar to the English stereotype of Ireland in days gone by. And, like the Irish, the Calabrians, for a good few generations, emigrated *en masse* to escape the desperate conditions in their own land, seeking work and a future for their children. Francesca and her husband Salvatore, Ciccio's father, packed up all their belongings and headed for the rich North of their own country at around the same time that Domenico made his trip down to Calabria: in the 1950s.

Calabrians had gone hungry all through the Second World War: and five years later, ten years later, none of the government's promises had been fulfilled. There was still no work, still no money— and they still eked out a living on rented land which they paid for in kind, handing over half, or sometimes even three-quarters, of what they had grown to their absentee landlords. Adding insult to injury, in that semi-subsistence economy, where shops hardly existed, where people still made most of their own necessities and grew most of their own food, they lived surrounded by acre after acre of unused agricultural land, which they were denied the use of. Here is local landowner Baron Galluccio, speaking in the early 1950s, quoted in Paul Ginsborg's *History of Contemporary Italy*: 'My Calabrian estates bring me 40 million lire a year from grain, and the same again from beans . . . With 80 million lire annually I live extremely well, and the rest of my land I choose to leave uncultivated, in order to hunt on it.'

Meanwhile, from the same source, at around the same time the Minister of Agriculture, Fausto Gullo, himself of Calabrian origin, was announcing to the Chamber of Deputies that 'in my homeland . . . there is not a single popular song that has a sense of joy about it; they are all laments, pervaded by a most profound sadness, a harrowing melancholy which . . . borders on despair'.

America had closed its doors: the New World, Calabria's safety valve for the last two or three generations, was no longer an option. There was anger and violence: there were stories of people arming themselves and occupying the land: of their being driven out by other armed men, by the marauding private armies of the landowners, or by hired-in Mafiosi; of the wild inaccessible hills of the Sila and the Aspromonte filling up with desperate outlaws and brigands.

Calabria's reputation hasn't improved too much in the intervening decades. The *latifundia*, the massive properties of absentee landlords like Baron Galluccio, were finally outlawed and broken up in the mid-fifties: but the next fifty years of special taxes to help the South out of the isolation and backwardness created by centuries of this feudal-style agriculture, fifty years of government subsidies, of attempts to industrialize, to launch and to re-launch its economy, have made no difference. All that money, it is said, has vanished into a sea of corruption, negligence, nepotism and incompetence. Embezzlement scandals, trials for corruption, have involved politicians of the highest rank. Anyone who publicly stands up against all this will surely be assassinated within the year, armed guards or no: the forces of law and order are

20

just as implicated as anybody else. There is still no work in the South. And these days there is plenty of Northern resentment at the parasite in the body politic. The Mafia, according to many, are the only people who have benefited.

Meanwhile Calabria languishes, wild and inaccessible still, at least in the perception of the outside world; its deep forests, high mountain ranges, and untamed shoreline virtually undiscovered by tourism.

2

As far as Francesca and Salvatore are concerned, their North Italian life, all fifty years of it, is but a pale shadow of the Southern Italian reality from which they spring. The Old Country is what counts. I will never know what I am Really Part Of, according to Francesca, nor will my relationship with her son be properly signed, sealed and delivered, until it has been witnessed and approved by the relatives and neighbours back in Calabria. Of course, it would be better still if we'd just buckle down and get married. But what can you expect these days?

Oddly enough, in spite of this, Francesca and Salvatore have not made it back home for well over twenty-five years. Or maybe it isn't so odd. Ciccio and I have been promising to go for four or five years already: and we still haven't managed it, not even with the enticing prospect of going to see the bit of land that one of Salvatore's brothers left Ciccio in his will. The trouble is that the entire

Ligurian branch of the family insists on being included every time we try to organize ourselves down there. Not just Ciccio's parents, but also his five sisters and their many and various husbands and offspring. Everybody wants to come: and whatever date we fix upon, some sister or niece or nephew will be mortally offended because it's their Roots too, and they've never been either, and they have work or school or interviews or hospital appointments or what-have-you, so they can't possibly go until . . . well, usually until August, when the whole of Italy is on holiday, with all the schools and factories closed for the month. And I'm afraid I'm the one that balks at August in Calabria. The place is a thousand miles closer to the Equator, and thirty degrees of heat is perfectly normal down there in August. Night as well as day. If we went then, I would see nothing at all. I would just spend the whole time lying in a darkened room. Or, of course, in the sea. Which might sound attractive, if it wasn't for the fact that there is a beautiful palm-lined sandy bay right here on our doorstep, down in Diano Marina. I can lie in the sea perfectly well here at home: and moreover, I am sure to be able to get back across the beach without dying of sunstroke.

*   *   *

Alas, what has finally precipitated the long-planned trip—very long-planned in Francesca and Salvatore's case—and moved us to just get up and go, regardless of protocol, is a death in the family. Enzo, Francesca's only remaining brother, died last month, aged seventy-eight. There was no chance of

22

organizing ourselves down to the South in time for his funeral—funerals in this hot land take place the very next day—so we are going for the memorial Mass that is said a month to the day afterwards, preceded by a kind of second wake, so that those family members who couldn't make it to the real one can say farewell in style.

For the sake of Francesca's nerves, we're planning to take the train. Francesca's last trip down was made when her six children were all still tiny: she and Salvatore loaded the lot of them into their Fiat 600, and slept two nights on the road, all sardined up in the car, one night by Rome, the next by Naples, finally making it on the third day, exhausted, to their ancestral home. The return journey back to Liguria was even worse: Francesca still tells the tale of how Salvatore was so tired that somehow, somewhere near Naples, what with there being a lot of confusing signs and piles of building materials lying about the place, and there being no other traffic about to give him a clue, he drove on to the wrong side of a stretch of motorway that had been opened before it was quite finished—a common enough phenomenon in the South of Italy in those days, apparently—and if it hadn't been for a police car that spotted his mistake, and came after him, sirens screaming, at the speed of light, the entire family would have been mown down by the juggernaut bombing towards them along the same stretch of road in the opposite direction.

The *Star of the South*, we find out at Diano Marina station, will get us to Calabria in eighteen hours: about the same time as it would take to drive there, admittedly, but at least you can move about on a train, eat and drink in comfort, have a

23

nap when you feel like it . . . and Zia Annunziata, who will be putting us up for our three-week stay, says we can use poor Enzo's car, bless his soul, once we're down there, because it's no use to her, she says, she can't bear to drive it.

So far I've never travelled by rail any farther than Rome—a mere third of the full journey to the end of the line that we're about to embark upon— and I'm overcome with excitement at the prospect of this thousand-odd-mile train journey. Ciccio and the rest of the de Gilio family find this hilarious. Do I imagine it's still the great event of the Good Old Days? Am I expecting the train to be full of migrant families with all their worldly goods stuffed into tattered brown cardboard suitcases tied together with string? Unshaven men in ill-fitting suits, grannies in shawls, wives in headscarves with a clucking chicken under each armpit? Brown paper ration-parcels dribbling garlic and olive oil?

Well, yes. I am. Something like it, anyway. That very same train, which also goes (naturally enough) in the opposite direction, back up Italy and across France to Paris and eventually Calais, used to be the best way home to England before the advent of cheap air travel—and I've certainly travelled on it more recently than any of the family has. The ambience in the snug eight-person compartments, packed with Southern Italian migrant workers heading back to their jobs in France and Germany after their summer holidays back home in Calabria and Sicily, was always a cross between an intense family get-together, the aftermath of a wild all-night party, and a refugee campsite. Oh, and a sort of travelling cornucopia of unknown and delicious foods and drinks, with every person in your compartment loaded down with those silver-foil and greaseproof-paper packages of snacks prepared by the loving relatives to keep home in their hearts—or in their digestive systems, almost the same thing in these parts—for another few days. Each of them, naturally, keen to show off how much better their own home cooking or olive oil or wine was than anyone else's, and insisting on sharing it with all and sundry. Including even the pair of daft foreigners—me and my sister—with nothing better than a couple of limp ham rolls and a bottle of shop-bought wine to contribute.

Francesca, on hearing our travel-by-train plan, is rather pleased that her sufferings of the past are being taken into consideration—but not at all happy with the idea of taking over the car of her beloved brother Enzo, God rest his soul. What will people think? Can't we hire a nice new car in Palmi? We'll look like a bunch of vultures scrambling to snatch up his scraps. What sort of *figura* is that, after twenty-five years? And then, after a lifetime spent in the rich North, to give the folks back home the impression that we're desperate to get our hands on her brother's old banger? No, no! We need something more fitting!

Marisa and Ciccio roll their eyeballs. Fitting to what, *mamma*? We've already started fretting about what the Calabrian neighbours think, and we haven't even started the trip yet . . . !

At a family mass meeting held in Francesca's garden around the table under the tangerine tree—my choice of location, because when the de Gilios all talk over the top of one another, as they are bound to do, you are much better off with no walls for the sound to bounce back off—the final roll-call for the trip, after much panic and argument, is as follows: Mamma Francesca, Ciccio, his sister Marisa—the only one of the five sisters not too busy with work and family to travel—and her son Alberto, aged sixteen, who has a gap between secondary school and college to fill. And me, of course. Just the five of us in the end. Salvatore has always said he would come, if ever we actually got ourselves organized to go on this trip; but now that the chips are down, he says he can't possibly leave his *campagna* and his vegetable garden. There are things about to ripen: other things that need hoeing over or pruning or constant watering or whatever.

The nearest city to our destination is, the sisters tell me with glee, a town called Seminara: a place whose very name reeks, to the Italian nose, of Mafioso crime and violence. (The *'ndrangheta* of Calabria has close ties with the Sicilian Mafia, and is equally feared and abhorred by upright citizens—and, indeed, I gather from Ciccio and his family, equally relied upon for job opportunities and rough justice on its own territory.) Marisa, cranking up the action, has bought me a T-shirt at our local market: one made down in the South of Italy. To wear on the trip! she says. Take a look at the label in the neckline!

I do. The logo says, in the intriguing apostrophe-filled version of English often employed by Italian fashion folk, 'Seminara's Casual': the text is superimposed over the image of a smoking sawn-off shotgun. The gift doesn't have the menacing effect that the evil Marisa intends, though. I am more relieved than terrified. If the locals go around making jokes about their Mafioso reputation, I reason, then things can't be that scary down there.

Can they?

*   *   *

I am looking forward to meeting the Southern relatives, several of whom sound deeply fascinating. I answered the phone to one, a cousin or aunt or something, who rang up to commiserate with Francesca on the death of her brother the day after Enzo passed away. Tell Francesca not to be bothering her head about it, she said. What is there to death, anyway? Nothing. It happens to everyone. Just shove the man under the earth for the worms to eat, have a good feed yourself, a good drink on top of it, wish him God speed, and that's that!

Upon reflection, I thought it best not to pass on this unusual form of condolence; but I am looking forward greatly to meeting this relative in person, if I ever manage to identify her. She called me *bella mia*, 'my beauty', all through the conversation—which I thought for some time was another sign of eccentricity until Ciccio informed me that this is a perfectly normal way of addressing people down in Calabria. Ciccio also tells me that when you speak to Important Men (not sure if this is code for Mafiosi, or rather *'ndranghetosi*, but will find out when I get there) you address them as *''a bellezza'*—'Your Beauty'. Something like calling people 'Your Highness' in English, I suppose, only leaning more to aesthetics than to mere physical stature, as you'd expect in a land of short but attractive folk.

Privately, next afternoon when Francesca has sent me up to the family land to collect any vegetables that need eating, Salvatore tells me, as

27

we move slowly along the rows of tomato vines, me picking, him pinching out the side-shoots, that the thought of Calabria may fill him with nostalgia and longing—but it also gives him a terrible feeling of *angoscia*—a word suggesting a mixture of fear and anguish. Why should he force himself to go and face today's realities in his long-lost homeland, he says, whatever they may be, good or bad? If he went there and regretted having left, that would be tragic: but then, if he saw that he'd been right, there was no hope for Calabria, that would be tragic too. If I see what he means. No, no, he'll just stay here and keep the tomatoes watered.

3

Hoping to make sense of the South somewhat quicker than I managed with the North, and to go about it in a rational and systematic manner this time, rather than by trial and error as I did here in Liguria—and how many trials, how many errors!— I have gone to our county town, Imperia, to buy myself a history of Calabria. And ended up buying a whole series of the things, five robust school-pamphlet-style volumes, all strapped together with a narrow thong of pink tape. No, *signora!* You certainly cannot just buy volumes two, three and four! Why do you think they're tied together in a bundle like that? All five, or nothing!

Still, I wanted something a bit heavyweight. Apart from this history-bundle, there were only a couple of annoyingly gushing tourist-guides, or a dry-as-dust tome full of esoteric details on the construction techniques of religious buildings. The authors of the bundle claim to be Historical Materialists, too: my favourite philosophical flavour. You can always rely on a Historical Materialist to tell you all sorts of gripping and sensational stuff that nobody else bothers to mention. It is called, naturally enough, *Storia della Calabria*, History of Calabria, and forms part of a series of regional histories covering the whole of Italy. Possessing, as I now do, all five volumes, I shall soon be well-informed not only on the more recent past of Calabria, but also on its role in the Stone Age. The region was a major exporter of obsidian around 5000 BC, I learnt downstairs in the shop, while flicking through Volume One—the rest of which will take me on through the colonization of Calabria by the ancient Greeks, the takeover by ancient Rome, and up to the High Roman Empire. And when I finally get to Volume Five, if I ever do, I shall also, I gather, gain a firm grasp of Post-Millennium Potentialities for Calabria.

So here I stand, on the pavement outside the Imperia bookshop in the warm early autumn sun, wondering whether to throw the unwanted volumes into the bin on the corner of the street. Please do not imagine that my attempt to avoid purchasing the first and last volumes was inspired by contempt for the great Classical civilizations, or indeed a lack of interest in Calabria's future well-being. It is just that the matters that are likely to perplex me in Calabria will, I expect, be rooted in the more recent past—and I'm sure there will be no shortage of information down in Calabria about the ancient Greeks and Romans. From all I've heard, the place is still positively heaving with archaeological evidence of their presence, from lonely columns to ruined temples, from great amphitheatres still standing to whole cities that still bear their Greek and Roman names. And I am a luggage-phobic, can't stand being burdened down with unnecessary stuff.

I take another look at Volume One. No, I can't do it. Roles have certainly been reversed since classical times, and with a vengeance. Here is the portrait of a cultured Calabria standing at the very heart of civilization. At a time when, as I happen to know from earlier research, the Liguri up here in the North were a wild and barbarous people, ferocious forest-dwellers, impervious to the soothing influence of the South. The Romans did manage, just, to colonize this part of the peninsula—removing their armlets before leaving their tents, I daresay, and not setting foot outside camp after dark—and to build themselves a road through these harsh hills, linking far-flung Marseilles with the heartlands of their Empire. They also succeeded, for a time, in convincing the scary Liguri that they had something, at least, in common with Rome: their hunting god Bormano was, in essence, the same celestial being as the Roman goddess Diana. But the honeymoon didn't last, and maintaining and defending the Roman road in such a hostile land was too troublesome. It was cheaper and easier to take ship at Savona and sail on to Marsilia, cutting out the land of the Liguri completely. The Romans may have given up on the road: but the Liguri kept Diana, merely changing her sex to masculine, her name from Diana to Diano: giving their god back his virility and, incidentally, leaving us the name of our valley.

That name is all there is to show for the passage of ancient Rome through these parts—except for a couple of stunted columns way up in the hills, markers on the margins of dusty, twisting tracks, once part of the ill-fated Roman road.

*   *   *

Anyhow, the matters that will be perplexing me—if experience in Liguria is anything to go by—will be rooted in the history of the more recent past. When we first arrived here, for example, Lucy and I couldn't understand what the locals found so strange and disturbing about our living in our isolated *rustico* up in the hills; we fondly imagined ourselves pioneers of a return to farmhouse dwelling in these parts. Utterly mistaken. There had never been such a thing. People here had always lived sociably in villages, and travelled to work their parcels of land up in the hills as and when necessary. Our house was never built as a full-time home: but for camping out for a couple of months in the heat of summer, when your beasts could find no pasture down below.

Then again, we could never work out why, whenever the inhabitants of the other villages in this valley felt the need to abuse the people of our own village of Diano San Pietro, they would bring up, as irrefutable proof of San Pietro's utter idiocy, the fact that the place was built on a broad flat bit of alluvial plain by the river, rather than perched high on a hilltop, or on the steep flanks of Mount Evigno, like all the other Diano villages. The San-Pietro-folk-are-fools notion is so firmly entrenched that we even have a local legend wherein Jesus,

31

travelling the land with the task of distributing a gift-of-God to every town, accidentally leaves a Sack of Ignorance behind when he stops for a rest in San Pietro.

But what is wrong with building your village on a nice flat fertile bit of land, a place you can walk about with ease, instead of a horribly steep and rocky place? Ah, we would be told by the inhabitant of the superior steep-and-rocky village, with a knowing wag of his head, everybody knows you're much better off uphill, where the air is clean and healthy . . .

Are you? This might be convincing if we were talking about, say, the Swiss Alps compared to the smog of Turin: but San Pietro is a quiet olive-farming village just like all the others, and what it lacks in the way of mountain air—not a lot, given the way the winds sweep straight down the valley—it certainly makes up for in sea breezes. The Good Air theory makes no sense at all.

But lost in the mists of history—or lost, at any rate, in our own Sack of Ignorance—there was a perfectly sensible explanation. The clue is in the language: the precious Good Air, the *buon'aria*, up in the hills. Down below, of course, you get the opposite of good air: Bad Air. *Mal'aria*.

Eureka! The coastal plains round here were riddled with malaria until it was eliminated in the late 1800s. The sickness is long gone and forgotten; but the notion lives on that the low-lying river plains are bad-air places, where only an idiot would go and make a home. And there's more to it than malaria: all through the early centuries of the last millennium, Saracen ships roamed the shores of the Mediterranean, raiding any town or village

32

within easy reach of the sea, looting and pillaging. Relative riches were being achieved, at long last, on these steep hillsides: the land had been terraced, the olive groves established. There was plenty to lose, and anyone with half a brain would have whisked themselves off, well away from any river estuary, up the nearest defensible steep rocky bit of hill. Yes, there's no getting away from it: in the good old days, you would have had to be a complete idiot to build your home in San Pietro. A simple primary-school history book was all we needed to work this out.

*   *   *

Still, learning this Ligurian tale has given me a bit of a head-start in matters Calabrian: because, as it happens, the exact same thing happened down there. Saracens, malaria, run for the hills. Except that down in the South, that much nearer to the Saracens' homelands, the attacks were more frequent, and their effects more devastating. Coastal cities were picked off one by one, their inhabitants fleeing far inland for safety: and complex, sophisticated cultures were destroyed, wholesale or piecemeal. Now, naturally enough, the survivors, settling into their isolated villages perched high in the hills, began clearing forests to grow their food; causing, over the centuries, massive soil erosion, landslides, and the silting up of the once-fertile coastal plains below, which slowly turned to sour bog and marsh. The anopheles mosquito moved happily into this ideal new environment; and soon, nobody in their right mind would even have considered building a city

33

down there by the sea . . . You were much better off staying up in the hills, where the air was good.

How much more to find out! And when we get to Calabria, I shall be wasting no time in pointless puzzling: I shall have the Pamphlets of Knowledge at my side. Following the Good Lord's example, I shall have left my Sack of Ignorance behind in Diano San Pietro.

4

Proudly bearing my bundle of pamphlets in their fetching pink ribbon, I arrive fifteen minutes early at Francesca and Salvatore's for our weekly family dinner, which tonight is also a goodbye dinner: we leave for Calabria at dawn tomorrow.

I have done well: Francesca's joy is boundless if you get here a bit early—while she becomes seriously agitated if the whole family is not assembled at the table by seven-thirty.

I find her in her kitchen, a sea of rustling supermarket carrier bags swirling around her feet, busily packing the various trophies from the North that she is planning to take back home to the South. Mostly foodstuffs out of her larder, by the look of things, and a rather worryingly large amount of them too, in my opinion. She is laying six big jars of her little round red chilli-peppers stuffed with anchovies out on the table, her silver hair wildly tousled with the excitement of it all. This one for Zia Annunziata, one for Cousin Antonio, the smaller one will do for Giuseppa . . . Should I bring one for Carmela too?

34

As is her wont, she is packing each jar into three layers of carrier bag. She always does this. Knots the first bag with a tight double knot, then puts it, with its knots to the bottom, inside another; and knots that one at the top; now into its third bag it goes, sideways on. More knots. Result of this procedure: it takes you a good ten minutes to get at anything Francesca packs for you. Her daughters give her exasperated lectures on the pointlessness of all this wrapping at least once a week—because, with Salvatore growing the vegetables for all the family up on his bit of land, and Francesca bottling and pickling anything there's a surplus of, we are all in constant receipt of large numbers of these frustrating packages. Francesca always agrees that we are entirely right, one layer of plastic bag does just as good a job as three, yes, yes: but she carries on triple-wrapping regardless.

Apparently, if you grew up, as she did, in a place where people still made many of their own containers, out of pottery, or rushes, or willow-basketry, or wood, depending on the nature of their putative content, the meeting with your first multi-purpose carrier bag, aged about eleven, is an almost mystical experience. You take it in your hands, said Francesca: and you are amazed. How can it be so light and so strong? Palms up, she presented us an imaginary feather-light plastic bag, resting weightless upon her hands: then closed her fists and gripped it tightly, as if to try to rip the thing apart . . . but no, she couldn't! Scrumpling the invisible bag now, she squashed it down to a tiny handful . . . So small!—and so big, too! she added. Not made for anything in particular, is it? But you can use it for almost anything!

Having first come across the plastic bag so relatively late in life, it seemed to Francesca a magical object, possessing supernatural powers, I gather; and of course, in the world of sorcery and superstition, three repetitions are de rigueur—and common sense has no place at all.

Once Francesca has finished her current package, we exchange kisses, and I ask if I can give her a hand with anything.

Of course you can't!! The dinner's been ready since seven o'clock! Sit down!

I do, squeezing on to the sofa between the mounds of plastic packages.

Look, I say, at all these books about Calabria I've just bought!

All those books? All of them about Calabria? says Francesca, in a somewhat disapproving tone. They've got a lot to say for themselves, haven't they?

She pauses to tie another knot or three.

You can get the water on for the pasta, though, if you want, she adds. In about five minutes.

Fine. I lean back, somewhat uncomfortably, among the parcels, flip open the first volume. And begin to fear that I may, perhaps, not be up to Italian historical-materialist linguistics. The introduction informs me that 'localistic bigotries' and 'apparent supranational homogeneities' have made speaking of 'territory' a troublesome theme in our times . . . but that the series hopes to provide me with the tools I will need to analyse it as a complex process: one that weaves together 'diverse spaces and multiple senses of belonging', while avoiding setting the wider dimensions against those of the infinitely variegated localities which compose it.

Hard work. 'Multiple senses of belonging', though: that's good. Exactly the sort of thing that my Ligurian/Calabrian fellow-travellers have had to deal with all their lives. And will be meeting in a whole new form, no doubt, when we arrive in the Diverse Space of the Old Country. I shan't give up yet. And I shall, of course, do my level best to stop them setting the Wider Dimensions against the Locality: or, indeed, vice versa.

Aha! I see now that the remark about localistic bigotries and troublesomeness is aimed, if somewhat obscurely, at the bigots of the *Lega Nord*, the Northern League: the right-wing-radical federalists who have made some headway in Italian political life over the last couple of decades, and whose aim is to break Italy up into its component regions, freeing (as they see it) the commercially viable and upright North from the deadweight of the hopelessly corrupt and poverty-stricken South. Which, the more eccentrically racist among them occasionally go so far as to claim, is really part of North Africa, and not Italian at all.

Francesca comes over to deposit another pair of packages on to the pile at my side. It's a good job really, she says idly, that Ciccio never did get around to taking me down to Calabria without her. How could he have been expected to know what was what, or show me the right places, or introduce me to the right relatives; or indeed explain away any odd foreign behaviour of mine that might otherwise be misunderstood and get our branch of the family a *brutta figura*? Because of course, her son may be a Calabrese up here; but down there he'll be nothing but a Northerner with strange

37

Northern ways, won't he?

Mind-reading? I note that Francesca has rephrased the multiple senses of belonging, perhaps more realistically, as multiple senses of not-belonging. She vanishes into the larder again.

Back to the book. The body of the text is a much easier read than the introduction, praise the Lord, and in no time at all I am well past the Stone Age and on to the Greeks. Many of the favourite haunts of the Greek heroes, I read—Hercules, Ulysses, Jason and his Argonauts—were in fact in Southern Italy, which then formed part of Magna Graecia, Greater Greece. The real-life navigators upon whose deeds those of the Heroes are loosely based would, I read, in reality have been hunting for new supplies of the raw materials—mainly metal ores— that the Greeks and Myceneans badly needed as their civilization, and hence their metal production, went on expanding. Interesting. A literal Golden Fleece, then. Didn't I say historical materialists were hot stuff?

Francesca returns to my side of the room, this time to add a few more bits and pieces to the lunch picnic bag for tomorrow's journey—a couple of jars of her olives in *salamoia*, by the looks of it. She spots the map of Calabria with all the ancient Greek cities marked on it.

What's the matter with it? she wants to know. The towns are all spelt wrong! Are they English books, then?

No, I say, they're Italian—but this is a map of Calabria in 700 BC.

Francesca is overwhelmed. Seven hundred years before Christ? But these are towns she used to know in her youth—Locri and Reggio and Gioia

Tauro—were they already there all that time ago, but just with their names spelt wrong? And look, there's Sibari, too!

Like many people of her generation, Francesca likes to run a finger along under the words as she reads; and so fascinating is this map—Look! Would Kroton be Crotone? And Mamertum—is that Mamertina, Oppido Mamertina, maybe?—that she soon has it positively smothered in fingers, as well as half-way off my lap, making it rather difficult to read. I give up with good grace, hand the book over, and dig my way through the burgeoning piles of mysterious objects firmly double-knotted into their triple bags to disinter Volume Two.

Good. I was only reading Volume One out of a sense of duty—I've been dying to get on to the bit about the Normans. Every time you meet a fair-skinned blue-eyed Southerner in Italy, which is surprisingly often, you will be told that there is a lot of Norman blood down in those parts. Also quite a few Norman castles. But how come? First there was the Classical period, the Greeks building their Calabrian settlements; followed by the Romans, doing likewise. The Roman Empire, on the wane, moved its capital to Constantinople: so now you had a Byzantine Calabria. Much later on, in the 1400s, after a series of royal marriages between the Angevins, who held the Kingdom of Naples, and the House of Aragon, rulers of Sicily, the Spanish crown inherited Calabria and kept hold of it right up to the 1750s. (Many people blame Spain for the way feudalism lasted right up to the twentieth century in Calabria, rather than dying out several centuries earlier, the way it did in the rest of Europe.) But what was going on, in that long gap

39

between the Byzantines and the Spaniards, round about the time of the Crusades, that attracted all these Normans—not merely to go to Calabria and build castles, but to go in such numbers, and breed so busily, that there are still genetic signs of their presence to this very day? Surely blue eyes are a recessive gene, aren't they? Meaning (if I remember my school biology aright) that you need three out of four blue-eyed grandparents to produce a blue-eyed baby, and only two out of four brown-eyed grandparents to get a brown-eyed baby. Those Normans must have gone at it like rabbits to get so many blue eyes into circulation that the evidence is still around seven centuries later, in spite of all the competition from the brown-eyed boys of indigenous Italy.

Look at this! I say some moments later, following Francesca, who has abandoned Volume One in favour of more research among her vast collection of preserves, into the larder. There was an actual Norman kingdom down in the South of Italy in the eleventh century!

Of course there was, says Francesca. That is why her son-in-law Giovanni, the traffic cop, is tall, fair and blue-eyed. A Norman if ever there was one. And, speaking of Giovanni, we should start getting the pasta on.

Giovanni? I ask, alarmed. The sons-in-law don't usually come along to these dinners: if they do, we can't all fit into the kitchen, and the meal turns into a major operation. But it's OK. Only Giovanni is coming, he's working a late shift and just popping in for a quick bite.

Under orders, I put the book down, fish out the biggest saucepan, and fill it with water. Handful of salt, lid on, and on to the range with it. Back to the Normans. Calabria was famed throughout Europe in those eleventh-century days, writes the author, one Filippo Burgarella, as a sort of Eldorado: a land of untold riches, rolling in gold . . . Was it? An Eldorado? Rich? This is startling enough in itself. But now Filippo waxes lyrical about the land itself. I have only heard tales of poor, eroded soil, of villages perched high on rocky outcrops above those malarial marshes, tormented by earthquakes, floods and landslides; but here is a lyrical description of green and fertile plains, of waving cornfields; of vineyards and olive groves going strong since the time of the Romans, of pear and apple trees, chestnut and oak, of good reliable streams and rivers watering the crops and providing the power to turn the corn-mills and the olive-mills. And of course, providing the ideal environment for the many willow coppices you needed to make all your basketwork receptacles before the advent of the magical plastic bag . . . Well, all right, that bit isn't actually in the book. I was distracted by the build-up of the things around me on the sofa. Positively mountainous. Are you sure we'll be able to manage on and off trains with all that stuff? I ask Francesca.

Mah! A couple of dozen carrier bags are, it seems, a mere bagatelle to a woman who managed, in her prime, to get everything the family possessed, not to mention half-a-dozen or so infants—Marisa as a mere babe-in-arms, Ciccio aged three, and the three bigger girls—on to the train from here in the North of Italy, right down past her Calabrian homeland again, over the Straits of Messina and on to Sicily: thence to the port and the Australian immigrant ship. Single-handed, too, because Salvatore had gone on ahead to find a job and a place to stay, and was awaiting them in Melbourne. Then, of course, there was the trip back again, once she and Salvatore had decided that Australia was not the place for them. No friendly piazzas or *passeggiata* of an evening, where you would get to know the neighbours, according to Francesca: just isolated houses strung out along an endless dusty road. And no games of cards or other civilized behaviour in the pubs after work, according to Salvatore. Not so much as a chair or table in them: Australians just stand at the bar and pour beer down their necks till they fall down drunk and crawl home on all fours, vomiting and dribbling. (Salvatore does a particularly fine imitation of an Australian in this state, upon request.)

So I bow to Francesca's superior experience of these matters. We'll worry about the luggage tomorrow.

*   *   *

It was the booming silk trade, I go on reading, on top of its naturally generous set-up, that had taken Calabria into the Eldorado bracket, coveted among Northern European adventurers. The place was an ideal enviroment for the silkworm, and for the mulberry tree it loves to snack upon. All over Europe, says Filippo, people would have heard tell of its fabulously wealthy cities—cities constantly under threat of sack and pillage from across the Mediterranean, with no protection forthcoming from their Byzantine overlords, whose Empire was seriously on the wane by now: but whose citizens were well able to afford paying out the huge bribes the Saracens demanded, on a regular basis, to leave them in peace and go away. Not only this, but the Saracens had a healthy kidnap racket going on too, since so many people were able to afford to pay massive ransoms to get back their prisoners. The place was in a state of chaos, rich, defenceless, and up for grabs, it seemed, to any comer with the courage to take it on.

Interesting. So the kidnap-and-ransom business is nothing new in Calabria—it's been going on for centuries. And it began with the Calabresi as victims, it seems, until they finally learnt to turn the tables and become the perpetrators . . .

Whoops. Seven-twenty-nine. The pasta water has come to the boil, and Salvatore has arrived home. He is already off filling the wine bottles from the demijohn in his shed. Time to throw in the *penne rigate*. The sisters and their offspring will be arriving any minute. Dinnertime.

5

As we start on the sizzling pile of aubergine and zucchini fritters, cooked by Francesca, grown by Salvatore, Marisa and Alberto are doing their best to persuade Salvatore to come to Calabria with us after all. He can still change his mind! Just throw a few things into a bag and go! Get the neighbours to water the vegetables. What could happen to them in a couple of weeks?

He didn't make it down there when his own

brother Lino died, says Salvatore grumpily, so what would he be going down there for now, when he hardly had anything to do with Francesca's brother Enzo?

Come on, *papa*, says his son. See what the old friends and relations are up to, help us check out the inheritance . . .

Bah! All the companions of his youth, says Salvatore, except for the occasional brain-dead one without the nous to get away, have either emigrated or died.

What about the last remaining uncle, Salvatore's youngest brother, Fantino? He's still down there, isn't he?

Exactly, says Salvatore. Brain-dead. Which means, he adds after a moment's thought, that there probably won't be anyone left in the village to help us find the *terreno*, the parcel of land, that Lino left Ciccio in his will.

But won't Fantino know?

No, no, says Salvatore dismissively. No, Fantino'll be no use to you. Never had anything to do with the land. He was at school for years, wasn't he? Then he went off and learnt to drive lorries. (Salvatore, the eldest son, only ever got a couple of years of schooling: his parents sent him away, once he had reached the age of seven, to work as a sheep-and-goat-herd up in the wild hills of the Aspromonte—seven was perfectly old enough to be expected to contribute to the household budget in Calabria in those days—where he was left to fend for himself among a bunch of rough and illiterate mountain folk, while his younger siblings stayed on at home to finish their schooling. The injustice still rankles.)

44

Still, maybe the place isn't worth finding, Salvatore adds. It's nothing but a piece of scrubby pastureland at the top of a hill, when all's said and done, with a dozen walnut trees on it.

Ciccio wants to see it, he says, because it's his. And he loved the Uncle Lino who left it to him.

The feeling can't have been too mutual, can it, if all he left you was that white elephant? responds Salvatore with a wicked grin.

It's lucky, in a way, that the *terreno* isn't worth bothering to look for; because, as it turns out, once Salvatore starts trying to give us directions, he can't remember exactly where it is, either. Or even which road out of the village you took to get to it. This just confirms how useless it is, though, he explains. Even in those long-gone days of poverty and hunger you would hardly bother with the place.

I should think not! says Francesca, whose attitude to her husband's home town, Santa Cristina d'Aspromonte, has always been on the dismissive side. Your whole village wasn't worth ten *lire*, she adds rudely, never mind some bit of wasteland up some faraway hill outside it!

Salvatore is goaded by this into changing his tune. Well, he says, you would never be staring starvation in the face as long as you had that *terreno*! The walnut trees were good and big, great croppers, you'd get a good few sacks of nuts off them every year—and the pasture was fine for keeping goats on . . .

Yes, says Francesca, doling out the pasta sauce, except that by the time you were that close to starvation, you'd have no goats left anyway, would you? You'd have sold them all. Or eaten them. So there you have it! A few walnuts that you'd have to

45

walk miles to gather. How would that keep body and soul together?

Stung by his wife's derision, Salvatore decides that we must be given a clue or two to help find the inheritance. He demands silence while he concentrates on bringing back the days of his youth: elbows on the table, he leans his head in his hands, shuts his eyes tight, and . . . some minutes later, he returns to the present with a cry of triumph. Yes! The exact road you took to get to the place will not come back to him, but once you were up there, he remembers, you could see the Aeolian Islands, Etna and Stromboli and Vulcano and Lipari, and the Sicilian shoreline as well on a good day; and not just the Tyrrhenian sea, but the Adriatic too. And there are bits of old stone columns lying about on the hillside nearby . . . in Salvatore's grandfather's day, people used to say, some sort of mad rich foreigner—an Englishman, probably, he adds, giving me a nudge and a wink and refilling my wine-glass to the brim—started digging them up, even paid people to help him. But then your man just vanished, never came back to finish the job. He said they were the ruins of a temple. There! That should narrow it down a bit, anyhow.

*   *   *

Salvatore's description of the Lost Terreno has got his second-eldest daughter Rosi, the business brain of the family, she who has her own travel agency in San Remo, extremely excited. Northern Italians may turn up their noses when Calabria is mentioned, but according to Rosi the foreign tourists love its mountainous landscapes, its tumbledown hilltop towns and its wild beaches, and find its millennial history, the tracks of ancient Greece and Rome, of Arabs and Normans and Spaniards, positively inspiring . . . Some day soon, Calabria will be the next big unspoilt holiday destination. With a view like that, and atmospheric ancient ruins too, his inheritance might make Ciccio's fortune! Holiday villas? *Agriturismo*? Luxury campsite?

I've got a better idea! says Alberto, frivolous youth. Don't let's abandon family tradition! We'll keep goats on it. Feed them on the walnuts . . . it shouldn't be hard to create a niche market for fillets of Calabrian walnut-fed goat.

Francesca, tutting at her grandson, puts the meat course in front of us—spare ribs *in umido*, simmered slowly in the pasta sauce, one of her Calabrian specialities—and is now serving herself the plate of plain boiled vegetables she always has instead of the meat. She is also visibly bridling at all this excitement over a paltry bit of land in Santa Cristina. Because there is another inheritance to be viewed down in Calabria: the house her own brother Enzo left her. It is in her own, proper, civilized town, Melipodio: and infinitely more valuable, probably, than Lino's old bit of pastureland. But for the moment she has to hold her tongue: thanks to her son's incompetence, she's not sure, yet, which house it is.

It was Ciccio who took the message over the phone from a tearful Cousin Carmela, Uncle Enzo's daughter. Tell Francesca that Enzo has left her the house that Zia Maria used to live in, she said. Alas, Ciccio did not realize that there had

47

been, once upon a time, two Aunt Marias: and he enquired no further.

So now Francesca is on tenterhooks, hoping that she's got the big place with the orange grove round it, on the edge of town where farmland starts, and not the tiny three-rooms-one-above-the-other house in the centre of the town and with no land at all. Still, tantalized though she may be, Francesca has so far refused, through all the phone calls to Calabria that have beeen made in the last few weeks, to ask which Zia's house is now hers. It would look mean and grasping, she says, and we'll find out soon enough.

As usual, she picks up the olive oil bottle to dress her vegetables: carrots, broccoli and fennel today. And as usual, her three youngest daughters all start telling her at once that she will never get slimmer if she drenches the stuff in oil. Yes, and as usual, Francesca, looking a bit furtive, and pouring a good strong dose of the stuff over her vegetables, muttering that olive oil is good for you, everybody says so, concentrates on avoiding her daughters' eyes while she gets them down her neck as fast as she can: because once the plate is empty, the filial lectures stop. Francesca has been on this diet of her own devising for over a year, and is always mystified that in spite of all her suffering she's hardly lost more than a couple of kilos.

6

In Italy, a surname with a separate 'de' at the head is often an aristocratic name: and eldest sister

48

Grazia is keen to discover some blue blood in the family. She has come across references to a noble family of Andalusian extraction bearing the name de Gilio. Could her family be scions of the Hispanic nobility fallen upon hard times? This is faintly possible, I suppose, given the Spanish Connection. We promise Grazia to do some research into the Family Tree while we are in Calabria.

And then, if we could look into the correct spelling of the name? I groan aloud. Various older members of this family own documents on which the name is spelt 'de Giglio' with an extra 'g'. If you are unlucky, you can spend an entire dinner with the de Gilio/Giglio family where nothing but this topic is discussed. Major emotions unleashed, major decibel count . . . Which is the real spelling? Nobody knows, or ever will, as far as I can see: because the great majority of the population of Calabria was illiterate right up until the 1930s. They would have just said their name aloud to some bureaucrat, who would have spelt it as he thought best . . . and the word *giglio*, meaning a lily, is pronounced almost the same as *gilio*, which means nothing in particular, so it would be an easy mistake to make.

Salvatore is appalled, anyhow, by Grazia's desire to claim kin with the nobility. Why would a child of his want to be related to a band of leeches and *sanguisughe*, bloodsuckers? As far as he knows, his family have always been good kind folks, honest day-labourers and peasant farmers. Well, as honest as you could afford to be in Calabria in those days. But as people always used to say, '*Chi ara dritto muore disperato*'—'He who ploughs a straight

49

furrow, dies desperate'—or 'dies in hopelessness'.

Sounds good, but what does it mean?

Honesty will get you nowhere, of course, explain the rest of the de Gilio/Giglio clan, who have heard it before. I still don't get the metaphor. What benefit, I ask, could the ploughing of a wonky furrow possibly confer on its creator?

Simple, says Salvatore. In his day in Calabria, when all the land was owned by the noble families his daughter loves so much, hundreds and hundreds of square kilometres all in one person's hands—not that you'd ever see them, they'd be away in Naples or Venice, lounging about in some big mansion paid for by their tenants' sweat and blood—you had to rent yourself a bit of land each year from the *sanguisughe*, he says, with a sly look at Grazia, and then half kill yourself to grow enough on it to keep your family. Because three-quarters of whatever you managed to wring from it was your rent, and had to go to the landowner. So, to cut a long story short, if your plough happened to swerve a little on the borders of your bit of land, and if you happened to gain an extra couple of furrows that weren't included in your rent, well, those few pounds of grain you'd grow on the sly, and keep to yourself, could make all the difference. Ah, those were bad times! And as if only leaving you a quarter of your harvest wasn't enough, the landowner's bailiffs and agents would be loaning you money for your seed and tools, which of course they supplied themselves—and you had to buy it from them, because where else would you get it? There weren't any shops in those days. And they'd charge you ruinous rates of interest so your debt would just keep growing . . .

A kind of early credit card company, then, says Ciccio. I know just how you felt.

Alberto giggles at the very thought of his grandfather possessing a credit card.

I Owe My Soul to the Company Store, Italian style, I say.

What did she say? Salvatore doesn't know what I'm on about. I translate it to him: and the sisters, who all speak perfect English thanks to their childhood sojourn in Australia, sing him a few bars of the song. And a few more. And a few more . . .

All right, all right, you'll deafen me! says their father. Well! Is that what that song is about? But isn't it American? Salvatore thought they didn't have aristocrats in America?

Ciccio, Marisa and I promise Grazia, Salvatore's opinion notwithstanding, to continue investigations: the town halls, the parish registers, whatever . . . though it might be hard, says Rosi—a lot of stuff has been lost, scattered, moved, what with wars and fascism and occupation.

It would be great, though, wouldn't it, says Grazia, to find a connection . . . even if we are, most likely, from the wrong side of the blanket . . . ?

No, it would not, says Salvatore, tearing a piece off the loaf before him and cutting himself a savage wedge of pecorino cheese.

Francesca, who has passed round the toasted pumpkin seeds, and is now nipping-and-cracking her way through a handful of them, is not at all sure that she wants to find out that her family is descended from a line of bastards: not even blue-blooded ones. Still, the worry is outweighed by the joyful prospect of getting her most important

51

connection back home, Anselmo the lawyer, involved in our researches. Little Anselmo will surely help, she says. Anselmo, the little neighbour boy whom she carried in her own arms to his baptism when he was a tiny baby—on foot, too, because in those days you didn't use cars for important religious rites of passage the way you do now—and who has ended up, against all the odds, a lawyer, and a Big Man in the town. A lawyer, an *avvocato*, she repeats, her voice breathless with respect. And working for the *Comune*, where they keep all the records. So that will certainly smooth our path!

Why on earth, I ask, do we need someone to smooth our path? Surely the public are allowed to inspect public records without needing to personally know a VIP ?

But this is an incomprehensible, alien notion to all three of the generations seated round this table. The need for personal connections, especially in any matter involving the state and its bureaucracy, is self-evident to any Italian, bred in the North or in the South; and my remark produces a resounding silence. How on earth can Northerners complain about the South being corrupt? It is only a matter of degree—and pretty infinitesimal degree, at that, you'd say.

Francesca snaps open another few pumpkin seeds, while her grandson passes round the fruit bowl. Giusi reaches for the *ricotta*—does anybody else want another taste? It's lovely and fresh! Anna gets up to put the espresso pot on for the coffee. What about an almond biscuit or two with it? Some *grappa* on the side? A *limoncello*? asks Rosi.

Now that the wine-bottles are well emptied, the

coffee and digestive liqueurs on the table, and we only have tonight left before we leave for Calabria, the sisters surprise me by starting a what-do-you-remember-of-the-place competition. I've always imagined that the family left so young, and visited so seldom, that Calabria hadn't made much impact on them. In spite of the whole lot of us meeting up at least once a week to eat at *la mamma*'s, where the food on the table is all as Calabrian-style as Francesca can manage with the North Italian ingredients at her disposal (otherwise Salvatore makes a fuss—what are these tomatoes doing in the fried green peppers? Have you turned Ligurian on me?), and in spite of the way we always linger, for our last course, over bowls of nuts and pumpkin seeds and dried figs and apricots and plates of salt-roasted chick-peas and dried fruits, a truly Southern habit, the members of the younger generation hardly ever mention Calabria around this table. But tonight they are inspired. We've had Salvatore's doom-and-gloom version of the homeland; now, along with the coffee and *limoncello*, we get the exiled children's happy memories of Zion.

We're off tomorrow to an enchanted place: a land flowing with cool almond milk sold fresh by the roadside, with honey cakes formed into spirits and demons; a place whose towns are overrun one day by the wild worshippers of the Black Madonna, the next by papier-mâché giants on stilts, striding to the boom of a hundred drums; or by the crazed performers of the *tarantella*, whose heart-pounding rhythms will dance you off into a mystic spider-bitten trance. But no! It's too late in the year: we've missed the giants on stilts: the Black Moor Grifone only dances through the streets after his Princess Mata one day of the year, in the second week of August. Still, we might catch a *tarantella*. We will be drinking Zia Annunziata's knock-you-out *amaro*, made from wild liquorice roots, which Ciccio will teach me to find and pick, and a fierce home-made red wine so thick and dark that you call it *'nchiostro*, ink; we will be eating all sorts of unlikely-sounding things—chick-peas cooked in sea-sand, fritters of sun-dried aubergine peel, sea-urchin pasta, white snails, goat kebabs—and *peperoncino*, chilli, with everything. Not to mention the fabulous *'nduia*—the local salami made with equal quantities of chilli paste and minced pork. Terrifying. You even get sweets made with chilli, it seems, when the *Festa del Peperoncino* is on . . . There are miraculous statues and dried saints to pay our respects to, and many nutty relatives to visit—and of course the Piazza of the Fourteen Crosses, so called because the *'ndrangheta*, some time last century, arranged the severed heads of fourteen slaughtered enemies in a neat circle around its central fountain . . .

Disturbingly, in the annals of this Northern branch of the family, which eats, as far as I'm concerned, unimaginably huge amounts of food, the Southern branch turns out to be famous for, yes, eating unimaginably huge amounts of food. And for never letting you leave the house till you've finished all of it. Think of that. On the other hand, though, one of the few pluses on the Calabrian tally, as far as Northerners are concerned, is the healthiness of the diet. Northern Italians chide themselves for over-using meat, animal fat, cream, oil, and suchlike bad things;

54

while the 'Mediterranean diet' eulogized by would-be healthy eaters in my own land is known, down here on the Mediterranean, as *'cucina povera'*, 'poor cuisine/cookery of the poor'—and is seen as a specifically Southern Italian tradition. Still, Mediterranean diet or not, it sounds as if there's plenty to worry about where the figure is concerned. As the almond biscuits are passed round and dunked in the coffee cups, the conversation turns to *dolci*. Down South, it seems, Arabic, Greek, Turkish influences are strong. We will find delicacies stuffed with pistachio nuts, dates, figs, honey . . . melt-in-the-mouth *ricotta* pastries . . . As the list goes on, it begins to seem horribly likely that, unable to fit my vast bulk into any form of transport yet devised by man, I shall never return from this trip at all. But then, at least there'll be some kind of a home, as yet unknown, for shelter, and a campsite/goat pasture to support us, if such a thing should come to pass.

*   *   *

Ciccio and Marisa are a lot less than enchanted when, the washing-up over, we come face to face with the vast array of luggage that Francesca has now assembled in the back porch. Cases, boxes, packages, canisters, a small crate of bottles, overflowing carrier bags. The live chickens may be missing, but we have all the rest of the classic Southern-train scenario. The dribbling olive oil and the perfume of garlic are much in evidence: Francesca has even managed to dig out an old cardboard suitcase.

What is it all? asks Ciccio, horrified. Does

Francesca think she's away to Australia again? How on earth are we supposed to get on and off trains with that lot? How will we change at Genoa? And again at Naples? No way. Some of it has to be left behind.

Francesca is disgusted. What a weakling her only son has grown up to be! Why, she and Salvatore made it up here on the train from Calabria with twice that amount of stuff! And she was pregnant, too!

But according to Ciccio, in the 1950s everybody travelled like that: it was normal then . . . but these days it cannot be done. Or maybe it can, but it would be deeply embarrassing. Nephew Alberto agrees. He has no intention of traipsing around the mainline stations of Italy as if he was playing a bit part in some New Realist film about poverty-stricken Southern migrants, hung about with parcels and packages and cardboard suitcases and aged grandmothers.

Well, says Francesca, she is certainly not going to turn up to stay with her family empty-handed, not after an absence of twenty-five years! Nothing to put on the table for her own brother's *veglia*, the night before his memorial Mass! What a terrible *figura* we would cut! Moreover, you never know what might happen on a long journey, do you? You have to be prepared for anything . . .

Anyhow, says Marisa, why on earth have we got to take a twenty-litre canister of *papa*'s wine? And the crate of mineral water? The Southern relatives can't be short of either! They make their own wine down there too, don't they? And surely there are places to buy mineral water down there?

It's not mineral water! says Francesca, giggling at

the thought. Mineral water! You don't pay for mineral water down there anyhow, the whole of Melipodio is full of natural springs, a fountain on the corner of almost every street. No, no, that's olive oil that she's decanted from the store for the relatives to try, a litre each . . .

But why? asks young Alberto. They have their own olive groves down there, don't they?

Of course they have, says Francesca, but what's that got do with it? They'll want to taste ours, won't they!

Marisa sighs deeply. And don't you think they're bound to give us a whole load of their own wine and oil to take back with us? she says. It's ridiculous!

Francesca does her famous puzzled look. Of course they will, she says, that's the point. We take them some of ours, they give us some of theirs.

And of course, Ciccio, dyed-in-the-wool food-victim that he is, can't help agreeing with *la mamma*. The Southern family's wine and oil will be completely different—different grapes, different breed of olive tree, different climate, different techniques—of course they'd want to taste ours. And we theirs, come to that.

You see, Marisa! says Francesca triumphantly. Listen to your brother sometimes, why don't you! Still, she adds, turning to Ciccio, if you really think we can't manage it all on the train . . . We could always drive, couldn't we? That jeep of yours is very nice and comfortable . . . and there's plenty of room in it . . .

Oh well, says Ciccio, wavering. What's a thousand miles, after all? I suppose we could take turns at the driving . . .

Marisa accuses her mother of plotting this outcome: and gets a bravura repeat performance of Francesca's puzzled look. Young Alberto, just as keen as his grandmother on cutting a fine figure, looks very pleased at the prospect.

So that's that. Ciccio has fallen neatly into the trap, talked himself into it. Francesca will arrive in style in Melipodio, riding in her son's big shiny silver people-carrier, and impressing the neighbours in the Old Country no end.

7

As dawn begins to break, the steep terraced olive groves of Western Liguria are already well behind us. We are driving straight into the rising sun: until just past Genoa, the coast runs eastwards, then, once we're into Tuscany, it curves south for the rest of the journey. The Mediterranean continues cobalt blue to our seaward side, but by now the foothills to landward are no longer the tail-end of the Maritime Alps, stretching on from Provence, but the beginning of the Apennines, the backbone of central Italy.

We are all still half-asleep. Francesca insisted on leaving at 4.30 a.m., to be sure of not keeping Aunt Annunziata, with whom we shall be staying, waiting for her dinner. We are already almost out of our own Province of Imperia, where we said a sad goodbye to Salvatore, who leapt into his three-wheeled *Ape* truck and zoomed off to drive the three miles to his beloved piece of land just as we were climbing into the car, the darkness still almost complete. He needed to water his five terraces of almost-ripe tomatoes before the sun got on to them, he said. He wanted to be the leaver, I think, and not the left-behind. And, of course, to commune with those five hectares of paradise whose produce is one hundred per cent his own, and over which no aristocrat, of Spanish origin or otherwise, has any right or dominion.

*   *   *

My travelling companions are soon having lots of fun playing the traditional Italian game of spot-the-local-numberplate regional stereotypes. We've left behind the country-cousin skinflints of Imperia and Savona now, and are skirting round Liguria's regional capital, Genoa. To listen to Marisa, Francesca and Ciccio—young Alberto is remaining aloof from all this, thumbs flying nimbly across his Game Boy, ignoring the idiot antics of the older generation—the Genoese spend their entire time trying to rip one another off, surviving on a starvation diet of chick-pea flour and spring onions while stuffing their mattresses with all the banknotes they're saving. Because they wouldn't trust a bank, would they, and they're too tight-fisted to pay bank charges . . . What does a Genoese use for toilet paper?

I groan at this hoary old chestnut. The answer? Confetti, of course!

As the motorway from the big cities of the industrial North of Italy joins our own Autostrada del Sole, carrying a wave of cars with Milan, Turin and Cuneo numberplates, we move on to the *mangiapolenta*, the polenta-eaters of the high plains, a greedy, cold and suspicious-minded bunch . . .

Some years ago, the Italian State almost ruined this form of entertainment by deciding to abandon the provincial prefix on car number-plates. Older cars, like our own, of course, still had theirs—we are bearing the old IM prefix for Imperia—but a new generation of cars came rolling off the conveyor belts with no indication of their local identity: just a generic Italian-ness. Good idea, I thought, imagining that this was a government move to undermine the forces of separatism, or, as the *Storia della Calabria* puts it, localistic bigotry, that were aiming to tear Italy apart. But the move soon proved a miserable failure. Think how comparatively little enjoyment there is to be got, when road rage strikes, from simply shouting, 'You cretin!'—when, with just a little more geographical information, those extra two letters on the plate, you could be shouting, 'You tightfisted Genoese cretin!' or 'You polenta-eating Milanese cretin!' After only two or three years of this tedious anonymity, an optional regional ID appeared, by popular demand, at the side of the national number. And we are back where we started.

Which is, at the moment, covering the falsely courteous Piedmontese of the Northern countryside, *'Piemonteis, fauss' corteis'* as the saying goes in Ligurian dialect; now, spotting a Cuneo car with its headlights full on in spite of the bright sunshine, my companions cackle delightedly at this confirmation of all they've heard about the Cunesi—who live, according to tradition, in an eternal fog on their sodden rice-growing plains, and are obliged to keep their headlights on day and

60

night. Moreover, no local woman in her right mind will ever marry a Cuneo farmer, their womenfolk just run off as soon as they get the chance, and the men have to buy in mail-order brides from even more miserable places—Russia or the Philippines, apparently.

I give my usual speech about the absurdity of all this Italian internal racism. What about what they say about you Calabresi, then?

All to no avail. Much of the fun comes from knowing that they're driving me mad, anyhow.

Somewhere slightly to the south of Rapallo, after a period of silent thought and furrowed brows in the back seat that has us all worried, Francesca announces that she will, of course, have to speak Calabrese while we're down in the Old Country. Because, she explains, if she goes around speaking Italian, old friends and neighbours are bound to think that she is *toscaneggiando*.

Doing what? I ask. What is this *toscaneggiando* word? Sounds like it should mean 'Tuscanating'?

Yes, you're right, that's exactly what it does mean, said Francesca. Carrying on like a Tuscan.

But how do Tuscans carry on, exactly? I ask humbly. We are about to cross the border between Liguria and Tuscany at any moment, and I feel I should be prepared.

How do they carry on? repeats Francesca, frowning. Why, they show off, of course! Give themselves airs . . .

And what on earth possesses them to load their main dishes with salt like that, contributes Ciccio, and then to put no salt at all in their bread? Have you ever tried Tuscan bread? No taste at all! Like chewing an old bath sponge!

61

They're absurdly big-headed about their great literature and their so-called correct Italian, too, says Marisa.

And, says Francesca, that's exactly what people would think of her if she turned up in her old home town and went around talking Italian! Big-headed.

So from now on, as she mentally prepares herself for the return to Calabria, Francesca lards her conversation with more and more Calabrian turns of phrase. Mile by mile, province by province, the Francesca I've known and loved for years begins to turn, slowly and inexorably, into a foreigner.

And here we are in Tuscany: golden rolling plains, the landscape all curving horizontal lines, lovely and restful on the eyes after the zig-zag verticals of the Ligurian mountain-and-valley landscapes we've been driving through all morning. This almost reminds me of England, I say, smooth and gentle and relaxing after all those spiky hills . . .

Relaxing!? Francesca repeats in tones of amazement, staring disparagingly out at Tuscany from her back window. *Ma no!* Imagine having to look at all that flatness day after day! Just going on and on the same like that! What *angoscia* that would give you! Still, some people must like it . . . she believes Sting has a house round here somewhere, doesn't he? Or is it George Clooney?

Nearly seven o'clock in the morning: time to ring Zia Annunziata, who will be up and breakfasted by now, to tell her that we're on our way and all's going well. Marisa pulls out her mobile phone; and while she's dialling the number, Francesca starts to list the things that need to be said to Zia Annunziata. There seem to be so many of them that by the time Annunziata answers, Marisa has given up trying to remember them all.

Here, *mamma,* you speak to her, she says, passing the phone over to the back seat, where Francesca is sitting enthroned among the trophies from her adopted land.

Francesca recoils from the mobile in terror.

No, no, she says, I don't know how to use it!

Just hold it to your ear, *mamma,* it's only a telephone!

Eventually Francesca accepts the offending object, holding it gingerly as if it might blow up at any moment; but as soon as she hears her sister-in-law's voice, fearfulness is forgotten: she rattles joyfully away in Calabrese as if she'd never spoken anything else. Through the Fog of Unknowing I manage to pick up the odd phrase.

. . . No, no, don't worry . . . a simple girl . . . eats the same as everybody else . . .

(Francesca is talking about me, I deduce. Whenever you hear that phrase, 'a simple girl', you know Francesca's on about me: simplicity is her highest accolade.)

. . . Just you prepare the vegetables the way you always do, and we'll do the meat when we arrive . . . she's normal, yes, eats just the same as us . . .

Really! Of course I'm normal! What sort of monstrosity is this aunt expecting?

Road signs for Pisa now.

Pisa! Worse than all the rest of Tuscany put together! *'Meglio un morto in casa che un Pisano all'uscio'*: better a death in the house than a Pisan in the doorway . . .

Hours of innocent entertainment. The de Gilios carry on remorselessly as we traverse the length of

63

their country, province by province. Not long now till Emilia Romagna, and time to hear all about the overweening Romans, who don't even bother to name their city, just call it *'La Capitale'* . . . And after Rome? The sayings seem to run out. Apparently South of Rome everything is so bad it beggars description. Or is it just that the description is too long? I have gathered that as far as the rest of Italy is concerned, although the South, from Naples on, may have many attractive and life-enhancing qualities—its inhabitants will, it is said, sing, dance and make merry at the drop of a hat, are great company, famous story-tellers, great cooks—on the minus side of the stereotype, its people have too much Sense of Rhythm for their own good and not enough Work Ethic or Respect for the Law; they make their wine too strong and their olive oil too rough; they are feckless and improvident; their famous religiosity is more heathen myth and superstition than true Christianity, and they are prone to every sort of antisocial behaviour, from simple boisterous noisiness to drunkenness, thievery and mindless violence: and on to sinister, politico-Mafia organized crime.

Yes. On second thoughts, it's enough just to say 'Napoletano' or 'Calabrese' in the right tone of voice: that covers the lot. So, onwards into the deep South . . . the heart of darkness.

We're well past Rome now, and in the last hour or two Francesca has not only managed to transform herself into a virtually incomprehensible alien; but, worse still, into a rather cross incomprehensible alien, who can't grasp that full-blown Calabrian is completely beyond her idiot

English daughter-in-law-type-person. Francesca is used to her children understanding what she says in either language, Calabrese or Italian; and they do understand, of course, even though they may not be very fluent at actually speaking Calabrese. They grew up listening to her and Salvatore speaking both languages: Calabrese inside the home, and Italian outdoors, for shopping and talking to the neighbours and suchlike. (But, once they had started school, hating to be the odd ones out, like all children, they began always to reply in Italian. It has to be said that this improved their parents' grasp of the national language no end; and eventually, with six children to two parents, Italian became the main language in the home, with Calabrese spoken only by the parents, at moments of deep distress or high drama. Ciccio and Marisa may have a good passive understanding of it still, but their Calabrese is hardly fluent. Thus do dialects die out; linguistically, a tragedy, but a good thing, you can't help feeling—something like losing your regional number-plates—as far as building any sense of Italian national unity is concerned.)

Anyhow, in Francesca's mind, the borders between the two languages are vague and blurred. Either will do. The same does not apply to my mind, alas. Address me in full-blown Calabrese, and I will gape at you like an idiot.

After I have gaped in just this manner several times, Francesca realizes that I am in dire need of a crash course in Calabrese; as is her grandson Alberto, who was raised dialect-free, his father being a Ligurian—which meant, since his parents had no dialect in common, that the lingua franca in his family home was ordinary plain Italian . . . So

Francesca entertains us all for the next hour or two by thinking up amazingly obscure remarks in Calabrian, phrases which are (as far as I can see) highly unlikely ever to come in useful on this trip, which she forces me and Alberto to repeat over and over again, while Marisa and Ciccio roar with laughter; refusing to tell us what they mean until we're word perfect. *'Vi ca iu che iuma,'* I say twenty-five times. Now, what does it mean, please?

'Look over there, it's on fire.'

Irritated? Moi?

8

By the time we are skirting Mount Vesuvius, the outskirts of Naples clinging to its lower slopes, gold and white in the early afternoon sun, we are starving. We have only stopped twice all day, for a coffee and a snack in an Autogrill, as they call motorway service station cafés here. We'll get off the motorway now, says Ciccio, and find somewhere pleasant to have a proper picnic lunch.

No! says Francesca. We mustn't waste time. Annunziata will have a banquet prepared, there are fifteen of us at table tonight, we don't need to eat much now, and we can't be late! Let's just park round the side of the next Autogrillo and eat a quick sandwich in the car.

Marisa is appalled. All this beauty around us, and her mother wants to eat her lunch amid petrol fumes in a motorway service station! And anyway, it's not called an Autogrillo, *mamma*, it's an Autogrill.

Well, says *la mamma*, if we do go somewhere else to eat, we'll still have to stop at another Autogrillo for our after-lunch coffee, and to use the loos and wash our hands, and that'll be two stops.

Autogrill, *mamma!* says Marisa again.

Bah! says Francesca. It's a stupid word anyway. Grill, *grillo*, what's the difference?

The difference, says her daughter, is that a grill is a place where you eat: and a *grillo* is a grasshopper. As you very well know.

Why doesn't Marisa leave his granny alone? says Alberto. Who cares about correct Italian? He, for one, would much rather eat at an Auto-grasshopper than at an Auto-grill.

Naturally, half an hour later, we are doing as the matriarch wishes: stuffing our picnic in a motorway car park.

*   *   *

Once past Naples the motorways have got less and less motorway-like; they may still have motorway signs on them, but they are more often than not covered in roadworks, or down to a single carriageway, the oncoming traffic funnelled over on to what ought to be the fast lane on our side of the road. I'm already finding it quite a lot easier to imagine how Salvatore could have got on to the wrong side of one. Now, just over the Calabrian border, the mountains of the Sila range looming ahead, and only another three or four hours to go to Francesca's old home, I get to see the first signs of one of the great Calabrian traditions I have heard so much about up in the North. Ciccio and

Marisa gleefully point out to me the famously unfinished and/or pointless bits of motorway, the entrances, exits, and (this looks to be a favourite) half-built access bridges across the motorways, bridges that lead nowhere and never will, just connecting one piece of empty scrubland to another, surrounded by piles of rusting girders and crumbling concrete pylons, slowly vanishing under scrubby vegetation. Dotted around the landscape we are soon passing assorted half-built factories, warehouses, unfinished *palazzi,* none of which ever got further than skeletal traceries of concrete and reinforced steel joists, now gently rusting away against their backgrounds of woodland or hillside . . . Not having much of a business brain, I have some trouble grasping how you could make money by not building something, rather than by actually building it. But of course it's quite simple: just enough work gets done on these projects to raise the subsidies, out of the various special funds that have been being allocated to lift the South out of its centuries-long depression, ever since Garibaldi's time: these days there is EU cash for deprived areas as well. Once whatever-it-was has passed a preliminary inspection, my informants explain, the work may well stop. Now the rest of the cash gets shared out between Mafia-building-company folk and the local friend-and-relation bureaucrats who helped get the deal nodded through; the project is abandoned for ever . . . and, Ciccio points out, by the strange logic inherent in the situation, the more senseless the project was in the first place, the less fuss anyone is going to make when it doesn't materialize. A few local workmen are grateful to have made a few months' wages out of the job; and if nobody needed the access bridge to get from somewhere to somewhere else, if nobody was expecting a job in the factory, a home in the *palazzo*, why would they complain when they didn't get it? Apparently, one of the juiciest scandals of this type involved a fish-processing factory built thirty miles inland . . . The mind boggles.

I am marvelling at this new concept, a landscape dotted with crumbling ruins of things that nobody wanted, and that have never actually had an existence, while Francesca stands up for her native culture, in a contradictory sort of way, telling us that this sort of thing doesn't only happen in Calabria, you know, and anyway it's nothing like as bad as it was when she was a young girl, that's why she and Salvatore left to bring their children up in the North . . . when, all of a sudden, our car, which has been behaving perfectly until now, decides to break down. Terminally. The gearbox seems to have disconnected itself completely from the motor, says Marisa, who is driving, in one of those special ultra-calm voices you use when you're in a complete panic.

Porca miseria! says Ciccio. *Lurida vacca! Madonna lupa!* The first of these expressions renders literally as 'pig misery': the rest are untranslatable, so I won't try. Marisa concentrates all her powers on drifting us, engineless, off the motorway and on to a slip-road in the middle of low scrubby hills, while her brother goes on providing the soundtrack with his traditional picturesque monologue on the topic of the Madonna and her many shortcomings. Marisa succeeds, by the skin of her teeth. No sign of habitation for miles; and now the car glides gently

69

to a halt on the hard shoulder. Worrying. Who knows if this slip-road actually leads anywhere? It may well be just another Mafia money-spinner, a road to nowhere. There's not a sign of another car anywhere about. Still, we've got breakdown insurance. Someone will find us eventually. We fish out the mobile phones. One of us will walk back to the exit, where there must, we hope, be a sign naming the place this road supposedly leads to— none of us noticed what it said in the heat of the moment—and we'll ring Europ Assistance.

Francesca, who has never been one for keeping abreast of modernity, is not at all reassured by any of this. Whatever the name of this place may be, she reasons, we don't know where it is, do we? So how are we going to explain to our would-be rescuers how to find us? She is convinced, it seems, that any rescuers who may appear will be coming from our own part of Italy—and if it's taken us all day to get here, how long will it take them? If they ever find us at all . . . !

She is deaf to her children's explanations about the role of breakdown insurance companies, their use of local garages, the function of maps and other tedious and unlikely matters, all of which involve the outlandish notion that people with whom we have no personal connection at all would be at all likely to bother finding a place they don't know either, just to rescue us. Alberto rolls his eyes at his granny's usual nonsense, sighs deeply, picks up his Game Boy and takes a nonchalant seat on the sun-shrivelled grass verge, disturbing a cloud of tiny grasshoppers. He switches the game on as if none of this had anything to do with him, and starts to play. Causing his mother to fly into a rage: is he just going to sit there and wait for everyone else to sort this crisis out, then, as if he was a three-year-old?

Well, says Alberto reasonably, what else do you expect me to do?

They say they'll be here within the hour, announces her brother from his telephoning-perch on a nearby rock, stuffing his mobile phone back into his pocket.

Francesca tut-tuts. If he'd believe that, he'd believe anything. She bustles off round to the back of the car to set about checking our supplies. Somebody has to behave sensibly, after all, don't they? We may well be stuck here till tomorrow! Thank the Lord she didn't let her children dissuade her from bringing along the canister of wine, and the bag of loaves of good Triora bread, she says, cock-a-hoop at being proven right; and the dozen jars of her own little red peppers stuffed with anchovies and bottled in her own good olive oil will come in handy too, and what a good job she brought those cushions and her travelling blanket . . .

Marisa sighs loudly from the front seat, from which she has refused to budge. We wouldn't be in the car at all, as we know, if it wasn't for Francesca's supplies. Chickens and eggs, *mamma*, she remarks cryptically. We're going to have to be very careful with the water . . . says Francesca. She turns to me, since her daughter is being so unsympathetic. How much water have we got with us? she asks.

I'm sure I saw a crate of bottled mineral water in the back somewhere, I say.

But no, of course I didn't. Those bottles contain

71

water no longer, but our own good Ligurian olive oil for impressing the Southern relatives.

Digging around between the seats we come up with just one big bottle of mineral water, untouched, and two small ones, already partly drunk.

O Lord, says Francesca. How will we manage?

Don't be ridiculous, says her son. They said they'd be here within the hour.

*   *   *

But will we really be rescued within the hour? Truth to tell, even the most optimistic and technologically up-to-date of us can hardly take the claim seriously. Efficiency is a highly fashionable pose in Italy these days, but alas, it often turns out to have little connection to concrete reality. More like two or three hours, we guess. If not four or five.

Ciccio pulls his feet up on to his rock, hugs his knees dejectedly. Marisa, still in the car, unwraps a boiled sweet meditatively, sticks it in her mouth.

Francesca will have none of this defeatism. Pulling a crumpled carrier bag from her coat pocket, she stumps purposefully away across the bumpy tarmac. Off foraging for her family, no doubt. I defy anyone to take Francesca anywhere she will not find something to eat. Barren rocks, concrete jungles . . . it makes no difference, within minutes she will be gathering something-or-other, nibbling away at some edible leaf or fungus or berry or what-have-you. And with amazing prescience, she has even brought a spare carrier bag, in case of emergency hunting-and-gathering

72

expeditions *en route*!

Before us is a scrubby bit of woodland planted with young pines: a triangle the size of a small field, presumably intended as a motorway-entrance island to separate the exiting from the entering traffic. If, that is, there ever was any traffic. No sign of any so far. Francesca is already over there, poking about at the bases of the trees. I follow her: I never can resist a good bit of hunting and gathering. And with Francesca in charge, you learn a lot.

Yes! Within minutes she has found a variety of *porcino* mushroom, a russet-brown coloured one, orangey-yellow underneath, which only grows beneath pines. *Ecco!* she says. Here we are! As soon as I saw the trees I thought we might find some *pinaioli*!

We start collecting. Ten minutes later, we have a good kilo of the things; mostly found by Francesca. But I am not dismayed. I am performing a lot better than when I first met Francesca; the bad old days are gone, the days when I might spot nothing at all, and find Francesca following in my footsteps giggling away to herself as she gathered up vast quantities of whatever-it-might-be that I'd completely missed.

Doing well! says Francesca, giving me an encouraging pat on the shoulder; and adds several remarks that are almost completely incomprehensible to me. I catch the words 'olive oil' and 'eat' and that's about all. She's gone off into Calabrese again. Wouldn't want me to think she was putting on Tuscan airs, I daresay. I get her to say whatever-it-was again in Italian. She was just telling me, she explains patiently, that you can eat

73

these mushrooms raw, the same as proper *porcini*. We could use some of the oil we'll be draining out of the peppers: that's already got salt in it. They're nicer with a few flakes of parmesan on them, but what can you do? Or did she bring some pecorino cheese, maybe, in the picnic bag? And if we could just find a something-or-other, she says, using some word I've never heard before, that would do nicely instead of lemon.

A what? I ask.

She repeats the unknown word.

But what is it? I ask. If I don't know, I can't look for it, I add helpfully.

A plant, of course, replies Francesca, giving me one of those how-daft-can-you-get looks. Its leaves taste of lemon, she adds, exasperated, when I still look blank.

Well, whatever it may be, we can't find one.

Once we're on the tarmac again, Francesca is able to raise her eyes momentarily from the ground in front of her—only to spy something even more gripping than mushrooms, up on the hillside above us. Look up there! she says excitedly.

I do. A pair of plump sleek creamy-beige buffalo, the kind whose milk you use to make the true mozzarella cheese, are grazing happily there. Is Francesca thinking of a nice juicy steak dinner? I wouldn't put it past her to turn a buffalo into a pound of sausages and a nice tidy barbecue roast with nothing but a penknife, if push came to shove. Or is she just planning to milk the creatures and toss off a mozzarella or two . . . ? I could almost wish we really were going to be stranded here for several days, with Francesca at the helm, just to see how we did. Better than any of those survival programmes you see on the TV, I'm certain.

Back at base, Marisa has dragged the great twenty-litre container of wine to the back doorway of the car, and has it balanced precariously over the back bumper. She starts tipping it, doing her best to fill an empty mineral-water bottle from it.

What on earth are you doing? her mother asks, as wine splashes on to the road.

Trying to decant some wine, says Marisa. We've got no cups, and how could we drink from a canister this size? At least we can take turns swigging from the bottle!

But what, asks Francesca agitatedly, have you done with the water that was left in the bottle?

Emptied it out, of course, says Marisa. It was only water.

Only water! Francesca goes ballistic. Has Marisa no brain? Does she not realize that you can't survive without water? Whereas it is perfectly possible to survive without wine? And only the Lord knows how long we may be here . . . *Mamma mia!* Do her children not have the sense they were born with?

Ciccio's mind, at any rate, has been working along lines that his mother would approve. Problem to solve? Make some food.

Ciccio has spread a couple of large brown paper bags on the bonnet of the useless car, transforming it into a handy picnic table; he has split one of the big flat Triora loaves horizontally, and with Alberto's help is now spreading a jar of Francesca's anchovy-stuffed red peppers lavishly on to the bottom half of what will soon be a gigantic sandwich, a good foot-and-a-half across. One of the bottles of olive oil stands beside it on the car

75

bonnet. He'll just sprinkle on some extra oil, Ciccio says, brushing away a couple of inquisitive grasshoppers that are doing their best to join the anchovies, and then we can share the loaf between us.

Alberto swoops on the nearest grasshopper, catches it in cupped hands. Here, he says, look, Granny, it's a grasshopper! An Autogriller, look *mama*! Granny was right!

9

In the nick of time, as war is about to break out among the de Gilios, we are saved by the hooting of horns, the flashing of lights, and the squealing of brakes. Our rescuers have arrived, in not one, not two, but three vehicles. And they have come several hours earlier than expected. Several days earlier, indeed, from Francesca's point of view. We have a tow truck, which is doing the flashing-lights part, and two vans, one of which is doing the hooting and the other the squealing. The first van bears a gigantic luminous red triangle on its back, presumably to warn other traffic of our existence; having driven right up to us, checked us out, and asked how we're doing, the driver roars off in reverse and takes up position twenty yards back up the road. Now, out of the squealing van jump two energetic men with flags, who shout out a greeting and dash off to guard our front and our off-side respectively. Not too necessary, perhaps, what with the distinct lack of traffic about, but a kind thought anyway. The tow truck pulls up ahead of us; the

76

driver jumps out, followed by a young assistant; and now our saviours start working out the finer details of our rescue. But what is it they're saying, exactly . . . ? I'm finding it very hard to make head or tail of it. Of course. They're speaking Calabrese.

It takes Francesca herself a second or two to register this fact, to realize that she really is at home at last. Talking her own language, in her own land. And you can actually see the realization hit her: she does a kind of happy shake of her whole being, and launches joyously into a blow-by-blow account, in Calabrese, of the trials and tribulations of the last hour. So joyously, in fact, that you'd hardly believe it was an account of trials and tribulations at all. Listening to it, I become aware that this Calabrian-speaking business may not be too bad after all. Now that Francesca's telling a story I already know, I can understand what she's on about, even though it's like understanding through a thick fog. The process is hard to explain to monolingual English people, used to a language with no real dialects left, only accents . . . it's as if, in some parts of the English-speaking world, you might find a region where, instead of counting 'one, two, three', people would count 'one, a pair, three'; while elsewhere it might be ' single, couple, triple', or 'solo, double, treble', or 'uni, bi, tri'. You would be confused to start with, but it isn't so incomprehensible that you would have no idea at all what people were talking about; and you learn to understand it quite quickly. Italians get enormous amounts of fun out of their dialects— other people's expressions sound wildly metaphorical and poetic, or picturesquely antique. In Cuneo, for example, a wooden spoon becomes a

77

spoon *'a't bosc'*—'made of woodland'. And even though some words may be completely different, you will soon get the hang of what kinds of changes or sound-shifts are likely. In Ligurian, when somebody first tells you to go slowly—*chang, chaning!*—you will see no connection with the normal Italian phrase, *piano, pianino!* But once you have grasped the rules of the dialect—every *pi*-sound in Italian has become a *ch*-sound in Ligurian; and all *'ano'* and *'ino'* endings have shifted to *'ang'* and *'ing'* respectively—not only does *'chang, chaning'* make sense, but you are well on your way to understanding dozens more Ligurian expressions.

. . . So here we found ourselves, Francesca is now concluding in Calabrese, the car stone dead, hardly a drop of water left to drink, stuck by the side of the road *comu maccaruni senza pertusu:* like a bunch of macaroni with no holes.

Our saviours now agree to celebrate the rescue with us by taking a short break to share our giant Triora sandwich and swig with us from the decanted wine, earning brownie points with Francesca for praising Salvatore's this-year's-vintage.

Some twenty minutes later, we have been thoroughly welcomed home to Calabria, and our car is now trussed up in all manner of chains and ropes, aligned just right, and ready for winching up on to the truck.

In you get, then! says the tow-truck driver.

What? Into the car?

Yes, says the driver.

Brilliant! says Alberto.

What, say the rest of us, we're going to travel in

78

it? On top of the tow truck?

Of course, he says. He and his helper are travelling in the truck already, so where else would we all fit? And the vans belong to the motorway, they're not coming to the garage. So in we get, and up we are winched, with Francesca, who is not taking the thing in her stride at all, reciting a whole string of Hail Marys and keeping her eyes tight shut. Once we are settled on and chained in, though, she is rather taken with our new transport. Talk about arriving in style. We've left the building-scam eyesore zone behind now, and here is Francesca, proud and happy, riding high on the roof of a lorry through the hills of her own Calabria, gazing out from this eagle's perch as we drive through a landscape tree-clad and furry in the afternoon sunshine, the road winding around spectacular screes of bare rock that swoop vertiginously down to deep boulder-strewn rivers.

Well, I say, that was amazingly efficient! Ten out of ten for Calabria. Look how many people came to our rescue, and in no time at all.

Look how many people, exactly! says Ciccio. It's called under-employment.

These must be the Sila mountains, are they? asks Marisa a few minutes later, her voice all wobbly with emotion. How beautiful they are!

She has been overwhelmed, she says, by the strangeness of returning to a homeland she has never really known. It's weird, but she feels such a mysterious connection to the place? As if . . . as if she's come home . . .

Home! Don't be daft, says her mother. What home? This isn't even the right province, we're in Cosenza here, miles and miles away from home. It certainly would be mysterious if her daughter had a connection to Cosenza!

Well, says Alberto, standing up for his mother for once, but it's still Calabria, isn't it?

Irrelevant, apparently. After the Province of Cosenza, says Francesca, we have to get across the whole Province of Catanzaro before we're at home in our own Reggio! When you're up in the North, I gather, a stranger in a foreign land, your loyalties may lie with the whole of Calabria. But once you're back on home territory, you belong to nowhere but the few square kilometres around your old town, and the rest of the Regione can go hang.

And what, I ask innocently, are the people of Cosenza and Catanzaro like?

Well, says Francesca, launching into the thing with a will, the Cosentini are all . . .

But now she catches my eye, laughs, and stops herself.

Calabresi? says Alberto.

How refreshing the younger generation can be!

And so much for romance and the soul. Marisa's fancy firmly stamped on, she is reduced to silent contemplation of her Roots. Or of the high peaks of the Sila, at any rate. We are heading over a narrow mountain pass now, precarious on the swaying lorry, all five of us reduced to silent dwelling on questions of life and death . . . three perilous hairpin bends more, and we're safe among pine and beech trees again.

I'll tell you why you feel at home here! says Ciccio to his sister, piling on the coals. He knows, because he felt the same thing himself, that last time he came down for the summer, when he was twenty. He and Dario drove down the whole length of Italy, rolling plains, craggy mountains, gentle hills, lakes, volcanoes, you name it . . . every kind of landscape, all strange and different—and when they arrived here, he felt as if he'd come home! Do you know what it is? Liguria! That's your mystical link. Calabria reminds you of the place where you really grew up! The parents chose the only bit of Italy that reminded them of home!

This is not perhaps the right moment to say it aloud, so I don't, but Ciccio is right. We have seen nothing at all like the place we left at dawn this morning, our own steep and rugged landscape, the terraced olive groves running down to the sea, the hilltop towns, the chapels perched perilously on high outcrops of rock half-way up mountains . . . until we arrived in Calabria. Though here the scale is much grander, almost Himalaya-like, the mountains higher, the valleys deeper.

Could this really be the reason so many Calabresi ended up putting down roots around the Province of Imperia? Best not to ask just now, though, with Ciccio and *la mamma* in such firmly unromantic mood. I daresay I'll just get a flea in my ear.

The garage we are taken to is a deserted place, a wasteland right out on the edge of a town, lying on a wide plain at the foot of the hills. Nothing much to be done here, while the mechanics take the car to pieces and put it back together again, except sit on the sofa in their office and wait. There's a lovely little automatic espresso machine in the corner—compliments of the house, they say, drink as much as you like.

Marisa and I tuck in. Ciccio and Alberto go off and do the Men Thing, where you hang around the mechanics and pretend to have some idea what's wrong with your car. Francesca goes off to stretch her legs. Marisa pulls a magazine out of her bag. I dig Filippo the Historian out of the depths of mine. May as well pursue my studies. Where were we? Ah, yes, Volume Two, the Norman Conquest of Calabria. It turns out to be a most enjoyably gung-ho tale, if you can manage to overlook its tragic consequences for later centuries. Here it is.

A certain Robert Guiscard of Normandy, with an eye to the main chance and nothing to his name but a bunch of merry men—four Norman horsemen and thirty-odd camp-followers, to be precise—arrived in the North of Italy some twenty-odd years before his kinsfolk took over Britain at the Battle of Hastings. He began his Italian career by putting in a stint as a highwayman up in the Lombard hills—a 'pitiless brigand', according to Filippo—and did rather well, quickly filling his coffers. By now he'd accumulated quite a few more followers and had built up his forces into something worth hiring out. So, in 1048, off he headed down South towards Eldorado, and offered his services to the Duke of Salerno, who was planning to take Calabria for himself, ousting what was left of the Byzantines for good: Robert had heard word on the street that he was looking for a good bunch of mercenaries to do the job. The Duke took Guiscard on—little knowing that he hadn't got himself much of a bargain. Nobody knows if Robert was planning the thing all along, or only noticed how desirable Calabria was once he'd arrived. But in any case, Robert Guiscard, victorious, dumped his employer and kept Calabria and all its riches for himself.

And so it came to pass that Calabria got its Norman Conquest eighteen whole years before we English did. And there Robert Guiscard and his fellows stayed. Breeding, as I mentioned earlier, like rabbits: and building Norman-style cathedrals and fortresses and castles all over the place, wherever they could find a space not already occupied by the ruins of ancient Greece, Rome or Byzantium—or occasionally on top of them. From which bases they set up a system of feudal dues and lands held in fief, of barons, lords and knights, presiding over a peasantry trapped in serf-like conditions, and owning no land of its own. A system that died out three centuries ago in Robert's land of origin; but which lasted so long in Calabria that people are still alive today who lived under it. People who hated it with an undying hatred, emigrated because of it, and get an attack of *angoscia* at the very thought of going back there. They would rather stay at home and water their tomatoes.

*   *   *

We set off again at last, car fixed, rather a lot poorer and several hours behind schedule. Once we get back off the bendy country roads and back on to the motorway, loud rustling noises begin to emanate from the back seat. I look round to discover Francesca unloading from her handbag quantities of large green olives, which she is piling into the mushroom bag. She just had to collect a few off the big tree on the road by the garage gates, she couldn't help it, she says, they were only going to waste anyway, and look how big and juicy, the

83

first proper Calabrian olives she's seen in twenty-five years! Nothing like Ligurian ones, are they? How could she leave them behind?

Marisa is mortified. *Mamma!* Really!

This kind of olive is lovely cracked and roasted, Francesca goes on, ignoring her daughter. We'll do them at Zia Annunziata's. With a bit of tomato and a touch of garlic and chilli, maybe . . .

Heading southwards on smaller roads now, not enough motorway left to bother with it, we are going through a much gentler landscape, an area of broad plains, fields of rough stubble, though with the sun setting behind them it's hard to make out what might have once been growing there—maize, tomatoes?—when my eye is drawn to a bonfire burning in the middle of the field we're passing, set some twenty or thirty feet back from the road; and to the small group of people standing around it. Not just people: they're all women, I see now. And this is obviously a hallucination. Ciccio was right, I shouldn't have had that third espresso on an empty stomach. Because the women gathered around the bonfire in the dusk appear to me to be Black African women, dressed in traditional African clothing, brightly-coloured wrap-around dresses of batik cloth and high-knotted headscarves. There seem to be a dozen or so of them, laughing and chatting among themselves, ebony skin gleaming in the firelight. I look away: look back again. No good. They are still there. Now we are past the field. Nothing beyond but gathering darkness. I check my fellow travellers for any sign that they too have just seen a clip from some documentary about African village life, inexplicably projected on to the Calabrian landscape. No joy. Francesca and Marisa are asleep. Alberto's eyes are glued to his Game Boy. Ciccio is quietly driving, showing no sign of having seen anything at all untoward recently.

Did you, um, see a bunch of African women in that field we just went past a minute ago? I ask him, diffidently.

No, says he. A long pause ensues. Maybe I should just drop it? I take a deep breath. I did, I confess.

Probably just here for the tomato harvest, says Ciccio, as if it was the most natural thing in the world. Too late for the grapes, isn't it? But the Senegalese do the peaches round Cosenza in June and July, definitely . . . and all the tomatoes around Naples . . . Do they? Well, that's quite a relief. I wonder what they were waiting for? A lift home? To wherever they're staying, that is. Not Senegal, evidently. Seems a very long way to come to harvest tomatoes. Or peaches, for that matter. Are there no local people to harvest the stuff? Where are all the simple Southern farming folk you always imagine down in these parts, working the land alongside one another in those big happy extended families . . . ? I give myself a mental slap on the wrist. Was I really expecting to see troupes of olive-skinned damsels, young Antoniettas and Francescas in ankle-length skirts and laced broderie bodices, tripping across the fields down here? I suppose I was, at some level. Carrying earthenware jars of wine balanced on one hip, naturally . . . Must have been looking at too many tomato-tin labels. Next time I open a tin of tomatoes or a tube of purée, I shall make sure I concentrate on visualizing the much more modern and likely picture of a bunch of West African women standing at dusk around a bonfire in some strange Italian field, far, far from home.

*   *   *

Through lots of small towns, now. Towns that look oddly poor and drab, vaguely Eastern European—hardly any colour about them, no brightly-lit shopping streets or advertising hoardings or even shop- or bar-signs. Many of them have clusters of modern buildings on their outskirts, half-finished and then abandoned, like the stuff we saw in the countryside earlier—creepers growing up the sides of their raw brick walls, weeds and shrubs firmly established in among the building-site rubble that surrounds them. More Mafia scams, I suppose. Except that as dusk wears on into darkness, it is slowly borne in on me that these places are actually inhabited. Lights have begun to come on in them; and now I come to look more closely, there is washing hanging out at their windows . . . Are people so desperate down here that they squat building sites? Or do the migrant fruit-and-vegetable pickers get put up in them, maybe?

My fellow travellers laugh at the idea. Not squatters, certainly not! Nor seasonal workers. It is another scam, surely, but of a different variety. You don't have to pay tax on a building while it is still unfinished. So down here the tradition has developed that you never do finish it. A place can stay unfinished for twenty or thirty years, with people living in it and all. And the authorities, as long as you keep on the right side of them, just turn a blind eye to the fact.

10

We're several hours late by now. We're never going to make it by dinnertime; it'll be more like ten o'clock by the time we get there. Annunziata will be away to her bed long before we arrive, Francesca tells us.

And yes, the next phone call establishes, after much agitated squeaking at both ends, that there's a reception committee of fifteen already assembling at Annunziata's. The Zia is afraid they'll all be gone home by the time we get there. Cousin Carmela will wait up for us, though, and feed us . . .

Should we just give up for tonight, then, stop rushing and get a hotel? suggests Marisa.

Certainly not! says Francesca. Give away our hard-earned cash to some bunch of unknown strangers, with all those good beds at my brother Enzo's, God rest his soul, going to waste? I don't think so! All that space Aunt Annunziata and Carmela have just for the two of them, because no one is going to make Francesca believe that Carmela's husband Pino really lives there! Not at all! He's away in Sicily, that one, has been for years. When he's not away in Naples! . . . They have the whole place to themselves now, and all that land too, though how they think they're going to keep it going now that Enzo's gone is anybody's guess . . .

This is an intriguing new feature of the journey: the closer we get to her home town, the more scurrilous hints about the lives and times of the Calabrian branch of the family Francesca is letting drop. Nothing of the kind ever got mentioned in Liguria. Obviously Francesca is much better informed than she lets on back at home . . .

It's getting on for eleven o'clock at night when we finally hit the first signs for Seminara; only another fifteen or twenty miles beyond that, and we'll be at our destination. Or so we think. But now we get lost.

Seminara itself is in almost total darkness, just a couple of tiny bars lighting the far corner of the main piazza; beyond that, a smaller piazza where the road forks. We take the left-hand fork, clearly marked 'Melipodio'.

No, no! says Francesca, not that way! It's the right-hand fork! You always took the right-hand fork here.

Ciccio groans. Francesca has been asleep for the last hour, she probably has no idea where we are, even . . . and she hasn't been here for over twenty years.

Still, he backs up to take another look at the sign, just to humour *la mamma*.

See! she says, once we get the headlights on to it again. Look, it's not a proper road sign, it's only wired on to that lamp-post. What did I tell you? Take the right-hand fork!

She's right, the sign is printed on that kind of rigid corrugated plastic that estate agents use for their For Sale signs, and fixed on with wire. Still, it is definitely meant as a road sign . . . and the arrow clearly points to the left. They've probably built a Seminara bypass since Francesca was last here, says Marisa. Or they're doing road works or whatever.

Ciccio takes the left-hand fork again, despite his mother's protestations.

And we drive on and on, the road getting narrower and narrower, the darkness more and more impenetrable, not a street light for miles, headlights picking out the occasional derelict-looking homestead by the side of the road, barking dogs in the silence the only sign of life, Francesca getting more and more agitated. For the next twenty minutes our lights show nothing but the trunks of gigantic olive trees looming twisted and ancient through the darkness, olive trees bigger than any I've ever seen before, the size of an English oak tree. The terraced earth rises above the road on either side, a tunnel of silver-green foliage meeting above our heads and cutting out the night sky completely.

It shouldn't have taken more than fifteen minutes from Seminara, says Francesca, glancing nervously out at the pitch darkness beyond the windscreen. Not if we were on the right road. We're lost, we're definitely lost, let's turn back . . . we could just wait in Seminara till daybreak . . . Couldn't we? Her voice has gone all quavery, old lady style. And old lady is not Francesca's usual style at all.

What? says Ciccio. We've driven getting on for two thousand kilometres across unknown terrain, and suddenly, right near Francesca's own town, she gets terrified! Why would we turn back when we're almost there? Don't be daft, *mamma*! We'll just press on.

Francesca lets out a moan of despair. Has this long trip been too much for her? Maybe she's been overwhelmed by emotion? The *angoscia* of homecoming that Salvatore feared? Marisa, sitting beside her in the back, has taken her mother's hands, is gently massaging her wrists.

But we should be going uphill, says Francesca, and we aren't, are we? We're going along the foot of a valley . . . I'm sure this is Castellace . . . (she pronounces the double l in that oddly Spanish way, Castey-yace).

Well, there you are, says her son soothingly, if you know the name of the place we can't be too far from home—next house we see, we'll stop and ask.

(Very optimistic, this—there's been no sign of human habitation for miles.)

No, no, says Francesca, panic in her voice. Don't stop, not in Castellace! This is *mala terra*—Bad Land! We'll be in the fog soon . . . there's always fog in Castellace!

We drive on and on. There's nobody to ask, anyway. Nothing but gnarled trees and blackness. Minutes later, as predicted by Francesca, our headlights are picking out swirls of mist lacing the narrow black strip of road and the darkness between the tree-trunks on either side of us . . . soon we have slowed to a crawl, the fog almost impenetrable. And now, ahead of us . . . what is that in the road? A pile of rocks? Has there been a landslide? Are we going to have to turn back after all?

We creep up towards the obstacle. A pile of huge boulders in the middle of the road. Quite a tidy pile, though, that looks as if it might have been put there on purpose. Why on earth would anyone have done that?

If we have to turn back, don't stop to turn round! says Francesca urgently. If they've put them there on purpose, that'll be the moment they're waiting for! Just reverse away at top speed!

90

And now, just in case we weren't unnerved enough, she shuts her eyes, raises her face heavenwards and starts to pray, clasped hands pressed tight against her bosom.

She's got Marisa and me into a panic too, now. Does she really think it's an ambush? Who? Why would anyone want to ambush us?

Francesca pauses in the middle of her prayer. Not us especially, you cretins, she says. Just any *forestiere*, any outsider, who's fool enough to follow that made-up sign at Seminara!

Porca miseria! says her son expressively. He is getting ready to slam on the brakes and go into reverse—yes, he's joined the panic too, now—when, at the last moment, we spot a gap at the end of the boulder barricade: a gap just big enough to fit through. We squeeze past and accelerate away.

Francesca opens her eyes again, finishes off her prayer, and breathes a sigh of relief.

Five minutes later we're sure we're on the right road: this one, Francesca says, enters the town the back way. Could be worse: Annunziata's piazza is this side of town anyway. Once we have seen the glow of street lights beyond the olive groves, and a few human habitations, *la mamma* returns to her normal self. Soon she has even cheered up enough to Tuscanate a bit.

Look at the olive trees! she says. Have you ever seen such huge olive trees? Calabrian ones are ten times bigger than anything Liguria has to offer, but ours are the biggest in Calabria! Lots of the trees are hundreds of years old: did we know that they were planting olives here centuries before they ever arrived in Liguria? There's one tree they say is a thousand years old, down on her brother's land . . .

And you get twenty times more olives off these trees, too . . . What you'd call a good harvest up in Liguria would be a disgrace down here. A catastrophe!

As we begin to squeeze our way between the cars parked on the narrow cobbled roads into the town, it starts pouring with rain, a thing you don't see much of in Liguria either . . . but who cares, we've arrived at last. There! says Francesca all of a sudden. Take the next turn-off to the right, now, that's it, takes us right up into Zia Annunziata's piazza.

The piazza is tiny, just twenty or thirty houses round it, and there is some kind of big stone fountain in its centre, dimly visible through darkness and sheeting rain . . . as we open the car doors, the roar of the rain is backed up by the loud splashing of the water cascading into the circular trough around the fountain. Here is Cousin Carmela at last, opening the door to us in ample flannelette pyjamas—we glimpse a round currant bun of a face, thick black hair streaked with iron grey and tied at the nape, then she steps back in out of the rain. We run for the house through rivers of water, clutching a few vital bits of baggage, and hurl ourselves into the narrow hallway. Carmela throws herself straight into Francesca's arms and bursts into tears; Francesca promptly bursts into tears too.

Now someone who introduces herself as Vincenza, masses of dark hair, age around thirty, appears from within: she shepherds the rest of us past the grieving pair, into a big warm kitchen with an open fireplace. She is here to do the honours in place of Zia Annunziata, she tells us. Annunziata was exhausted by the welcome-home dinner party; she said to tell us she hopes we won't take it amiss, but she was up at five, she'll see us in the morning . . . Vincenza, giving Ciccio the usual hug-and-kiss of welcome, bursts into tears too, burying her head in his shoulder. What sad circumstances to be meeting in after all this time, she says, when she finally manages to let go of him and resurface. Ciccio can't have been more than twenty last time she saw him, can he? She was just finishing school, herself . . . but what a fine figure of a man he has become!

And Marisa! It's even longer since she and Marisa met, they were both just little children . . . and now Marisa's a mother already . . . So this must be Alberto? What a grand big lad he is! And this is Antonio's English fiancée? A lovely girl! she says, giving me a rather perfunctory squeeze in my turn.

Antonio. I am going to have to get used to this. I know perfectly well that Ciccio was baptized Antonio, but nobody has ever, to my knowledge, addressed him by this name. His sisters occasionally call him Tony, or rather Tonny, pronounced to rhyme with Bonny, when they are reminiscing about their childhood years in Australia—but otherwise he has always been Ciccio. I'm going to have not just a foreign Francesca, but a new Calabrian Antonio-person to get to grips with as well. What will he be like?

Will you be wanting pasta? There's plenty of lasagne left. . . ? Though it would probably be best, wouldn't it, if we just took some minestrone, since the hour is so late, and a soup is more digestible? asks Cousin Carmela, rising heroically above the joy of reunion to concentrate, as people always will

93

in this country, on the matter of keeping our bodies and souls together.

(Did I happen to mention that Volume Four of my history of Calabria contains a whole section on Alimentary Culture? Only nine pages each are devoted to matters such as Long-Term Economic Structures: Latifundia and Pasture, the Napoleonic French in Calabria, and so on. But food, or rather Alimentary Culture, gets eighteen.)

We all agree to soup, and Vincenza sets about getting us seated at the big kitchen table. Vincenza is some sort of distant cousin, I gather, and although the complexities of the family tree, explained half in Calabrian and half in Italian, elude me for now, I manage to grasp that she lives next door. I also notice that, somewhat oddly for a next-door neighbour, Vincenza too is in a nightdress and bathrobe. Her house connects to this one on the first floor, Carmela explains, she won't have to take a dousing running through the streets in her nightwear, don't worry!

Connects on the first floor? I didn't get much sense of this place at all, through the darkness and the rain. The buildings looked all joined together on the circular piazza side, with a jumble of outside staircases and verandas and balconies, and a steep hill to the back.

Carmela insists on our taking our wet shoes off before we catch our death from them, Vincenza collecting them all up from round the table like a gym mistress while Francesca relates the awful tale of being lost in Castellace, of how sure she was that the rocks in the road had been put there by *malavitosi*, criminals, who would burst out from among the trees to rob us of everything we

94

possessed the minute we stopped . . . *Malavitosi*! Not at all! says Carmela cheerfully, disappearing through a door beside the open hearth into a side-room, whence she goes on talking. No, no, it's just that there are road works on the main Seminara road, and they're doing their best to send people round the Castellace way to keep the traffic down. Trouble is, most people don't want to go through Castellace.

I should think not! says Francesca.

No indeed! says Vincenza.

Why, say I, what's wrong with Castellace?

Ah, says Francesca, it's always been *mala terra*. Bad Land. Nobody wants to go through there if they can help it! You never know what might happen . . .

Oh, there's nothing to fear these days, things aren't like that round here any more, says Carmela, reappearing with a two-foot length of sausage in one hand—sausage nearly as thick as my wrist, and of such a deep orange-red colour that there's no chance it's not packed full of chilli—and some sort of grilling device, a thing that looks like a cast-iron tennis racquet, in the other.

Aren't like what? I ask.

Carmela gives Francesca and Vincenza a quelling look.

Well, they've got the road through Castellace half blocked up with rocks, just to start with, contributes Ciccio, who seems not to have picked up on the strange tenor of the conversation. Too busy focusing on the exciting sausage, no doubt. Why have they done that, then, he adds, if they actually want people to go that way?

Oh, they're doing work on the bridge just before

95

Castellace too, answers Carmela, relieved, it seems, to get off the topic of the *mala terra*. They had those big metal barriers to start with, she says, the freestanding ones, so they could close off whichever side of the road they were working on. But people kept pinching them. Too useful for penning sheep. The workmen got fed up with nearly getting run over, so they just threw the rocks there to slow everybody down . . .

She is putting the racquet-thing on the table and opening it up as she speaks—it turns out to be hinged at the top—and, rolling the sausage into a big fat whorl, she shuts it up inside the two halves. We got these specially for you, she tells Francesca, plumping the contraption on to the olive-wood embers in the fireplace, where it hisses and sizzles and lets out a delicious porky perfume, making me realize that I'm starving hungry.

They came all the way from the old butcher up in Spilingo, she adds—still as good as ever they were all those years ago—so you'll just have to try a bit, however late the hour!

Castellace, I repeat tenaciously. What, I ask, is the thing that we are not worrying about any more?

Nobody answers. Vincenza busies herself with getting all our shoes laid in a neat ring on the hearth-bricks, where they form an intriguing counterpoint to the sizzling sausage-bat in the centre of the fireplace; while Carmela picks up a large wooden spoon and disappears through the doorway into the side-room again. I lean round to get a glimpse through the doorway. There seems to be a sort of secondary kitchen through there in the shadows, even bigger than this one, where Carmela is giving a stir to something bubbling on a range

96

just inside the door. I now notice that the only means of cooking in this room is the open fire—maybe it's not really the kitchen? Is it a dining-room? Living-room? But then there is a sink and draining board in here . . . and a fridge, and hanging strings of garlic and onions. Do they perhaps divide up their room-functions differently in Calabria?

Why would anyone want to ambush people in Castellace, particularly? I carry on dauntless. Or at all, for that matter?

Francesca gives me a little why-don't-you-shut-up wag of the finger and a warning look.

So I shut up.

Silence falls.

11

Vincenza has put out the plates and spoons, glasses and wine-jug; now she goes over to the tall window to the side of the fireplace and throws it open to the piazza. The rain has stopped now, and delicious cool damp air wafts across the room, filling it with that lovely autumnal wet-leafy fragrance. She brings on the condiments for the soup: a hunk of cheese and a grater—you don't grate parmesan, a Northern cow's milk cheese, on to your soup and your pasta in these parts; you use pecorino, a Southern sheep's cheese—and a dribbling bottle of olive oil. No chance of talking about anything but food for the next half hour or so, then. Carmela nips back into this room with a huge pot of steaming minestrone, doles out the soup and bread. And notices the open window. Vincenza! she says sternly. We'll all catch our deaths! How many times do I have to tell you?

Vincenza stomps over and shuts the offending window, muttering to herself about how you could easily suffocate round here, and nobody would turn a hair . . .

I am amazed. Vincenza must be the first Italian I've ever met that wanted a window open. To most Italians an open window represents draughts and colds and stiff necks, rather than wholesome fresh air. A kindred soul at last. Not that Vincenza seems to be doing any better than me at getting her own way.

Carmela pretends not to hear, anyhow: and we all begin to eat. Francesca is in ecstasy, rediscovering the long-lost flavour of the minestrone of her youth—and is soon doing her best to name each of the half-a-dozen varieties of bean in the soup.

All our own home-grown stuff, says Carmela. Every bit of it.

There are lots of chick-peas in it, too. Do they even grow them themselves? I've never seen a chick-pea plant.

Yes, of course we do, says Carmela. *Qua non ci manca niente!* We lack for nothing here! But you'll see no chick-pea plants here till next year, now. You're too late.

Ah, yes, we lack for nothing here, echoes Vincenza. *La terra è generosa!* The land is generous! she adds in an oddly poetic manner.

The pecorino and grater go round the table, followed by the olive oil bottle—the last lot of oil that *papa* made, bless his soul, before he passed away, says Carmela as it gets to me. I put on plenty, in his honour, even though I never had the pleasure of meeting him.

Francesca's right, the minestrone is delicious—but there is some secret ingredient, something that reminds me vaguely of Greek food. Or is it Indian? A flavour I certainly don't identify with Italian cooking as I know it, anyhow. Eventually I get it. Coriander. Is there coriander in it?

Si, coriandolo, Carmela agrees.

Coriandolo? The word unleashes great confusion among the Ligurian branch of the family. Up in the North, the confetti you throw around at weddings is called *coriandolo*; and our Marisa, who has never heard of *coriandolo* as a cooking ingredient, stops in the act of raising the spoon to her mouth and stares at its contents, suspecting for a horrified moment that she will find little bits of coloured paper floating in it. Causing Francesca and Carmela to fall about giggling.

(Strangely, the word *confetti* in Italian—closely related to the word 'confectionery' in our own language—means sugared almonds; essential at any wedding in this country, indeed, but to be given out as presents to the guests, tied into little gauze bags with satin bows, and certainly not intended for throwing about the place.)

Carmela obligingly disappears again into the other-sort-of-kitchen behind the hearth, and returns with a sprig of fresh coriander, which Marisa sniffs and bites at with great suspicion. Not bad. Why has her mother never used it at home in Liguria, then? she asks.

And where would I find it, for goodness' sake? says Francesca. Try asking for *coriandolo* in a

99

greengrocer's up there! They'd just send you to a stationer's! Sneering at you for being an ignorant Southerner, into the bargain!

Now that I have enough minestrone inside me to keep body and soul together, I try getting back to the intriguing, if unpopular, topic of the Bad Lands. What is it, I ask, that is so Bad about them?

Ah, says Carmela, smokescreening again. There's nothing to worry about these days. That was all years ago.

Castellace always used to be a place where *briganti* hung out, says Vincenza, breaking rank.

Briganti? Brigands? I imagine red bandannas, gold earrings and flintlock pistols . . . Sounds as if it was a very long time ago, then.

A long time ago! Not at all. Why, says Francesca, throwing discretion to the winds in the name of accuracy, she remembers the police launching Operation Marziano not long after she was married: they were hunting down sixty-seven outlaws in this area . . . Weren't they, Carmela?

Carmela looks as if she's sucked a lemon. But Francesca is away now. Sixty-seven outlaws, she says, all of them on the run! And how did a man keep himself when he was on the run? Nothing for it but to hold up passers-by. Though the families did try to help out with food and clothes and a few *lire* when they could . . . Castellace was a good place to do it, if you had to do it, what with the mist and all the big trees.

Not just hold-ups, though! says Vincenza enthusiastically, abandoning the PR job completely for a good tale. On down the Castellace road is where they held that American millionaire's boy that got kidnapped for ransom, they kept him for months, what do you call him, John Paul something, all those years ago, do you remember him?

John Paul Getty Junior? I say, suddenly taking this a bit more seriously. Not so long ago after all, then. Forget the bandannas. Think balaclavas.

Yes, that's the boy! she says, crouching down at the fireplace and turning over the sausage-bat resting on the embers. What names these foreigners have! How's anyone supposed to remember them?

Got one of his ears pruned in the end, eh? adds a new voice from the hallway. Zia Annunziata has come to join us after all. I turn round to see a big bony powerhouse of a woman, sharp features, bright blue eyes, nothing like her round cuddly daughter, except that she is wearing identical flower-sprigged flannelette pyjamas.

Yes, says Vincenza. They certainly did! Pruned his ear!

She and Annunziata laugh uproariously at this happy choice of word.

Zia Annunziata does the rounds: a hug and a kiss for Francesca; an extra pat on the cheeks for Marisa, who has grown into a lovely girl, hasn't she; a squeeze and a poke in the ribs for Ciccio. Hope you've brought plenty of jewellery! the Aunt says to him with a wink, and cackles with laughter. (Incomprehensible: I've never known Ciccio to use any jewellery at all. Still, he seems to find this remark as entertaining as she does.)

And this is Marisa's son? *Che bel ragazzo!* Alberto gets a massive squeeze, a chuck under the chin, and a pair of vicious-looking pinches to the cheeks. And now Francesca introduces me:

Annunziata stops talking a moment to take stock.

Already saw her photograph anyway, she says.

Photograph? She's seen a photo of me? Francesca certainly does keep in much closer contact with the Southern branch of the family than she ever lets on back at home.

Annunziata gives me one of those weighing-and-measuring looks that I'm familiar with from my first encounters with Francesca. I brace myself. She is already testing the flesh of my upper arm. Something tells me that Zia Annunziata will belong to the Old School of Italian *mammas*. I am about to be told that I need fattening up. Yes, here we go . . .

Not as thin as you look in the picture, she says, grudging approval in her voice. In fact, now she's seen me in the flesh, I look like a good strong girl. A bit skinny, but a nice-looking girl, she repeats to Francesca, as if I was deaf. Or as if they were discussing some head of livestock about to go to market. And that's the ceremony over. I suppose family is just taken for granted round here; you'd never believe Francesca had been away for twenty-five years. They're all behaving as if they'd been in one another's company day in day out for ever.

So it was round here that they, er, pruned John Paul Getty's ear? Ciccio repeats, keen to get back to the gripping topic of the kidnap victim.

Sent it off in the post to his *papa*, didn't they? says Annunziata with relish. And he paid up then, all right!

The kidnappers were lucky the parcel got there at all, that's all I can say, contributes Carmela, who is now adding a bright yellow bowl full of bright red *peperonata* to our dinner table, next to the napkin full of bread rolls. The way stuff goes missing in the post round here! You'd hardly believe it! Carmela herself sent a whole cheese off to her daughter in Milan a couple of months ago, she was desperate for some real Calabrian pecorino, the spicy one, bought from Ercole, do you remember Ercole, Francesca? He's still making the best pecorino around . . . And the thing never arrived at all! Just vanished completely! It's a scandal!

So the kidnappers kept John Paul Getty in Castellace, then? I say, hoping against hope that the gripping question of the inadequacies of the local postal service is not going to get in the way of the rest of the story.

Yes, for a time, says Annunziata. But then . . . she adds, suddenly looking very vague, . . . then they took him somewhere else.

Hard to avoid getting the distinct impression that the locals knew rather a lot more than they ever let on to the authorities about the movements of the kidnappers. And it looks like that's all we're going to get. Time for the next course. Carmela serves up the sausage, flipping it out of the bat and on to a wooden board, passing us a knife to cut off our own chunks.

As I suspected from the look of the thing, my namby-pamby Northern European tastebuds can't cope with it at all. More an explosion of agony than a foodstuff as far as I'm concerned—though Francesca, Marisa and Ciccio are all ah-ing and ooh-ing as if they've just found the Holy Grail. While my fellow eaters delve into the intricacies of exactly why North Italian butchers are unable to reproduce this ferocious delicacy correctly, and which of the neighbouring villages is best at

103

creating it down here, I abandon the sausage, mopping beads of perspiration from my brow and upper lip, and concentrate on the bread and *peperonata* instead. I notice that Alberto is with me on this: he is just picking at the sausage, stuffing plenty of bread in with each mouthful. It's obviously not entirely genetic, then.

Next, of course, we get nuts, seeds and fruit. At least this is one bit of Calabrian tradition I'm familiar with. Vincenza brings in a plate of enormous fat fresh figs and a chunk of fresh pecorino—soft, white, almost mozzarella-like stuff when it's just made, nothing at all like the *stagionato*, the matured version we've just been grating on the soup—from the other kitchen. Carmela begins piling bowls of walnuts, almonds, dried figs and salt-roasted pumpkin seeds on to the table, and puts out a pair of nutcrackers for each of us. Ciccio looks meaningfully at me as he passes me my pair; and generously decides not to entertain the company with the tale of my Nutcracker Disgrace. Coming as I do from a land of philistines who hardly eat any nuts except at Christmas, when one pair of nutcrackers does for the whole family, I once threw away a dozen pairs of nutcrackers he had just got hold of, in among a job-lot of ex-restaurant wares, at a bargain price. I naturally assumed that the ridiculous number of nutcrackers was just an unnecessary and space-wasting part of the booty, and threw them into the bin. A fact that was only discovered at the tail-end of Ciccio's birthday dinner a few weeks later, when eighteen members of his family queued up, sighing patiently, for the one measly pair of nutcrackers we now owned, till Ciccio was obliged to go down to the

104

toolbox in the *cantina* and bring up two hammers and several varieties of pliers. Took me weeks to live it down. Luckily for me, Marisa missed this event: and Francesca, who was present, is too busy communing with the Calabrian soul food on her plate to waste breath showing me up. The foolish foreign behaviour of my past remains concealed.

Anyhow, says Annunziata, rising from her seat, things aren't anything like as bad as they were when you left, Francesca. There's nothing much to worry about these days. As long as you don't go out too much after dark, and keep yourself to yourself . . . and know where not to stop in your car!

Annunziata gives a cackle of laughter, picks up a large morsel of the ferocious sausage from the chopping board, slips it into her mouth, and sets off for bed again, chewing nonchalantly.

Was that a joke? Is there any chance that Ciccio and Marisa will know where not to stop the car? Something tells me their local knowledge is not all it could be. I make a mental resolution to take at least one Aged Relative along with us wherever we go, just in case. I'd like to get back to Liguria with my ears intact.

12

As soon as we've finished our fruit-and-nut course, Carmela offers to take Francesca to her room. She's dying to get to bed herself. Francesca must be exhausted. Carmela has got a room ready for her down on this floor, next to her own. Vincenza will show us young folks upstairs to where we're sleeping—it's on her way home, anyhow.

On her way home? Ah, yes, of course, along the balcony.

Up we go with Vincenza, who shows Marisa and Alberto to a tiny snug room at the head of the stair; and sends Ciccio and me to the other end of the corridor, where we find a marble-floored mausoleum of a room, full of the biggest and most ornate wardrobe-and-chests-of-drawers set I have ever seen. Which is saying something in this land of enormous wardrobes. This one is a juggernaut a good eight feet high, well over twelve long, filling up nearly the whole of the back wall from floor to ceiling, a bevelled mirror on each door surrounded by carved and gilded cherubs. Cherubs, moreover, that match the other cherubs adorning the borders of each drawer in the black-marble-topped chest-of-drawers. Through the door in the corner, I discover a small bathroom. Lovely! Our own private washing arrangements. On this far side of the house, away from the piazza, a tiny window looks out on to a kind of ancient stone battlement ten yards off: a high terrace wall at the top of which, if you bend down and crane up, you can see a tall church beautifully illuminated in an underwater-looking bluish green light. Complete with bell tower lit up in orange for contrast.

Bell tower. Oh no! A bell tower right next to our bedroom. I decide not to mention this to Ciccio. Sufficient unto the day is the evil thereof. I myself, since I've been living in this land where bell towers are a constant hazard, have learnt to sleep through any amount of the things. But Ciccio, despite being born and bred here, is a sensitive plant who cannot tolerate a bell at dawn. Worse still, he always feels the need to awaken me so that I can share in his agony. Hopefully it won't be the kind of bell that rings the half hour as well as the hour. Better still, maybe it's not actually a clock tower at all. If we're lucky, they'll only ring the bell for Mass.

The room, now I come to look at it properly, is unusually full of doorways. A strange bedroom altogether, with as many entrances and exits as if it had been designed for a *Carry On* farce. As well as the door we've just come in through, and the other one leading to the bathroom, there is a set of French windows beside the bed that open on to a wide balcony running the whole length of the house, overlooking the piazza. At the foot of the bed, yet another door leads into a small room with a sofa and an ironing board in it (I said they divided their room-functions up differently here— what kind of room would you call that?), whence another set of French windows opens on to the same balcony. Little do Ciccio and I know what an impact these simple architectural facts are going to have on our lives for the next three weeks.

I start unpacking, looking for something to change into. Ciccio, Marisa and I have decided to go and check out the ancestral town's night life. Surely not everyone here will be in bed by midnight, keeping themselves to themselves? Ciccio thinks he remembers a bar just up the alley on the opposite side of the piazza. Maybe we'll bump into Paolo and Mimmo, the second-cousins-once-removed, or some such type of relative, that he used to hang out with last time he was in Calabria. He can't wait to see what's become of them, he says: and heads for the bathroom.

Seconds later, just as I'm pulling my blouse off over my head, there is a volley of raps at the landing door, and with a loud cry of *Permesso!* Vincenza bursts into the room, making me jump out of my skin and emit a loud squeak of terror.

Not to worry, she says, we're all the same once we're naked! She stops and takes a good look just to be sure. *Belle mutande!* she adds as she nips across our room towards the French windows. Nice knickers!

Ciccio, alarmed by the squeak, comes out of the bathroom to see what's wrong, clad only in a towel. Ah, good! he says, when he sees Vincenza. He wanted to ask her if she knows which house Francesca's been left in Enzo's will? He couldn't ask down there in front of everybody—his mother would have been mortified—but he's been dying to find out.

Zia Maria's house, of course! says Vincenza.

Yes, but which Zia Maria? The one in the town, or the one with the orange grove?

In the town, says Vincenza, just over the road, don't you remember it? Come out on to the balcony and I'll show you. See the alleyway leading up the hill, across the other side of the piazza? See the big house with the balustrades on the corner? It's the little one behind that, the next door down the alley, you can just see its balcony sticking out, the wooden one. It's in a state, though—you can look at it when you want, it's not locked up. Now, quick, get back inside, she says abruptly, bundling Ciccio back in through the French window. If someone sees me out there with a half-naked man

108

in the middle of the night, that'll be that. Shotgun wedding. You'll be carrying me over the threshold before you've even had time to get the place fixed up . . .

I'm away home to bed, then, she says, with another of her sudden changes of humour. My stairs are just at the end here. *Buona notte!* And she steps back out on to the balcony.

Ciccio's only just returned to the bathroom when Marisa appears in her bathrobe, whispering excitedly to me to come and see the rooms next to hers. She just looked into them, trying to find the bathroom—and she's never seen anything like it in her life! *Cabbala!* she says. Sorcery!

Seems unlikely on the face of it, and yet when I step into the first room I certainly can't think of any more reasonable explanation. A bedstead stands in its centre—but a bedstead you couldn't possibly sleep on, since it has no mattress or indeed base of any kind. It is being used to form a horizontal frame around a most bizarre collection of objects. A few pieces of clothing are spread neatly on the floor within it: a white and a red blouse, a white and a red skirt; an ivory fan, four oranges placed one at each corner of the frame, several hundred matches laid carefully out in a square around two non-matching shoes, their partners balanced on the window ledge across the room . . . Can't be accidental but it doesn't make sense either. Unless it's some piece of conceptual art. Is it a joke? A trap for nosy guests?

You need to see the next room, says Marisa, then you'll be sure it's not a joke.

The next room really is spooky: it is completely empty, nothing but a floor of beautiful old hexagonal terracotta tiles—on which lies, just below a peeling green-shuttered window, a large pile of beans. Those mottled-pink-and-black haricot beans, to be precise: the pile a couple of feet wide, spread on the tiles below the window, and surrounded by burnt-out night-lights. Not a pile, really, Marisa points out: but laid out in a design. It's a *cabbala* of a heart, she says.

Heart? It looks more like a lopsided apple to me. Then I see what she means. Not the stylized heart of romance, with two equal lobes above and a point below, but a horribly anatomical heart, one lobe bigger than the other: the sort of thing you'd see laid out on a butcher's slab.

We creep off down the corridor to find Ciccio. Tell me about it! he says. This whole house is deranged. He has just spent ten minutes unravelling a veritable cat's cradle of washing-line, knotted to and fro across the shower, before he could get into it for a wash.

He comes and takes a peek at the mystery rooms. Don't even think of asking, says he. It'll be something to make sure of a good bean harvest, maybe. Or to bring Carmela's husband home; or to find one for Vincenza. Or something to do with Zio Enzo's death. You're best off not mentioning it. Just leave it be and say nothing. He embarrassed Zia Lina, the one he stayed with last time he came down, horribly—by asking her about some weird thing she was up to with chickens' beaks and stuff, grinding them up into a powder in a pestle and mortar. He was really interested, who wouldn't be? But they think that, coming from the soulless North, you're bound to be sneering at them for ignoramuses, superstitious pagans, not proper

110

Christians. And they'll never tell you anyway.

*   *   *

But according to Marisa, magic and charms and potions are women's business . . . maybe they wouldn't tell Ciccio, but she is sure they'll talk to her. She will get one of the female relatives on her own and ask. About the beans, at least. The women down here are famous for their knowledge of *cabbala*, says Marisa. We could learn a lot.

I prod the *cabbala* gently with the toe of my shoe, causing a small herd of microscopic bean-dwelling beetles to appear and rush desperately about seeking new shelter. Learn what? Witchcraft? I point out to Marisa that she's hardly been here an hour and already the superstitious paganism in her wild Calabrian blood is beginning to show: the veneer of civilization is breaking down.

Quite possibly, she says. What she needs is a nice civilized shower to get her back to normal. Can she use our bathroom for now, till we find out where the other one is? She can't face any more weird surprises tonight.

*   *   *

Some days later I can't resist asking about the beans anyway.
Oh, those! replies Cousin Carmela, nonchalantly. They've been there since last year . . .

111

13

The wet cobblestones gleam in the light of the street-lamps: we stop in the mouth of the alley across the piazza and take a covetous look at Zia Maria's house. Vincenza was right, the place is pretty small—you certainly couldn't get the whole de Gilio family in here at once, we'd have to take turns at it—but it's beautiful too: a carved stone lintel over the door, old-style solid shutters instead of slatted ones, a wooden balcony on the first floor resting on hand-planed beams grey with age, the marks of the adze still on them. The alley is narrow, just wide enough to take a car at a pinch, so the first two floors aren't going to be very light: but the tiled roof only covers the back half of the top floor, making an outside room that must have a crow's-nest view for miles. Marisa gives the door a push, and it creaks open. Will we try going inside? No, it's much too dark in there to make out anything at all. What if there are potholes in the floor, or piles of rubble? We'll have to wait till tomorrow, come back in the daylight.

We thread our way on through the warren of tiny streets towards the centre of town, to where Ciccio thinks he remembers a bar. Lots of the houses have their whole first floor built of wood: carved and curlicued wooden balconies are de rigueur, strings of sweet peppers, chillies and tomatoes hung to dry in the shelter of the eaves, glowing a lurid red in the lamplight. The streets are full of the sound of water trickling and gurgling; some of it from the fountains on the street corners, but more of it sounds like it's below our feet. Was there really that much rain?

No, it always sounds like that here, Ciccio says. There's a whole network of underground streams and rivers running beneath the town. That's the free mineral water *la mamma* was going on about.

On to wider streets now, imposing merchant houses built of cut stone, room to park a car. Look at how few of them have local Reggio Calabria plates, says Ciccio, how many from the North of Italy! This is a town of emigrants: and what's the first thing an emigrant does with his savings? Buys a car to get home in.

Ciccio falls behind in the darkness, checking out his childhood memories: but Marisa and I have seen the bright light flooding across the street from the bar up the road. We press on, and walk into the Bar Z, alone and apparently unaccompanied . . .

*   *   *

Some time later, the three of us are declared Jewels in the Crown. Everyone in the bar insists on buying us round after round of drinks to compensate for their hilariously insulting presumptions of earlier on. We toast our homecoming, the fact that we are not Eastern European sex slaves, and our new-found jewel status several times; bowing to public opinion and changing over from beer—a drink known to be bad for the health and the physique, especially once September has arrived—to the good local beverage we are downing now, a kind of liqueur called Nocino, 'little nut', made, apparently, from the husks of walnuts. Which, we're told, strengthens

113

the constitution no end.

The husks? Really? I seem to remember the husks of walnuts leaving a revoltingly bitter flavour on your fingers. But this stuff is delicious and sweet.

Ah, say our informants, you have to pick them off the tree while they're still very young, before the nut inside is formed: that's when the bitterness comes.

Of course! Like the pickled walnuts we make in my own country, I say. You pick them green, and poke a needle into each one, I recall, to make sure the inside is still soft.

Everyone is fascinated by this notion—pickled walnuts, now, never heard of that!—and wants to know how you do it. But alas, I have no idea. My granny used to make them when I was a child. But I never followed the procedure at all closely, just joined in the bit where you chose the right ones by poking the needle into them. And the bit where you ate them, of course.

A tragedy, says Aldo. It's happening here in Calabria these days, too. Young ones don't bother to learn from their elders . . . and soon nobody will know how to make anything any more. Everything will come from factories. Mark my words.

Aldo, it seems, recently discovered that his daughter-in-law didn't know how to make the *salamoia* you use to bottle your windfall olives: he is still reeling from the shock.

Now that everyone has worked out who Ciccio is, one of the younger men at the bar claims to remember him from his last visit—he was with a friend, wasn't he, whose family was from these parts too . . . ? He remembers how proud Mimmo and Paolo, Ciccio's cousins, were of their Northern connections. They took Ciccio and his friend everywhere, introduced them to everyone—and then what did they go and do but make a spectacle of themselves. That market stall! The boys nearly died of shame.

Why, what's so shameful about a market stall? asks Marisa.

Not the stall, says Ciccio. The jewellery we were selling from it. A real man couldn't sell women's stuff round here. Not without bringing all his male relations into disrepute. They wouldn't let us set up a stall anywhere nearer than Palmi, twenty kilometres away. We'd make them a laughing-stock, they said, and ruin their prospects with the girls!

Mimmo's away in Denmark, the barman is telling Ciccio, working in his uncle's pizzeria in Copenhagen. But Paolo's in this bar every morning for his breakfast espresso. Come in around about half past seven, and we'll more than likely catch him before he goes off to work.

Work? says Ciccio. He's got a job, then?

There seems to be some secret subtext going on among our fellow-customers at the moment: some motive for hilarity that is not being shared with us.

The barman seems to be having trouble keeping a straight face. Two youths are positively snorting with suppressed mirth. Only Aldo, who hardly knows the cousin, is looking as mystified as us.

He has a market stall, says the barman, provoking an outbreak of giggles from the young ones.

Ciccio sees the light. Jewellery! he says. Don't tell me! He's selling jewellery!

He is right, of course.

No! I can't wait to see his face! he says. We'll pay him a visit at the market! And he makes the barman promise not to say anything, not till we catch up with Paolo.

I manage to snatch a private English-speaking moment with Ciccio, to investigate the earlier mysteries of the evening. Why did they have to call in Aldo to check us out, instead of just asking us who we were themselves? Has he understood? And what was all that about Poles and Bulgarians? Why would we be Poles and Bulgarians, for goodness' sake?

Ciccio turns out to have a grasp of matters Calabrian hardly to be expected in one who's spent less than six months of his life in the place. It's obvious, he says. They thought he was a foreign freelance, an interloper bringing his team of good-time girls in for a break from the streets. If he was, and the business hadn't been OK'd by the local lads, we probably needed to be run out of town. Somebody with the right connections had to be called in to check us out.

Well. In spite of having watched every episode of *The Sopranos* at least twice, I would never have worked this out for myself. So much for there being no Mafia around here these days, then, I say.

Not necessarily, says Ciccio. Far from expecting a cut of the action, for all we know, they mightn't tolerate that sort of thing in their town. You'd need to be a lot better informed than we are, he says, to know what Aldo's friends in high places might have in mind.

All very well, but this still doesn't sound, to me, like a description of a place where there is no

116

Mafia. Alas, before we get on to the topic of Poles and Bulgarians—do they come here for the harvests, like the Senegalese, maybe?—Ciccio is drawn back into debate in Calabrese, or his best approximation to it, by Rocco, the tawny-headed young man who first made the phone call to summon Aldo.

He wants to give us his condolences on the death of Uncle Enzo, he says, shaking Ciccio's and Marisa's hands, doing the formal kissing. Didn't he hear that Enzo had left Francescella's branch of the family one of his old places? You'll all be moving back down to the old home town, soon, then? he says, grinning.

Of course, says Ciccio. We can't wait. Just like all the other *emigrati*!

It's the old town house by the piazza, says Marisa. It's tiny, I don't think we'd all fit in! Seriously, though, she adds, she might think of staying, if she could find some work down here. She's sure this would be a better place for her son to grow up. Everything in the North is so commercialized, everyone so selfish, no sense of community left . . .

You're married, then, says Rocco, looking a bit disappointed.

Not any longer, says Marisa. And yourself?

Still looking, says Rocco. Anyhow, he adds, dragging his eyes away from Marisa, as it happens, he and his family run the builders' yard here . . . so we know who to come to now, don't we, if we decide to get the place sorted out? And if Marisa's really looking for work, he will see what he can do . . .

Hardly any jobs down here as it is, says an old

117

man sitting in the corner, earwigging. And the woman wants to come down here and take one off us, does she!

14

Behind all the good cheer, there are some odd undercurrents going on in this place. When our new friend Aldo first arrived, the younger men were all calling him *'mastro'*, the old-fashioned version of *'maestro'*, teacher or master . . . a sign of deference unheard of up at our own end of Italy, except in historical romances and costume dramas on TV. Now that Aldo is two sheets to the wind, though, some of the younger men, especially Rocco's two companions, have started to behave as though all this respect-paying is a bit of a charade. In fact, through the fog of incomprehension, I'm getting a powerful sense that the real top dog around here is Rocco himself. I check with Marisa: doesn't there seem to be a growing vein of irony whenever they address Aldo as *'mastro'*?

Yes, she's getting the same impression. We duck out of Ciccio and Rocco's building fantasies—Zia Maria's house has already gained an extra storey with panoramic views right down to the sea—for some social guesswork. Could it be that the earlier respect was mere deference to Aldo's age, whereas Rocco, who looks a good twenty years younger than Aldo, is actually higher up some social, or political, or even Mafioso, ladder than him? But if so, why would Rocco have called Aldo in to deal with the Bulgarian and his Poles, rather than doing it himself?

Marisa thinks it could be a job for a dogsbody, couldn't it, and Rocco is too important to dirty his hands with such matters . . . ? Or maybe there's some kind of power struggle going on? Rocco would be the young blood, and Aldo the old? Or are we letting our stereotype-fuelled imaginations run away with us? No idea: but how pleasant it is, again, not to be the only mystified foreigner. It's making me realize how much I've missed my sister's company up in Liguria since she left Italy for the Wild East. How much more enjoyment there is in being mystified when you have someone to share the speculating with!

Speaking of inheritances, Ciccio is saying now, does anyone in here know Santa Cristina at all well? His other Zio, on his father's side of the family, left him a bit of land up there a while ago . . . there are supposed to be some remnants of a ruined temple on it. Would anybody have any idea where it was?

Ciccio glances hopefully, as he speaks, at the most aged denizen of the bar, the grizzled gentleman who didn't want Marisa stealing Calabrian jobs: who goes on supping slowly at his glass of red wine, and gazing steadfastly at the wall. No response.

But Rocco and friends tell us that there is any amount of lost archaeology lying around this part of the world, poking out of pasture, tangled in tree roots, hidden in undergrowth. Classical ruins are ten a penny, and are not, as we'd imagined, all restored and tidied up and neatly signposted for the tourists, the way they would be in other parts of Italy. And how many tourists do we think come to

Melipodio, or go to Santa Cristina? says Rocco, laughing at our innocence. Not the major clue we thought it would be, then. We'll have to go up to Santa Cristina and ask. People nearby will know.

That's right! says the aged gentleman in the corner, raising a pair of rheumy eyes at last to glower over at our group. That's the only reason any of you lot come back here—to see if your forebears accidentally left a goldmine behind them. Which they didn't. Won't take you long to find out there's nothing here. And be off again just like your parents before you. Mark my words.

* * *

Two o'clock in the morning, and the bar starts to close. As we take our leave, Rocco takes care to place himself so that he's the last to shake Ciccio's hand. Keeping a firm grip on the hand, he stares long and hard into Ciccio's eyes.

You know me now, he says. Don't forget that I am at your disposition if you ever need anything. Anything at all . . .

Ciccio is most nonplussed by this. He spends most of our walk home through the labyrinth of cobbled alleys trying to decode it. It didn't seem like a simple offer of builders' supplies as required, did it? There was definitely an implication that Rocco was a man of some influence about the place. But probably he was just entertaining himself, playing on the fearful 'ndrangheta fantasies of the Northern breed of Southerner? Then again, maybe Ciccio was simply being offered some dope to smoke? Up in Liguria, if someone carried on like that, that would definitely be what they meant . . .

*   *   *

On our way down Zia Maria's alley, nearly home, Marisa gives a yelp of joy as we pass the old house. A Calabrian memory has come to her at last! . . . She hasn't forgotten everything after all! Not exactly a memory of this house itself, nor of the aunt who once lived there, but of an old lady in the house across from it, on the other side of the narrow alley . . . She stands staring at the house in question, even tinier than Zia Maria's . . . Yes, she was scared of this place: the feeling suddenly hit her as she passed it—she didn't want to visit Aunt Maria, because you had to get past this neighbour-woman, who always said *buon giorno*, so you had to say it back to her, and Marisa didn't want to: because although people said she was a nice old lady and you should greet her politely, she was just like a witch was supposed to be, she always had the door open on to this ground-floor room, all dark and cluttered, and a fire burning in the hearth, the only light there was inside . . . and chickens running in and out of the door, cats prowling around . . . and a pot standing on a trivet in the fireplace, just like a proper witches' cauldron . . . and she was all bent and bowed and toothless, with grey straggly hair tied back haphazard, strands escaping on all sides; and hung about with layers of shawls and cardigans and aprons above a long black skirt, like a big curtain gathered around her, but the black so old and worn it was a kind of dark green . . . it came down nearly to her ankles, but she always had one side of it tucked up somehow, so you could see a

121

pair of grimy ankles bulging above broken-down slippers . . . Unless she's made it all up? she says, coming out of her trance. A Nocino-induced mirage? No, it must be real: it's so clear.

Yes! Ciccio confirms that this is indeed a genuine memory . . . he recalls the woman in question as clear as day. He was afraid of her too: especially after the day she called him in to watch her wringing one of the chickens' necks. Marisa has not, as she feared, irretrievably lost all her Calabrian past: she can go to bed happy.

Soon Ciccio and I are tucked up too, under our own mountainous eiderdown on top of the billowing mattress in the marble mausoleum.

How things must have changed since last time he came, though, says Ciccio. Paolo with a jewellery stall! After all that performance! Imagine! He will fill me in on the tale for my bedtime story.

He had set off from Liguria, he says, with his friend Dario, who was also of Calabrian origin and also wanted to check out his Roots, in a Fiat van loaded up with cheap-and-cheerful fashion jewellery. Rather than be a burden on their relatives, they planned to earn their keep for the summer by setting up stall in the local markets. The goods were leftovers from a friend's seafront market stall up in Liguria—stuff that had been selling well the summer before, and would probably still be fine down in the South, where fashion should be running a little slow. They sold like hot cakes, as it turned out—he and Dario were on to a good thing. But they soon discovered that to sell Women's Stuff in public down here was to call not just their own virility into question, but that of all the male relatives they had come to bond with. What kind of a man would do such a job? The cousins were certainly not having them setting up stall here in the Home Town! Were they mad?

Most of these critical cousins were out of work themselves—no jobs to be had in Calabria, as usual—so towards closing time they would ride their Vespas the few miles to whichever town was holding the market that day, stand at a safe distance while Ciccio and Dario got the incriminating trinkets safely back into the van, and escort the Northerners to the bar for an *aperitivo* before dinner, and a good manly game of table football. They would rather be workless for the rest of their lives, they said, twirling the rows of miniature footballers with an expertise born of years of unemployment, than sink to such depths.

Even, asked Ciccio and Dario, if this meant staying at home for ever, doing bits and pieces of casual work, being kept by their long-suffering mothers and fathers for half the year?

Ah, said the cousins, but that was different. That was normal.

15

We are awoken, horribly early, not by the bell tower but by the sound of laundering. Squeaky female voices, taps being turned on and off, rushing water, scrubbing, splashing, all going on apparently on the balcony just outside our bedroom windows. I feel like a degenerate lounging here among the eiderdowns. They've probably been up since dawn, while the house guests snore away in their pits, sleeping off the Nocino. Oh Lord, should we get out of bed? I can't face it. Much too early. And why are they laundering outside the window, anyway? I could have sworn I saw a washing-machine in the bathroom last night.

Now comes another of those sudden volleys of raps, this time from the French windows, accompanied by a loud cry of *Permesso!* Yes, it's Vincenza again. She hurtles in from the balcony, makes a dash across the room, and vanishes into the bathroom.

Ciccio, who already has his head under a pillow—he is extremely sensitive, as I may have mentioned, to any type of commotion first thing in the morning—extends an arm, makes a grab for one of my own pillows, flips it on top of the pile and presses the lot down over his ears. Just in time—because now, adding insult to injury, the bell tower, which has so far remained silent, begins to ring out six-thirty: six long-drawn-out bongs, followed by a bing for the half hour. Now, a whole series of even more resonant bongs from another, larger bell begins calling us to seven o'clock Mass. Ciccio lets out a low moan of despair from beneath his pillows: then he suddenly goes rigid in the bed beside me. The bells! he exclaims, casting off pillows to right and left as he struggles to a sitting position. The bells!

Che cavolo? he adds angrily after a moment's thought, ruining the Hunchback of Notre Dame impression. (The phrase *'che cavolo?'* is usually translated into English as 'What on earth?' although I prefer the literal translation, 'What cabbage?')

124

I subtly edge the covers up over my own ears, and shut my eyes tight. It is always best, I find, to give Ciccio the impression that he has no audience. Shortens the performance quite considerably.

But this, it turns out, is not one of Ciccio's usual anti-bell tirades. In fact, it's almost what you might call a pro-bell tirade. These particular bells have, it seems, always been one of the highlights of his trips to Calabria. And he is demanding to know What Cabbage has happened to them? They have been ruined! Why are they doing nothing but a plain, monotone bong? These particular bells, he explains, once he has regained enough self-control to speak coherently, have always rung out the first few bars of 'Summertime' to call the faithful to Mass: and Ciccio has always loved them. Who wouldn't love coming from the kind of town where the church bells play Gershwin at dawn, reminding you that the living is easy? They gave him great joy in the early mornings—a time of day when, it must be said, hardly anything gives him great joy. And he was looking forward immensely to seeing my face when I heard them. He has taken great care not to mention the phenomenon, so as to make my surprise all the greater. And now look! They're just bonging away like any old bells anywhere else in Italy! What, he demands loudly and passionately, has happened to 'Summertime'?

As if on cue, there comes another outbreak of staccato raps, this time from the bathroom door; and the usual cry of *Permesso!* Vincenza, it seems, feels that she needs our permission to leave the bathroom, as well as to enter it. Not that she actually waits for permission: she is already half-way across the room. *Ah, buon giorno* she says,

125

seeing Ciccio awake at last.

But Ciccio is in no mood for frivolity. What, says he to Vincenza, has happened to the bells?

The bells? Nothing has happened to them! says she. Have you gone deaf?

But where has 'Summertime' gone? The rot of modernity is everywhere these days! Even down here in the South people have started changing things just for the sake of it!

Ah, the old priest died, God rest his soul, says Vincenza. We've got a new one now. And this one says 'Summertime''s got nothing to do with Christianity.

I can't believe it, says Ciccio. Is nothing sacred?

Well, says Vincenza, pausing in the doorway of the sofa-and-ironing-room, a lot of people complained at the time. But he doesn't like jazz. Go and talk to him yourself, you'll see. Anyhow, you'll soon get used to it. We have.

Ciccio sinks on to the pillows, weak with horror. Bong! he says tonelessly, in time with the call to prayer. Bong! Bong! Philistines! *Cretini!* Bong!

There being little point in trying to get back to sleep in a bed in which your partner is set on imitating a bell tower in Big Close Up, I climb down from the bed and head for the French windows, aiming to let in some fresh air. Only to find myself face to face with Carmela, who is standing just the other side of the glass, behind a veil of hand-crocheted net-curtaining, her hair tied up in a cotton scarf, pegging laundry out on to a washing-line that has been strung right across the windows. This is certainly not the most private bedroom I've ever slept in. And since the French windows open outwards, washing-line-wards,

126

there's not a lot to be done about fresh air just now, either . . . *Buon giorno*, Carmela mouths through the glass, chuckling at my surprised expression, and waves to me to come on out the other way, through the ironing-and-sofa room. I try doing this, only to find myself bumping into Vincenza again, now making herself busy plumping up the cushions on the sofa. Squeezing between her and the ironing board, I stick my head out through wet flapping pillowcases to greet the relations.

Buon giorno, I reply to Carmela, who is now back along the balcony, working away with a scrubbing brush at a sort of cast-concrete washing-vat, a thing on stumpy legs with a built-in ridged concrete washboard sticking out one side of it. Mamma Francesca *buon-giorno*'s cheerfully at me from a bit farther along the balcony, where it widens out, at the end of the house, into a fully-fledged green-tiled terrace, partly roofed over by the floor above; she is sitting on a three-legged stool under the grapevine pergola which shades the rest of the terrace, wearing a large flower-sprigged apron and shelling broad beans into a bucket, looking for all the world as if she'd never left Calabria at all.

The daylight is horribly bright out here, my head aches, and now I come to think of it the air is no fresher than it is indoors. It's steamy and humid out here, hot sun beating down after last night's rain. All too much to cope with this early in the day. Niceties having been observed, I shuffle back indoors, past the bed in which my partner is now snoring gently, having given up his bell imitations for the time being, praise the Lord, and into the bathroom. I throw some lovely cold water on to my face to help combat the effects of the Nocino. Yes,

127

there it is: definitely a washing-machine. They've probably decided not to use it so we can get a lie-in. Sweet of them. Unless it's broken down? Whatever. I certainly need the lie-in. I clamber thankfully back under the sheets. Peace at last.

There is no hope of a decent period of unbroken rest in this room, though. Another knock at the door. Marisa with her toilet bag, wanting to use the bathroom again. A fraternal squabble about privacy ensues—but what is Marisa supposed to do if she can't find another bathroom? Maybe there isn't one—maybe our relations only wash in here?

No, says Ciccio, they certainly can't be taking that cat's cradle of washing-lines down every morning before they shower, and then putting it back up again. Why doesn't she just go and look? There has to be another bathroom.

But Marisa needs the loo urgently. And for all she knows, down here in Calabria people only wash once a year on St Swithin's day. In fact, she's sure she's heard that not so long ago country people in the South would never remove all their clothes at once for fear of the *aria* getting to them . . . or was it for fear of sinful thoughts rearing their ugly heads if you saw yourself naked? Anyway, maybe the relatives stick to the old ways, don't shower or bath at all, just go for the bit-by-bit sponge-bath at the sink in the kitchen? So why doesn't her brother just shut up and let her get on with it? She vanishes into the bathroom.

An hour or so later, Francesca puts her head round the door to say that she's going off to see Graziella. Annunziata and Carmela went ages ago, and she's been waiting all this time for us to wake up . . .

I am surprised. We've only seen Zia Annunziata for about thirty seconds so far. It seems strangely casual behaviour for an Italian aunt, to go dashing off visiting whoever this Graziella may be, rather than staying at home to commune with family she hasn't seen for years. Aunt Annunziata must be as eccentric as her household would lead you to believe.

Unless you want to get up right away and come too? adds Francesca. You're not making much of an impression lying abed of a morning, anyhow.

Ciccio is outraged. Some of us have driven thousands of miles while others just relaxed in the back seat. And moreover, Ciccio knows the only reason she's so set on following Annunziata is envy. We're very tired, it's only eight o'clock, we'll be here three weeks, we can see Graziella any time.

Who is this Graziella? I ask, intrigued. And what is to envy about her?

But Graziella, Francesca reveals, giggling at my foolishness as usual, is not a person: it's a place. A piece of land, naturally. The best bit of the family land, in fact. And more important than family itself, obviously. Family members may come and go, be born and die, but the family land is eternal.

Anyhow, says Francesca, it's not envy—Vincenza says Annunziata was worrying about having left the irrigation system on, she wasn't expecting the rain last night, she might be needing a hand. But she does want to see how the Aunt and Cousin are managing the place without Enzo, God rest his soul, to run it . . . it'll be hard for them, neither of them's in the first flush of youth, are they? . . . and when you think about it, Ciccio is the only male relation left . . . Francesca wouldn't be surprised if

Annunziata didn't ask him to run the place for her, if he showed an interest. And it's always worth having another string to your bow, isn't it? Is he sure he doesn't want to get up and come, now?

Machiavelli had nothing on Francesca. Does she really have a secret plan to establish her son down here? She's never shown any sign of it till now. Maybe, though, now that she's finally back here she's discovered a desire for revenge on the forces that drove her away in the first place? Wants to prove that Calabria does have something to offer its children at last?

Ciccio does not rise to the bait. He needs coffee, he says, plaintively, before he can even start to think.

There's some made downstairs, says Francesca, ignoring the hint in her turn. And off she goes.

Coffee. Enticing thought. I'll go and get some, I say, throwing on the bathrobe and setting off down the stairs.

Easier said than done, though. I find the espresso pot relatively easily—in the second kitchen, the one behind the fireplace—but alas, it is nearly empty. A trip out to the first kitchen to refill the bottom with water. In again for the packet of coffee. Out for a spoon. Back to put it on the range. Now, where will I find the milk? And the sugar? How complicated this house is. No sign of milk anywhere. As I wait for the coffee to bubble up, I wander down to check the doorway at the far end of the room, the dark and windowless end where the house is built straight into the rock. Maybe there's another fridge in there? A long, narrow scullery: a fridge, but no milk; and a very loud sound of rushing water. On I go, hunting for its source; past another concrete laundry-vat, two more sinks, another range-size gas cooker; and there, behind a collection of dusty demijohns of wine, a gulley full of rushing water cuts right across the floor—a dangerous-looking rubble-edged gash, a couple of feet wide. You certainly wouldn't want to find yourself stumbling about in here in the darkness. It's more of a cavernous trench than a gulley at the far end, where it disappears under the floor, presumably to join the subterranean river system.

Beyond the gulley, against the rock wall, yet another sink lurks in the shadows—you'd think the plumber would have told them they'd gone far enough by now, wouldn't you?—and, even more oddly, a shower-base: plumbed in, but with no curtain or any other means of obtaining privacy if you happened to want to use it. Not that you would, I suppose. Maybe Marisa is right about the relations' bathing habits? Even once you'd removed the collection of gardening tools propped in it, you'd still be surrounded by piles of muddy potatoes, baskets and boxes of beans awaiting shelling, and something that looks like a mountain of mouldering apples.

Beyond the shower lies another doorway. It looks as though you can do a complete circuit of the house at this level. Yes, here I am back in the main hall. Maybe this door, opposite the entrance to the kitchens, will lead to the main bathroom?

No. It's not a bathroom. Talk about dividing up your room-functions differently! This is not any type of room I have ever come across in my life. I stand in the doorway and boggle. It contains three small upright chairs and a rough stool, which are

131

set in a circle in its centre, amid a golden-brown sea of—what is it? Nuts! Walnuts, to be precise. Wall-to-wall walnuts, still in their shells, piled waist high towards the far side of the room, low enough to paddle through at this end. Probably the relations hold wild walnut-eating orgies in here of an evening, when there's nothing worth watching on TV. A simple country pastime we have yet to be introduced to. Unless they use walnuts instead of water for cleansing purposes?

16

We've managed to drink our coffees in bed, and had a few minutes of peace. And Ciccio has solved the mystery of the walnuts for me. They are for stuffing into figs. Annunziata and Carmela make their living, or part of it, by creating these delicacies, which they sell from a stall at Palmi market. Food, drink, sweetmeats . . . walnuts certainly seem to be the staff of life in these parts. I'm beginning to see Ciccio's walnut pasture in a whole new light. No wonder his father thinks of it as a bulwark against hard times.

Some time later, Marisa and I head upstairs, off on a serious bathroom hunt. We'll try the floor above. Still no bathroom. Two more doors to try on this landing. Another bedroom, unused evidently, but with books and magazines piled all over its floor. No more *cabbala*, at least. The next door turns out to lead on to another balcony, this one about the size of a football field, a flat roof covering the entire building, extending over the narrower balcony below; and done out in acres of pale blue tiles. Faintly reminiscent of a bathroom in a general sort of way, and yet definitely not one. Strange, the way this house is full of tantalizing hints at a bathroom, without there actually being a fully functional one anywhere—apart, apparently, from the one you have to pass through our bedroom to get to. I remember reading somewhere about the invention of The Corridor, and being surprised that such a simple thing had ever required inventing. But it did: and it went hand in hand with the invention of the very notion of privacy. Until that, a room just led off another room, which led off another, and so on: even in royal palaces. You simply barged your way through whatever anybody else was doing in theirs to get to yours. This house must have been created at some intermediate stage, I deduce, when the concept of the separation of spheres was still in its infancy, and the corridor a new-fangled fad you could take or leave.

Another of those concrete washing-vats—how many of the things can one household possibly need?—stands in the far corner of the terrace, plumbed to discharge into the roof gutter. More clotheslines criss-cross above our heads. Between us and the washing-vat, half the terrace is roofed over in a ramshackle way in ancient terracotta; beneath the tiles stand row upon row of wooden racks covered in small round brown objects protected by panels of mosquito netting. Figs, of course, that's what they are. Thousands and thousands of figs, put out to dry, and waiting to meet their walnuts.

Voices from below. Vincenza, who didn't go to Graziella with the others, and a certain Uncle Antonio, who is really a cousin, but called Zio because of the respect due to his age (sixty-odd, I guess), and who is waiting at the kitchen table to meet us. I take to this Uncle immediately: he is all grey stubble and cigarette smoke, bouncing with suppressed energy. He is also extremely muddy. He has been planting olive saplings all morning, he says apologetically. His son Antonello should be here soon to say hello, too—he's about the same age as Marisa's boy, so they'll be able to keep one another company. Vincenza's in the back kitchen making coffee for everyone. We'll sit outside in the piazza in the sunshine while we drink it, so all the neighbours can get a good look at you newcomers, he adds. You'll have fewer house visits to pay that way!

In the distance we hear the gurgling of the espresso pot: Vincenza appears out of the back kitchen with it. Later she'll show me how to make Antonio's coffee, she says reprovingly, as if I'd been shirking. She deposits the pot on the table and vanishes off into the bowels of the house again. Wonder why she thinks I should be making Zio Antonio his coffee, especially, anyhow? I kick myself—of course, Ciccio is Antonio too, must get to grips with this. Even so, I can't see why he can't make his own coffee, though. Obviously Women's Liberation has made even less progress down here than it has up North. Which isn't saying a lot.

Zio Antonio is telling us all about our welcome-home dinner that we missed last night. Even the

134

relatives from distant America were there—they've made it over to pay their respects. That will be nice for me, having them around, won't it, because they all speak English too: they've been living in America for decades, he says, in Noo Joysey, Noo York. He sounds most convincingly as if he's sending the pronunciation up, and I laugh appreciatively.

Zio Antonio gives me a strange look: what could be so funny about an address?

Carrying our coffee cups, we step out into the piazza and are immediately accosted by a large lady at the next door, also laundering away in one of those concrete vats. Hers seems to be actually plumbed in on the pavement just to our side of her front door. It is fed by a tap in her outside wall, its water outlet a piece of hosepipe fixed to gush away into the gutter by the side of the road, just in front of us. Which it now does, causing me to leap a foot in the air.

Antonio? says the laundering lady to Ciccio, brandishing the plug. Is that you? *Ay per mia*, how you've grown! Is this your *affidanzata*?

Ciccio, I mean Antonio, introduces us. I am indeed his *affidanzata*: a handy word that officially means fiancée, but neatly covers all sorts of irregular liaisons. I am Anna: this is Giuseppa. (I often become Anna in this country, because *anni* means 'years' and the notion of its also being a name is much too confusing for many older folks.) Giuseppa knew my Antonio when he was this big, she tells me, giving him a big pinch on the cheek.

Two upright chairs sit on the pavement outside the house, as they do outside almost every other house in the piazza. Some even have a little table, too: their own personal pavement cafés. I leave the

135

chairs to the men, and sit on the stone doorstep, warm as toast after a morning under the hot sun. We left a mild early autumn up in Liguria; but here in Calabria we've come back to the tail-end of summer.

Are you only just out of bed, then? Not even taken your coffee yet? says Giuseppa to Ciccio, giving me a conspiratorial grin. I've been remiss in not getting my man caffeined up and into action before now, I gather.

Impressive levels of surveillance in this part of the world, says Ciccio—by tonight everyone in town will have heard about the lazy layabeds from the North, where the easy life weakens the character. Won't they, Giuseppa?

Maybe, she says with a grin. But you're looking well on it, anyhow.

Vincenza now appears, as if by magic, out of a tiny brown-painted doorway that you'd hardly notice, set in the wall between us and Giuseppa. My house! she says, spreading her arms. It's hard to see where a house could fit in between Annunziata's and Giuseppa's. Is her home only six feet wide? And how did she get here? She must have gone up the stairs, through the mysterious first-floor entrance into her own place, and back down again out of her own door. She is carrying a brown paper bag of biscuits in one hand, which she thrusts unceremoniously at me, and a half-drunk bottle of mineral water in the other.

There! Antonio's breakfast! she announces abruptly, and heads off again, back through our own door this time.

What a lot of Antonios there are round here, I say.

136

All of us named after the grandfather Antonio, says Zio Antonio with satisfaction. My son too— Antonio-known-as-Antonello. That would be your Nonno Lira, he adds, patting Ciccio on the thigh— Lira was his nickname, because he could turn a penny out of anything . . .

Ah, yes. Grandfather Lira. He's the one in the photo back home, with the big thick glasses and the donkey; the one who, according to family legend, died of despair once he was too old to ride it any more. He had gone on defiantly mounting his steed every morning, against the advice of his friends and relations, who had often warned him that at eighty-five he was well past riding age—until the day came when he lost his grip and fell, proving them right. A loss of *figura* that sent him, from that very day, into terminal decline.

Yes, that's him, says Antonio. Nonno Lira. He was one of the greatest at getting hold of bits of land! Some man! He had stuff planted everywhere! Tomatoes growing away down on the river banks, carrots and marrows and potatoes and all sorts in little tiny plots he'd found and taken over, by the sides of the roads or on the margins of the big landowners' groves, little corners of land the bailiffs wouldn't spot . . . He was a great one for marrows, he would train them up a tree or a bush anywhere so you'd hardly notice them . . .

But why did he need to hide them? I ask.

Because if the bailiffs found the stuff they'd root it all up, wouldn't they? says the Zio.

But, I mean, why did anybody care if he grew food on land nobody was using?

Zio Antonio raises his eyebrows and looks meaningfully at Ciccio. Some innocent female

137

you've found yourself! he says. You were only supposed to grow stuff on the land you'd rented from the big house, weren't you? But our Lira was too clever for them, they could never prove it was him, that was the thing. Otherwise the family would have been in bad trouble for stealing land.

But, I say, that doesn't really sound like stealing land . . .

Exactly! says Zio Antonio.

17

I am dying for Marisa to finish getting ready so we can go and check out the Zia Maria house by daylight. What on earth can she be up to? Leaving the men to their biscuits, I wander out into the middle of piazza to get another look at it: it looks rather worryingly decrepit in the bright sunshine. I stop off to check out the beautiful stone fountain in the centre: it is urn-shaped, floral swags carved at the top, with a set of shallow octagonal steps leading up to it, the outline of the carving softened and worn by centuries of weather and wear; and it has eight brass nozzles with lions' faces, very worn but still just recognizable, set into its sides, pouring a constant stream of water into its circular rim. Endless supplies of water right outside your front door! Eldorado indeed. How much easier life would be at home in Liguria if only we had this much water just lying about the place, proper rivers and springs instead of our miserable *torrente*, the huge wide river-bed in Diano San Pietro, filled by the sudden influx of melting Alpine snow each spring, but by the end of June holding nothing but a sad lost foot-wide trickle moving sluggishly down its centre. Not to mention our tragic well that these days always runs dry a good month before the autumn rains arrive to save us . . .

The fountain's from the Cinquecento, calls Giuseppa. Been here five centuries . . . Nobody knows who the artist was, though . . .

Look at that! I've spent so long starved of water that rather than seeing a work of art, I saw nothing but a utility that would make life an awful lot easier if only we had one just like it outside our own door. I am ashamed of myself. Still, upon reflection, I suppose that's exactly how most of the inhabitants of this piazza would have viewed the fountain when it was first put up all those centuries ago. No need to upbraid myself. I'm just more in touch with the realities of history these days than I used to be.

All the houses here used to do all their washing in it once upon a time, adds Giuseppa, starting to wring hers out and throw it into a large basket. Just you ask Francescella! It was us girls' job to bring buckets and buckets of it over to the house for cleaning, in the old days before we got taps indoors . . . No buckets these days, thank the Lord, but— *guarda come siamo ridotti*! Look how we are reduced! Since last year the *Comune* has decided the fountain is an important historical monument, and forbidden us to use it for the laundry any more!

And giving me another conspiratorial grin, Giuseppa picks up her laundry basket, brings it up the steps to the fountain, tips it out under one of the spigots and begins vigorously rinsing it out.

Who would use tap water for the last rinse when they had fresh spring water just outside the door?

she says. Who do they think they are, anyway? Men!

Whichever authority decided the fountain was of great historical importance seems to have had no qualms about covering the shallow stone steps leading up to it with brand-new sharp-angled speckly grey granite tiles that hardly sit well with the mellow weathered stone above. Still, maybe this is simply an acknowledgement of the impossibility of stopping the local inhabitants from going on brazenly using it as they always have done.

I dangle my hand into the lovely cool water, looking across the square. Tall narrow three- and four-storey houses clustered round an oval piazza, terracotta roof tiles every shade of orange and red, wrought-iron balconies and tall elegant shutters, climbing vines and wisteria. Above the piazza, the houses pile above one another up the hill, past the church that no longer plays Gershwin and on to the high point of the town, an imposingly ornamented stone building half-hidden by tall palm trees.

A beautiful view, as long as you stay on this side of the piazza. Slight problem, though, if you turn towards the side we're staying on. Aunt Annunziata's house is certainly not beautiful; some terrible seventies refit has been perpetrated upon it, a brutalist cement façade with shallow modern arches disfiguring a frontage that must once have been as lovely as the neighbouring houses . . . As if this wasn't enough, across the corner alley from Annunziata's stands an even worse eyesore— another of those raw-brick building sites, a four-storey house apparently knocked down, half-rebuilt and then, by the look of it, abandoned for years— windowless holes in its walls, clambering weeds sprouting from the protruding dollops of mortar, bags of cement biodegrading in puddles on the bare concrete floors within, rust dribbling from the steel joists in the new ceilings. And oddly, when you view it from Annunziata's balcony, which I found myself doing earlier while awaiting my turn in the bathroom, you see a substantial collection of washing-machines gathered together on the second floor, some rusting away, others gleaming pristine white. What on earth could that be about? And how did they get them up there?

One beautiful house, on the attractive side of the piazza, with wrought-iron balconies and climbing wisteria, tall pale green shutters, particularly takes my fancy . . . Look, Ciccio, I call over to him, isn't that one beautiful?

But this is not the right moment to discuss architecture. Ciccio has left his seat and is crouching by the car, prodding away at our front offside wheel, Uncle Antonio at his side. Apparently the tyre has developed a puncture. They're going to have to change the wheel, says Ciccio. How come nothing ever goes wrong with the darned car except when you really need it and are thousands of miles from home?

Still, Vincenza, who is now filling her half-drunk bottle of water at the fountain—she seems to have a terrible fear of going thirsty for someone who lives in a place so bountifully supplied with the stuff—takes me up on the topic of the lovely house.

The woman who lives in there, she tells me, has never been known to come out, not for years; she hasn't even been seen in daylight. Her relatives leave a basket of shopping outside the door twice a week and it's gone next morning . . . that's the only

141

way you can be sure there's someone still alive in there. She never married—know what I mean? she adds, giving me a nudge and a knowing look; and suddenly sets off at speed for the alley between Annunziata's and the building site, where the town houses trail off into cottages and sheds.

*   *   *

He'll walk on down to Graziella with us in a bit, says Antonio, if we want to go and catch up with the others; but maybe we just want to rest and get over the trip? Annunziata will be down there every day of this week anyway, because they still haven't finished gathering the walnuts, and there are the *pappaluni* to get in, too, so there's no rush to go today . . .

Pappaluni? says Ciccio. What are *pappaluni?*

See that? I'm not the only person who has to keep asking what words mean any more, either. A new life is dawning!

Zio Antonio doesn't know what *pappaluni* are called in Italian; they're a kind of bean, big and flat and white, that comes apart into two halves really easily . . . What do you do with them? Well, you boil them and then usually make a salad with them—with finely chopped onion and olive oil and maybe flaked tuna fish . . . or you can put them in the minestrone . . .

Ciccio has it. They're *fagioli di Spagna*, Spanish beans: what we English call butter beans. Interesting. I've never seen butter beans growing. In fact, like chick-peas, they're the sort of thing you're so used to meeting all your life in the dried form that you never even think of them growing at

142

all. I may be too late for a chick-pea plant, but if I'm lucky I'll catch a butter bean. Adding something, at least, to the sum of human knowledge.

*   *   *

Zio Antonio wants to know when we're going to go and check out our inheritance. We're just waiting for Marisa, I say: we tried to get a look at it in the dark last night, but we couldn't see a thing.
In the dark? says Zio Antonio, shocked. But how did we even know where to find it?

It takes a while, but we eventually establish that the house we looked at last night wasn't the right one at all. It was the other Zia Maria's. Vincenza was just having us on. Enzo left Francesca the house with the orange grove, three or four hectares of land, just on the edge of town. That girl Vincenza has a very strange sense of humour, says Zio Antonio. Take no notice of anything she says! No wonder she's never found herself a husband.

The place with the orange grove is horribly overgrown, Antonio tells us . . . he could take us over to have a look at it later, if we like, he has a bit of land of his own nearby, that's where he's in the middle of planting his couple of hundred new olives. He could give us a hand with a bit of clearing down there, too, once he's finished, later this week. Just so Francesca can see what's there. Not that oranges are worth anything these days. And maybe Ciccio would like to give him a hand with his planting?

The hunted look that comes over Ciccio's face at this prospect is evident to me, if not to the long-lost Uncle. This is the sort of thing his father Salvatore

143

has been springing on him since he was big enough to pick up a sickle. Olive-farming as a family duty. Though this is a new one: the extended family duty. At least we have a good excuse, for now.

We're not allowed to go there, says Ciccio, not till after the memorial Mass, in case we look grasping and get a *brutta figura* in the town.

Absurd! says the Uncle. Who told you that? Francescella? She's lost touch in all those years she's been away among the Ligurians. You'll get more of a *brutta figura* if you don't go—that would be bad, now, looking as if she didn't give a fig for what her own brother left her!

What's the house like anyway? I ask in my bald English way, not being much of an expert in the niceties of the Italian *figura*, North and South.

Oh, you know, it's old, says Antonio. An old *casupola* . . .

A *casupola* is an old-hovel sort of building. But is it big? Small? A ruin? Repairable?

No use. This is exactly the way countrymen carry on in Liguria, hardly interested at all in whatever buildings may stand upon the land—only in its size and agricultural potential. We'll just have to wait and see.

18

Suddenly the piazza is filled with the revving of motors and squealing of brakes. A bunch of youths on Vespas and *motorinos* appears: they roar twice around the fountain, and come to a halt before us. One of them pulls to the front, about an inch from

Antonio's toes, and is introduced to us as Antonio's son, Antonio-known-as-Antonello.

He has been sent here by his mother to entertain his cousin Alberto, he says, looking none too pleased about it. Where is this Alberto, then? he adds, revving loudly in neutral, while his friends gyrate slowly and noisily round and round the piazza, laughing and shouting to one another over the roar of their motors, all of which seem to have had their silencers removed.

Ciccio goes in to alert Alberto to his guests.

There is a series of bangs and crashes from the balcony above our heads, as someone struggles to open the French windows; it is Marisa, all dressed and ready, and full of the joys of holidaymaking. *Buon giorno, Calabria!* she shouts, as she disentangles herself from the washing-lines. Is there any coffee left for Alberto? He's just getting up. He'll be there in a minute . . .

Stop that terrible racket! shouts Zio Antonio above the roar of the bikes. All of you! Or else come back in half an hour when the boy's up . . .

How many more coffees? shouts Vincenza through the kitchen window. Are you taking one too, Antonello? Ah, this place is enough to drive anybody to distraction! *Qua non si può ragionare!* she adds angrily. You can't reason here!

Zio Antonio rolls his eyes and takes a biscuit. What airs Vincenza gives herself, he says. Alberto comes out now, coffee in hand, and sits on the doorstep, next to something I'd taken for a drainpipe, but now see is actually the stem of an ancient and massive grapevine. It climbs up to the balcony above, where it turns into the wide shady vine pergola under which Francesca was sitting doing the beans earlier on. It hadn't even occurred to me to wonder where on earth all those vine-leaves came from, up there in the air.

Anyhow, Alberto leans on this vine, grabs a biscuit out of the bag Vincenza left, and glowers adolescently while he dunks it into his cup and slowly munches his way through it, making like he's hardly noticed the boys on the bikes, who are now parked in a huddle on the other side of the piazza, heads together, toying defiantly with their accelerators. So they ignore Alberto back, in their turn. Oh Lord. Where has Marisa got to? I'm sure Alberto would not appreciate a busybody aunt with a silly foreign accent interfering, telling everybody to Be Nice to One Another.

Go and talk to your cousin, Alberto! shouts Marisa from the balcony. Alberto plays deaf, glaring into his coffee. Ciccio and Zio Antonio are taking no notice of the youth situation at all. I follow their lead, sitting and quietly munching a biscuit from the bag. A sort of rusk full of caraway seeds and pistachio nuts, very dry and hardly sweet at all. These are really serious Mediterranean *cucina povera*—hardly any sugar or fat or egg in them as far as I can tell; nothing, in fact, that makes a biscuit a biscuit to the Northern European mind.

Except for the name, says Ciccio when I share this thought with him, and generously give him what's left of mine, since he's finished his.

What does he mean, the name?

Biscotto, he says in Italian. Two words, bis and cotto. Think about it. You English say the same thing, but in French—bis-cuit.

So we do! Twice cooked. The dry, rusk-like

146

feature must, in fact, be the essence of bis-cuit-ness. Never thought of this before. Still, the unhealthy ingredients added by later generations have certainly improved the flavour and texture of the Ur-biscuit no end, in my opinion.

Alberto drains the last drop of his coffee and strolls off in the direction of the cousin and the bikes, cool and casual, well away from interfering relatives. Good move. I do my best not to look. Soon he is sitting on the newest-looking of the bikes, some kind of insect-looking Piaggio: now he's swirling round the piazza with great panache. All is going well. Until, that is, Marisa appears, coffee in hand, to join us—and has a fit at the sight of Alberto on a bike with no helmet on.

Alberto! Come back here immediately! Marisa shouts, to no avail, as he and the boys vanish in a cloud of dust. None of them, now she's drawn my attention to it, was wearing a motorbike helmet. Strange: back home in Liguria the police took to enforcing the helmet law—which had been on the statute books, ignored, for a decade or so—two or three years ago, and these days you never, ever see anybody without one. You get stopped and fined within seconds up our way if you try it . . . even on the hottest of days, when the last thing anybody in their right mind would do is to wrap their head in a great insulated plastic bobble—as I know to my cost.

How come, Marisa asks the Zio angrily, you let your Antonello go about with no helmet on? It's dangerous. And it's against the law!

Ah! From Naples southwards, says Zio Antonio, things are different. The other way round, you might say. Down here, the police prefer you not to wear a helmet.

Marisa snorts. Are the police not supposed to enforce the law? How could they prefer you to break it? And why would they, anyhow?

Well, says the Zio, because, down here, not wearing a helmet shows that you are an honest citizen going about your lawful business. People are scared of bike-riders in helmets—they're more than likely to be wishing to conceal their identity for nefarious reasons. The *scippatori*, for example, the bag-and-jewellery-snatchers on bikes who infest many Southern cities, always wear them—so the police (and indeed the public) have no interest at all in forcing people to put them on.

Well, just wait till he gets back, says Marisa. Never mind the law—he could at least learn to obey his mother!

*   *   *

Vincenza comes back up the alley, dangling a metal container full of milk, a kind of mini-churn. Do they sell milk wholesale round here, then, I ask her, like they used to do in England once upon a time? Vincenza looks at me as if I am mad. Or maybe, I say hopefully, you go to the farm to buy it? No, she says. She just went and milked the sheep. Down the side alley, she says. It lives in the byre there. Come and look.

The alley turns out to be mostly made up of abandoned cottages and barns. And at the end of it, a hundred-odd yards away, the town just stops dead and turns into countryside. We stop at the nearest building, a rough stone cottage, half derelict—and Vincenza points me to a door of roughly nailed planks. There she is! she says. In there!

I peer in: a long mournful sheep face stares back at me from the shadows, surmounted by a fine set of curly horns. And in there is where we keep the chickens, Vincenza says, pointing to a similar building across the alley. I look inside: the place is a mixture of garage, hay barn and chicken run. The river is just at the bottom here, she says. Do you want to walk on down?

I do. We are at the bottom of a valley here, I see as soon as we get past the tall houses of the piazza; a dip between the high hill at the back of Annunziata's house, surmounted by the church, and another more gentle slope to our left, terraced with gardens and vegetable plots, with villas surrounded by palm trees, agaves and ornate balustrades, rows of cottage-like houses with much more modest grounds; right next to us, on the lowest few terraces, is a paradise of an *orto*, a vegetable garden, with every vegetable you could imagine growing on it, cane frames bearing tomatoes, peas, beans, marrows, neat rows of salad leaves of every colour and texture planted between fruit trees, date palms, and even a couple of banana trees. Do they actually ripen here, then? I ask Vincenza.

They do. Lucky Calabrians. Up in Liguria banana trees and dates will grow all right, and even flower; but the fruits never set. And is that your garden? I ask, hopefully.

But no: it belongs, says Vincenza, to the Cavaliere Spinella. A rich man, who owns many, many hectares of land round here. And the grand villa with the stone balustrades and the palm trees

149

round it, the one at the top of the hill, just above the church.

We wander on down the lane to where the river crosses the road, wide and shallow, a set of stepping stones leading across to the far bank. There are orchards on either side of us now, apricots and peaches; across the river a grove of orange trees that seems to extend for a good mile towards the more distant hill. On the higher slopes in the distance, grove upon grove of those huge olive trees. Everything looks impossibly green and fertile: the Eldorado-phase Calabria described by Filippo the historian, you'd say, before the centuries of tree-cutting and soil erosion took their toll on the place.

It's beautiful, I say to Vincenza. Nothing like the way I imagined Calabria, parched and dry. Where are all those miserable villages perched on rocky outcrops surrounded by exhausted soil and mudslides?

Not far, says Vincenza. Wait till you go up to the high Aspromonte, and you'll see. These are just the foothills. According to Vincenza, this town was saved by its olive groves: they've been here since Byzantine times, and nobody was going to cut them down to plant corn or beans instead, were they, when olives and oil would keep them better fed anyway? Melipodio was already here long before people started running from the coast. That was the only reason people ended up in those high, steep places, land that was easy to ruin with a bit of carelessness: trying to get away from the Saracens and the malaria. But this place is a good way from the sea, and its inhabitants never needed to run. And the malaria wasn't as bad as in other places:

150

though they used to get bad floods, once upon a time, in spite of the olives. Still, the town was safe enough from bloodshed. There's been a monastery here since Byzantine times, too, Vincenza tells me. So we never sank into utter poverty, she adds. Or into benighted ignorance. Not until recently, anyway, she says, with an ironic gleam in her eye.

What a strange woman Vincenza is. I can't make head or tail of her.

She agrees with my History of Calabria, at any rate. Filippo too says that it was the olive-planting that saved this area from the terrible fate that befell much of the rest of Calabria: a long slow process of deforestation and soil erosion, begun under the Romans. First, the woodlands on the seaboard's lower slopes were cut down to plant the land, mainly for vineyards: that wasn't too bad for the ecosystem. But later, with people beginning to grow seasonal crops like corn, and the population increasing, the land was cleared further and further inland and uphill, and further still once the flight from the Saracens began. Treeless, the topsoil began gradually washing down off the slopes, leading to more clearing even higher up, and so on—and meanwhile, the once fertile and well-drained plains below, in the narrow space between mountains and sea, were eventually choked up with silt from above, and turned into marshland, which soon filled up with malarial mosquitoes . . . and the work of cultivating corn on it, where it was still possible, became positively life-threatening. Not that this stopped the *latifundia* landlords planting the stuff, or rather getting others to do so on their behalf; especially up round Cosenza, on the other side of this narrow peninsula, the side facing

151

Greece and Albania. Zio Antonio tells me, chatting about this later, that although the malaria had been conquered by then, in his youth you would still describe somebody who was looking badly under the weather as 'looking as if they've just got back from Cosenza'. Villagers from this area would walk two or three days, he says, to spend a month harvesting and threshing, half-suffocated by the damp miasma rising from the land, the dust from the corn husks lying in the close air of the hot, windless plains: like as not returning home to lie shaking and trembling in their beds for the next month, struck down by malaria. Of course they would: they were desperate to feed the hungry mouths back home.

19

Vincenza and I turn back at the river and head home to the piazza. She's just going to put her share of the milk into her fridge, she says, then bring the rest round to the Zia's. Why don't I come in and see her place?

Opening the tiny brown door, she sets off down a long narrow corridor; I follow her in, start to shut the door behind me—no, no, says Vincenza, leave it open, at least in my own place I can have some air if I want. It's so hard to breathe in this town. You could die asphyxiated . . .

We arrive in a small living-room that opens on to a kitchen beyond; there are books piled on every available surface. While she puts her milk away, I nose among the books, trying to get a few clues about Vincenza—but you'd never be able to guess anything at all from them. Every possible genre seems to be represented here, from Mills & Boon to Dante, from collections of religious tracts to knitting patterns. On the mantelpiece and the shelves, in between books, is a mixture of children's toys, bowls of boiled sweets, half-eaten chocolate bars, and very many bottles of mineral water, full or half-drunk. No further forward. There are a few framed photos inside a corner cupboard: two children in pride of place, a boy and a girl, seven or eight years old. I pick it up. Are they relatives? I ask Vincenza.

Zio Antonio has just wandered in through the open door to join us. Don't bother with that, he says. Come over here! This is the photo you really want to look at! and he points me over to the picture of a lovely young girl dressed up in late-eighties fashion, displayed on the wall by the window on to the hallway.

Our Vincenza when she was at university! he says. Wasn't she lovely!

Ah, um, yes, I say, trying to keep the incredulity out of my voice. I wouldn't have recognized her at all. Did she really go to university? That would explain a lot. I suppose it's only because she dresses the same as all the other women here, doesn't seem to have any noticeable job, that I'm so surprised. And why would going to university necessarily make you permanently adopt a new dress code? Or get you a job in a place famous for its massive unemployment levels? What a lot of idiotic preconceptions I have. And of course that would explain why her Proper Italian is so much more Proper than everyone else's round here. Vincenza either speaks purest dialect, or perfect Italian; she never falls into a jumbled, impressionistic hybrid of the two, the way everyone else does when chatting to us Northerners. Her perfect Italian is oddly stiff and precise, very formal-sounding—you'd almost believe she was reading aloud from a book when she speaks it. But I suppose books must be where she learnt it: university texts. And, alas, I don't always understand what Vincenza's saying first time around, even in Italian, what with the unfamiliar accent and the unusual academic vocabulary.

Lovely photo! says the Zio. And she still would be lovely, if only she took a bit of care of herself, eh, Vincenza? he adds. She'll get herself a man yet!

And who wants to be lovely? says Vincenza, shooting rays of hostility at the Zio. Who wants a man? She takes my arm. Come into the kitchen, she says, we'll give Antonio a bit of peace and quiet, he doesn't want to have to listen to us gossiping, does he?

Off we go into her kitchen, pressed right up against the church-retaining stone wall. Ah! she says, letting out a long breath of relief as she half-closes the door, shutting out Zio Antonio. *Qua, si, si può ragionare*, she says. In here, yes indeed, one can reason!

Well, I'm finding it very hard to think of this living space as at all conducive to rational thought: it is tiny and cramped, and I can certainly see why she spends so much of her time round at Annunziata's.

We'll make ourselves another coffee, she says. An English-style coffee this time, with milk in it. Lovely fresh milk.

154

Has she been to England, then? I ask.

Of course, she says. She's been to all the big capital cities—Paris, Rome, Vienna, London. Ah yes, she's spent time in all of them—and spent it well! London? What is there to the place? That— she clicks her fingers disdainfully—is all there is to London! To any of them. They may be great and famous cities, but when all's said and done, you're as well off here in your home town as anywhere else on earth, aren't you, however much you may like to dream of streets paved with gold and with romance . . . because here in Melipodio, *non ci manca niente:* we lack for nothing.

*   *   *

Vincenza clatters loudly away getting the espresso pot filled and on to the gas, lowering her voice confidentially beneath the racket she's making.

That photo, the one Zio Antonio didn't want me to look at, is of her own children, she says, her own lovely twins . . . Nobody likes her to talk about them. But they can't take the picture away from her, even if they can silence the words out of her mouth.

I am confused. I thought she'd never been married. Did she have these twins out of wedlock? Is that why we had to come into the kitchen before she could answer?

They're not living with you now, though? I say, eventually. Seems diplomatic enough. No, says Vincenza. They're far away, up in the North, with family—with some cousins of hers. It was a hard decision, but in the end, she thinks it's better for them to be brought up there . . . Because down

155

here in the South, she says, coming out with her catch-phrase again, *non si può ragionare*—one cannot reason.

Doing my best to decode all this—one minute the home town is a virtual paradise, the next it's no good for bringing up her own children in—I decide there must still be a terrible stigma to unwed motherhood down here; did she get pregnant while she was at university, maybe, away from the eagle eyes of the relatives, and have no choice but to get them adopted or give them to Northern relatives?

How old are they now? I ask.

No answer. The coffee is bubbling up, and Vincenza is busy with cups and sugar. She suddenly changes to a brisk, businesslike tone. Are you thinking of having children with Antonio? she asks, giving my belly an extremely sharp prod. Are you pregnant? No? Good! Let's take the coffee through! Enough nonsense!

Well, that seems to be the end of the intimate gossip . . . Back in with Antonio, Vincenza pours the sheep's milk into our coffees. Surprisingly nice. I try a cup of it on its own. Knock it back and get another.

So, Anna, have you been to visit the famous statue of the Madonna, borne miraculously to us on the waters of the flood? says Vincenza, who has now adopted the dulcet tones and flowery vocabulary of a tour guide. Maybe she really is a bit batty?

Unnerved, I reply, truthfully, that nobody has mentioned this famous Madonna to me at all. Not so far, at any rate.

What, nobody has mentioned the miraculous Madonna who came to give this town faith and

156

hope when all seemed lost, when Melipodio had been betrayed by its best friend, the river? Torrents of water, torrents of mud, overwhelmed the town; and when they had receded, there, lying in the filth, quietly waiting to be found, to bless us all, our new beginnings, our clean start, lay the Madonna . . . and no one has ever discovered where she came from, or who made her. Though the experts say she is from the Cinquecento, the fifteen-hundreds. And nobody has mentioned her to you? Vincenza lowers her brows. Well, she says, the priest has entrusted her, personally, with the care of the Madonna from the Waters and her chapel, she holds the keys to the sacristy—so we can go in the back way whenever I want. It's only over the road. Shall we go now?

Don't be foolish, Vincenza, says Zio Antonio. The guests need to be fed and rested before they start seeing the sights. They've only just got here.

All right, says she. I'll take you tomorrow morning.

Why not? I say.

And why on earth, he adds, did you tell them that Francesca had inherited the house over the road?

Vincenza dimples. Just so they would appreciate the other one more, she says.

*   *   *

A deafening racket fills the piazza again. Alberto and the motorbike gang have returned. The others go on riding, squealing round and round the fountain, while Alberto explains loudly, revving away at the accelerator of Antonello's Vespa, which he is now riding, that he needs his jacket—it's a bit nippy on the bike once you get up speed, will one of us go in and get it?

Never mind jackets, says Marisa, he shouldn't be going that fast anyway, and she forbids him absolutely to ride that bike without a helmet! Alberto hisses that he is not prepared to look like a complete idiot in front of people he's only just met, and anyway where is he supposed to find a helmet? And off he zooms, the rest of the company shooting off in his wake.

Che testa dura! says Zio Antonio admiringly. How hard-headed he is! A true Calabrese! He gives a couple of knocks with his knuckles on the wood of the empty chair beside him to show just how hard Alberto's head is—though we would call it mule-headed in English. Ah, yes, his father may have been Ligurian, but the Calabrian blood has won out! Antonio chuckles over this for a moment or two, then asks if we know the story of the Calabrese who decided to leave for Rome, a true Calabrese with a serious *testa dura*, and bumped into Jesus on the way?

No, we don't.

Well, he stopped to pass the time of day with Jesus, and Jesus asked him where he was off to, and the Calabrian said, well, Lord, down here in my own land there's no hope of making more than a miserable pittance in life, so I've decided to take to the road and try my fortune. I'm going to Rome.

So Jesus gave him a reproving look and said, come now, don't you mean, 'I'm going to Rome, God willing?'

No, said the Calabrian, I don't. I'm going to Rome. And I'm going whether God's willing or not.

158

So Jesus, outraged at this disrespect to his Father, raises his hand and turns the Calabrese into a frog; and away he hops into the ditch at the side of the road.

Exactly a year later to the day, the spell wears off, and the Calabrese finds that he's turned back into a man. So he climbs back out of the ditch and sets off on his journey again. He makes another mile towards Rome before he bumps into Jesus again.

Ah, says Jesus, nice to meet you again! And where are you off to now?

I'm going to Rome, says the Calabrese.

Have you not learnt your lesson? Do you not mean that you're going to Rome, God willing? asks Jesus.

I told you already, answers the Calabrese, I'm going to Rome, God willing or God unwilling!

So Jesus raises his hand again, turns your man into a frog again, and away he hops into the ditch, for another year.

Third time, and our Calabrese makes another mile before he bumps into Jesus again. And of course, Jesus asks him the same question.

Well, says the Calabrese, I've made three miles in three years, spent nothing on board and lodging, and as you see, I'll get there in the end, whether God's willing or not. And if he's not willing, he adds, pointing to the side of the road, well, there's the ditch, right there.

Jesus cracks up laughing: and since he's got such good entertainment out of your man, he gives in, and speeds the Calabrese on his way to Rome.

20

Right, says Ciccio, time to get this car unloaded. Now, right away, because how's he supposed to change the tyre with twenty tons of rubbish weighing the thing down? He can't even get the jack out.

Zio Antonio will give us a hand, he says, but he has to go and buy himself a packet of cigarettes first. Do we need anything from the shop?

Is it far away? I ask, not having seen a single shop between here and the centre last night.

Far away? says Zio Antonio. It's just there, in the corner of the piazza!

He is pointing at what looks like an ordinary house, the usual green floral curtain shading its open door from the hot sun—but once you examine it closely, there are indeed a few wooden boxes of vegetables lying on the pavement outside it, propped against the wall. Well, if this is what shops look like round here, we may have walked straight past any number of them.

Maybe a couple of rolls, says Marisa, who must be feeling, like me, that caraway-and-pistachio rusks weren't quite what she fancied for breakfast.

While the Zio is away, an aged gentleman, vaguely familiar-looking, joins our company. The grumpy old man from the Bar Z, of course, that's who he is, the one who told us to go home and leave Calabria alone. We have said *buon giorno* to him, and he has returned the greeting: but we're not quite sure what's supposed to happen next. He is just standing staring at us, as we go in and out of

160

Annunziata's house. Is he a bit senile? Should we say something else to him? We might just get another mouthful of abuse, though.

Zio Antonio returns from the shop and resolves the situation: he shakes the man's hand reverently and asks him how he's doing, calling him *'bellezza'*. Marisa and I nudge one another. Fancy that! People really do call one another *'bellezza'* here, then. Hard not to think it sounds rather rude— imagine saying 'How are you doing, beauty?' to a respectable aged gentleman!

A short exchange in dialect, and honour seems to be satisfied; this is Serafino, says Zio Antonio. He was worried, seeing all these unknown people going in and out of Annunziata's: he didn't realize you were family.

Obviously untrue: Serafino knows perfectly well who we are. Does he suspect us of being up to no good anyway? Or did he just fancy a closer look?

Serafino shakes our hands one by one, bowing deeply as he does so, and potters off.

Bellezza! says Marisa. Wonderful! Should we have called him that too?

No, says the Zio. You have to know the person first. You don't say it to just anybody. Only to important people. Serafino was a very big man, in his time. If someone was really, really important, he adds, you would kiss their hand as well.

Would you? Marisa and I can't wait.

So, on we go, in and out, unloading all Francesca's stuff from the car, piling everything on to the table in the first kitchen: who would presume to guess what was stored where, in a land where the exact function of rooms is so shrouded in mystery? We'll leave that to our hostesses, we decide. It would take us hours to fight our way through all Francesca's wrapping, anyway.

Ciccio is fretting about the wine—it needs to be got out of the plastic and into glass bottles before it's ruined. We females could get on with that while he changes the wheel. Where will they keep the bottles and the corking machine?

In the bathroom, probably, says Marisa, if we can just find that . . . And she opens the door just inside the hallway, opposite the kitchen, on the off-chance.

Madonna! she says. Come and look at this!

But I know already: I have been there. The Walnut Room.

This place is a madhouse, says Marisa, staring at the sea of nuts. I want to go and stay in a nice quiet predictable hotel! With a bathroom!

Don't be stupid, says Ciccio, who has stuck his head round the door to see what she's making all the fuss about. That's just Annunziata's workroom. Where she and Carmela get the walnuts ready. Crack them, and stuff them into the figs: thread them on sticks, and take them off to market. That's what they used to do last time he was here, anyhow . . . They're delicious, too . . .

*   *   *

Ciccio has dug out the jack; the spare wheel is lying in the middle of the road. He and Zio Antonio have already collected the small knot of spectators and helpers you always get within five minutes of opening the bonnet of a car in this country, and are battling to get the nuts off the wheel, when a handsome old man with a fine brush of iron-grey hair appears, crossing the piazza and heading for our side-alley to the river. He is leading an equally good-looking donkey: and he looks remarkably like the photo of Ciccio's grandad we have on the wall back in Liguria, the famous Nonno Lira, also with donkey. The newcomer makes a great performance of the wheel-changing circus and its paraphernalia getting in his way, dragging his donkey theatrically to one side as if it was about to trip over.

Buon giorno! he says, in a reproving manner.

Good day! replies Ciccio, standing up politely. Ah, he adds, grovelling, you wouldn't get problems like this with a donkey, now, would you? You've stuck to the wise old ways, *signore*!

The old man smiles grimly. Problems? he says. Problems? Do you have any idea how much it costs to get a donkey shod these days? If you can find anyone prepared to do it at all! Best place to look is the graveyard. You Northerners! he adds, with a disparaging glower at our Ligurian number-plates. You know nothing!

And with a bitter laugh, he stomps off up the road.

Bloody Northerners, he repeats to himself as if we weren't there. Think they know everything! And they know nothing!

Ciccio turns, businesslike, back to his wheelbrace. But anyone can see that he is in the throes of a deep identity crisis. Him? A Northerner?

As proposed by Filippo the historian, and amended by Francesca, a multiple sense of not-belonging has come upon him.

21

The jeep unloaded at last, and the wheel changed, Zio Antonio demands to be taken for a run in it as his reward. Let's go for a spin—he'll show us round the town. We could drive up towards his olive-planting maybe . . .

Melipodio by day is a bit run down, attractive in a slightly raffish way: once you are out of the medieval alleys where our piazza lies, the wider streets in the newer centre are an extraordinary mixture of ruins, beautifully restored buildings, and brand-new brick-and-concrete monstrosities, some really unfinished, others just giving that impression, as I now know, for taxation purposes: all standing incongruously right next to one another. Earthquakes, Zio Antonio explains. The town was badly hit by one in the 1780s: and then again in 1908, by the famous earthquake that killed twelve thousand in Reggio. It left half Melipodio in rubble all over again, too. He shows us the *Comune*, in a stuccoed eighteenth-century *palazzo* that the earthquake missed, and the home of the mysterious Cavaliere Spinella, the curlicued villa you can see from our piazza, perched right at the top of the town. It used to be a castle once, he tells us, but the family wanted something more modern, once the French had left. (That puts it somewhere in the 1840s, then.) There still don't seem to be any noticeable shops, not of the kind I'm used to anyway, with a sign outside them telling you what they're for; we have passed only one identifiable shop, just round the corner from our own piazza, whose sign bears the legend *'Polli e Stoccafisso'*—Chickens and Stockfish. Not a type of shop I'm familiar with, but must remember to check it out. Over the road from the chicken-and-stockfish sign, there is an equally intriguing road-sign. *'Grotta di Sant'Elia Speleologo'*, it says, its arrow pointing up towards the mountains of the high Aspromonte. Saint Elias the Speleologist? A holy cave expert? We need to see this grotto, and soon.

The rest of the town looks as green and fertile as the low-lying part that Vincenza showed me round earlier: the whole place is filled with climbing plants and trees of a size that would amaze a Ligurian. Out of the town and we're soon driving along under those millennial olive trees, much less menacing in the sunshine than they were last night, but still enormous. I am used to Ligurian trees a mere twenty or thirty feet high, but these ones must be double that, all gnarled and twisted with age like something from a fairy-tale forest. But then, olive trees only arrived in Liguria in the twelfth century AD. Which has always seemed like an extremely long time ago to me—until we got here. Byzantine olive trees! Zio Antonio says some of these trees really are over a thousand years old—can that be true? Can a tree live that long?

Flocks of sheep are grazing quietly beneath them, milk-sheep like the one Vincenza took me to see: a rather perturbing sight when you're not used to it, a flock of strangely tall, slim, long-legged sheep with big pendulous cow-style udders.

What a very good idea that is, I say to Ciccio, my partner in the exhausting twice-yearly job of clearing our own olive groves back home in Liguria. Why don't we get a few sheep? Save

165

ourselves all that work—and get a supply of fresh milk into the bargain. Silly idea, of course; these days the grass round our house has turned to shrivelled straw by mid-June, and there is no water to be had anywhere. What would happen to the sheep then?

We could always hire ourselves a good strong seven-year-old, says Ciccio, to take them up into the hills.

In among the grazing sheep, I have begun to notice a surprising number of those thin, pale blue carrier bags you get in Italian supermarkets, the ones people often recycle for their rubbish. It looks awful—old plastic bags just strewn about that beautiful tree-shaded pasture! They aren't blowing about empty as if they'd got there by accident, either, but are filled with something-or-other, and tied at the top. Do people just throw their garbage away into the countryside round here?

Zio Antonio laughs. The bags are filled with sand, not rubbish: and they're for holding down the olive nets come harvest time. Over the couple of millennia before the invention of the olive net, the land was thoroughly cleared of stones, he says, all carried away to build houses and walls, leaving the ground nice and smooth, easy to pick the olives off, come harvest. But then, once people started to lay nets down to catch the crop, there was nothing to weight them down with, stop them rumpling up or blowing away: till some genius thought of the carrier-bag-full-of-sand solution.

We're out of the shade of the deep olive forest now, and back into hot glaring brightness: a plain covered in miles and miles of orange groves, dark glossy leaves gleaming in the sunshine as far as the

166

eye can see. That was all only just planted when he was a child, Zio Antonio tells us. The whole plain had been nothing but useless marshland for generations, and till Mussolini got it drained you might manage to grow a bit of corn on the edges of it if you were lucky, but that was all. He remembers everyone in town being over the moon about it, their plain being usable land at last: a lot of Calabrians, he says, still speak well of Mussolini because of his great commitment to land reclamation schemes all over the Region.

Zio Antonio is not a Mussolini fan, though. He may have created a few more jobs round here; but who really got the benefit of all that government money being spent? The landowner, Cavaliere Spinella, of course, who was already rolling in it.

Was this place one of those malaria marshes, then? I ask.

Zio Antonio thinks so—but they'd got rid of the malaria by the time he was big enough to notice. He remembers these groves being guarded day and night, though, once the oranges were getting ripe. Once upon a time inheriting that orange grove of Zia Maria's would have made your fortune, he tells us, but nowadays you can think yourself lucky if you make anything at all from oranges. Not worth a dry fig.

He will show us now, he says, if only he can get his leg disentangled from my handbag strap on the floor of the car, the wound he sustained while stealing oranges when he was thirteen years old, even younger than Alberto is now—in the days when oranges were really worth something. Have we noticed his limp? Never been the same since, he says, struggling to pull up his left trouser leg in this

167

confined space, eventually succeeding in showing us a gnarled and scarred shin . . . That, he says, is where he was shot in the leg by an armed orange-grove guard.

Shot? I say, startled.

Ah, that's how precious oranges once were! And now look! You can't even give them away! But this was just after the war, and there were men with guns on every plantation, the Zio tells us. People were eating Hunger by the ladleful, as we say in Calabrese: *a fame si pigghiava c'a coppa*—but woe to the child who stole an orange! he says bitterly, rubbing the knee.

The landowners would hire in the local hard men to back up their bailiffs, it seems, once the oranges were nearly ready for picking, to guard the groves for them: although you never really knew which way round it was, according to Zio Antonio, because those same men, if they hadn't been paid to protect the harvest, would have been down there with a lorry stealing it. Still, he says resignedly, it all evened out in the end.

What, I say, and they just fired at you? At a child pinching a few oranges?

Certainly not! Just fired, indeed! The *'ndrangheta* were men of honour, in those days. They caught up with him as he tried to make his getaway, with half a dozen oranges stuffed down his shirt, took him just outside the big wrought-iron entrance gates—that was to protect the landowner, so nobody could say it had happened on his terrain—and they held him down on the grass, and carefully fired just the one bullet into his leg. A warning to the rest. Ah, life was hard in his youth, he says. But you took your punishment, glad to be left among the living.

And it wasn't long, he goes on, no more than a decade or two, till things went the opposite way, and the whole town was out watching those precious oranges just being thrown away, destroyed. To start with, according to Zio Antonio, they were just tipped straight out of the backs of the lorries and into the sea: but once people started diving in for them, even though it was just for the lark, the bulldozers were brought in. They were being dumped to keep prices up, so of course they couldn't be given away free: that would defeat the object.

This time, though, instead of the Mafia, it was the police keeping the locals at bay. Lorry-load after lorry-load of oranges, he tells us, dumped into piles as high as a house, and squashed to a pulp by big yellow bulldozers: the machines going back and forth, back and forth over them, leaving great orange-red stains all over the land.

How senseless the world is! says Zio Antonio. One day oranges are worth killing for: the next they're rubbish. But either way round, you can't have any! *Justizzia e sanità'—amaru cu 'ndi circandu!* he adds. That's an old Calabrian saying. But she won't understand that, will she? he says to Marisa. Tell her in Italian.

But I understood fine. Justice and health— bitterness to him that seeks them.

22

Here, says Zia Annunziata, dragging a sack of something over the threshold and shoving it towards me with a foot. Help us get the stuff into the house, would you!

I heave it down the hall a bit, out of the way, and step outside into the piazza, where a three-wheeled *Ape*, the classic peasant-farming transport, stands outside the door, its open truck-bed filled with baskets, carrier bags, sacks, buckets, which Francesca and Carmela are unloading. Francesca is looking very flushed and exhilarated. One of us needs to get thinner! she says, giving Annunziata a prod as she returns for another pile. Annunziata nods in her direction. You're right, one of us certainly does! she replies.

Francesca tells us that she rode home in the back of the *Ape*. There was no way they would all three fit into the cab at once. She hasn't had a trip like that in years, she was nearly shaken to bits, but she thinks it's done her good! And they bumped into Anselmo the lawyer, too, we've just missed him, look, that's his house over there across the piazza, the one with the little round table outside it . . . he's coming over to the house to say hello before dinner . . . there he is popping his head out now, go on, wave hello! (We wave to a dark-haired and rather cadaverous-looking man who is leaning out of the door in question: he waves back.) And did you hear the news? Enzo did leave us the house with the orange grove! She should have known Enzo wouldn't let her down!

170

Yes, we did hear that, eventually, I say. Though there was a bit of a hiccup first.

Wonderful, isn't it? says Francesca. We'll go and have a look at it first thing tomorrow!

Annunziata thrusts a particularly large sack of something-or-other at me.

Really, *mamma*! says Carmela. She's English! And she's a writer!

Well, call the others, then! says Annunziata.

Don't worry, I say, anxious to dispel any strange notions either of them may have about writers or Englishwomen. I can drag a sack all right.

Be careful, girl! says the Zia, as I bump one up the steps. That's your own supper in there. *Pappaluni!*

What? I say. *Pappaluni?* I can't eat *pappaluni*! I'm English. And a writer.

Carmela looks most alarmed. But Annunziata gives a bark of laughter. She's got a sense of humour, then, even if she is English, she says.

Ciccio and Marisa come out to join us. Alberto still hasn't reappeared—but he's probably round at Zio Antonio's with cousin Antonello.

What a lot of stuff! I say, as we heave buckets and bags—most of which seem to contain nothing but walnuts, leavened with the occasional lettuce or red pepper—into the hallway.

Ah, Graziella is good to us! We lack for nothing here! *Non ci manca niente!* responds Carmela, dragging another pair of overflowing carrier bags into the hallway.

This may be true, though the way everyone keeps repeating this phrase is enough to make you think that something must be lacking. Moreover, the most noticeable item we don't lack just at the

171

moment, I can't help thinking, is yet more walnuts.

Will I put them in here? I ask, efficiently opening the door to the Walnut Room.

No, no! Not in there, of course not! They need to dry out first! says Annunziata. The correct place for drying out walnuts, it seems, is in the back yard, under another bit of ramshackle roofing, hard up against the high stone terrace wall that prevents the church above from tumbling down on top of us.

Into the kitchen we go: where the big table is piled high with our offerings from Liguria. Rather than being surprised and delighted, as I'm expecting, Annunziata and Carmela are oddly off-hand and matter-of-fact about the mountain of Northern produce we've brought them: they're behaving more as if it was an expected tribute than a generous gift. I see what Francesca meant: she really did have to bring all this stuff. The olive oil is the only thing Annunziata and daughter comment on. They've given up on their own trees, they say, the price you get for the olives only just covers your expenses these days. How lucky you are up there in the North where oil is still worth something! The last straw here was when the miller stopped collecting your harvest, and you had to drive your olives over yourself to the *frantoio*, the oil mill. A fortune in petrol, two or three trips to the mill— miles away, too, now all the nearby mills have closed down—and Enzo, God rest his soul, decided it just wasn't worth it.

(I wonder, privately, why Zio Antonio is planting another four hectares of olive trees if there's no money to be made from them? I won't ask just now. Maybe Calabrians just love lamenting their lot?)

We've been keeping enough trees going just for the household's yearly supply of oil, contributes Carmela, but now my father is gone and we'd have to pay someone to do it, we're not even getting the harvest in this year.

No, says Zia Annunziata, we aren't. Because what menfolk there are left in this family are a bunch of shirkers who've left us in the lurch, every last man jack of them!

Carmela jumps up and starts nervously fiddling with dishes over by the sink.

The next bit of conversation is carried on between Carmela and her mother in impenetrable dialect.

I seize the chance to get a bit of background from Ciccio, who is doing his best not to laugh. It's a long time since he's caught up with the intricacies of the situation down here, he tells me in English—yes, we too can be impenetrable if we want!—but as far as he knows, the only menfolk left in the family are cousin Carmela's responsibility, if you want to look at it like that: which apparently Annunziata does. There is only Carmela's husband Pino, who has evidently taken no interest in agriculture for some time, if ever; and her daughters' two husbands, who work at office jobs in Milan and Turin and have never shown the smallest sign of interest in some not-very-profitable bit of land in deepest Calabria.

And what about yourself, Ciccio? says Marisa. Did you not think some of that was aimed at you? Go on! Offer to go and get the harvest in for them!

Oh Lord. Ciccio hadn't thought of that. Not looking so smug now.

Once our hostesses have sorted out their

173

disagreement, they begin to get on with the job of carrying away their booty from the North and stashing it in the secret innards of their many and various kitchens. Carmela is going to start the supper, now, she says, if anyone wants to help. Ciccio rushes to her side: nothing he likes better than being let loose in a kitchen.

Francesca settles down at the table with one of the sacks of beans at her side, and chucks a big pile in front of each of the rest of us; we'll get on with shelling the *pappaluni*, then, she says, ripping into her own pile at an impressive speed.

Marisa rolls her eyes skyward. *Pappaluni*! What sort of word is that? Sounds ridiculous. *Fagioli di Spagna*, you mean, *mamma*!

Anselmo will be round to say hello soon, says Francesca, ignoring this remark; and he says he'll help us sort out all the inheritance taxes and what-have-you, too. Why doesn't one of you get some of Salvatore's wine decanted for him to try?

What are we going to do with the place, then, *mamma*? asks Marisa.

Francesca doesn't know. We should get it done up, anyway, shouldn't we? Then we can think about it.

We met someone in the bar last night, says Marisa, a nice man—Rocco, you call him—his family has a builders' yard, and he offered to supply our building stuff, whenever we want to start sorting the place out.

Zia Annunziata, passing with another pile of Francesca's parcels, overhears this and laughs. It's a good job he did offer, she says, because you won't find any other builders' yard to supply you, not within fifty kilometres. No driver will come here to

174

Melipodio from anywhere else, not after what happened to the last one that tried.

Really, *mamma*! says Carmela. I'm sure they don't want to know about that!

But Annunziata seems to have decided that life is more entertaining if you give up on discretion.

He got a bullet in his tyres, says she, baldly. Rocco's lot didn't want the competition.

No! say we. But Rocco seemed like such a nice man!

And so he is, says Annunziata. There was nothing specially terrible about it. The same thing would happen to Rocco's drivers, likely as not, if he sent them delivering into someone else's territory. The competition were just chancing their arm, testing the ground. And the driver knew what he was letting himself in for all right. He'd been given two warnings; and even then, when he came back a third time, they only shot out his tyres. They could have shot him, couldn't they?

Bah! says Francesca. *Si mormora in paese!*

I haven't heard this expression before—'they murmur in the village' but I guess it means that this is just village gossip.

Si mormora! says Ciccio. Honestly, *mamma*! Either someone's had their tyres shot out, or they haven't. What's murmuring got to do with it?

Yes, says Francesca, but you can never be sure how it happened. Or why. No need to automatically think the worst.

Well, it certainly wasn't a hunting accident, says Zia Annunziata. It was out of season.

But you would never think Rocco would carry on like that, says Marisa. He's so *simpatico*!

Well, his family wouldn't keep their business for

175

long, would they, if he didn't do the same as everyone else? And he was very *simpatico*, very nice to the driver, as it happens, says Zia Annunziata, gathering up our beans and heading for the next kitchen. He gave the man a new job, working for him instead, a few weeks later. To show it was just business, not personal.

*   *   *

A knock at the door, and the famous Anselmo-the-lawyer appears; shortly followed by Vincenza, who tells us that Alberto won't be here till later: he's eating round with Antonello.

Anselmo has only popped in for a minute, he says, just to say hello, but we must all come round to dinner soon, his wife is dying to meet us all. Especially Francesca, the young girl who carried him to his baptism! he says, gallantly taking her hand and kissing it.

Francesca goes positively gooey at this. We are all introduced to him, one by one, with much hand-shaking and formal kissing: then Ciccio is despatched for a bottle of Salvatore's wine. Anselmo mustn't leave without drinking a glass with us, says Francesca, she won't let him! And put out a jar of the stuffed peppers, too! she calls out after Ciccio, as he heads for the stores-zone in Kitchen Three. So, how is Anselmo doing? she asks. How is life treating him?

Fine, just fine! he says.

Of course it is, says Vincenza. He's a lawyer, what do you expect? *Carta canta 'n cannolu!* she adds, swapping to deepest dialect.

'Paper sings in the tube'? No, I must have got it

176

wrong, that doesn't make any sense.

Yes it does, says Marisa. It means a legal paper, you know, a document, rolled up the way lawyers do it. Tied with tape.

A scroll, then. 'A parchment sings in its scroll.' Sounds more like a saying, at any rate.

It's an old, old saying, volunteers Anselmo. From the days when only the propertied classes would possess such a thing as a legal document, when almost nobody else could read or write. That's why the scroll sings, I think, he says, sipping appreciatively at his glass of Salvatore's wine, and raising it in a silent toast to Francesca. Because the writing goes on signifying, singing, even when it's rolled up and put away, doesn't it? Even when nobody's looking at it. Must have seemed magical stuff to illiterate people who had nothing but the spoken word at their disposal, fleeting sounds, no fixed, permanent power to them . . .

It certainly must! says Annunziata, returning from the inner kitchen. Especially when they came up against it in a court of law! Where would an illiterate man's word get him, eh, against a man of property with a few fine scrolls and a good, cunning lawyer at his side?

Ah, do you have to be so hard on a poor *avvocato*? says Anselmo, taking one of Francesca's voluptuous anchovy-stuffed peppers from the bowl that Ciccio is now proffering.

What poor lawyer is that? asks Vincenza. She has always imagined, she says, that the scroll in question was just singing along to the sweet music of the golden coins pouring into the lawyers' pockets. Is that not right, then, Anselmo? Still, whichever it is, she adds, turning to Francesca, life

177

always treats a lawyer just fine down in these parts. You've no call to worry about how Anselmo's doing, that's for sure.

But Francesca is not worrying. Not at all. Anselmo has risen from his seat to take another of her peppers: and she is basking in the golden glow of his compliments.

23

The first dish to arrive on the table tonight— though not to be actually eaten yet, Carmela says, not till after the *antipasti* and the pasta—is surprisingly un-Calabrian. A platter of *milanesi*: breaded veal escalopes. Also known as Wiener schnitzel: a dish that somehow migrated over the Alps from Vienna, to be adopted, nominally at least, by the people of Milan as their flagship foodstuff. Ciccio had to let Carmela cook them, he mutters into my ear. They were bought specially for us: modern stylish food for the delicate palates of Northerners—Milan being about as far North as you can go from here and still be in Italy. Luckily, our hostesses ran out of ideas for strange Northern food after that: the rest of the dinner is soul-food Calabrian. Red-hot anchovies for starters—you dip them in chilli powder, then flour, and fry them. That, explains Carmela, is why she couldn't do the *milanesi* second—the frying oil in the pan would have been flavoured with anchovy and chilli, wouldn't it?

Pity she didn't, mutters the ungrateful Ciccio. Might have given the *milanesi* a bit of flavour.

178

There is also a big bowl of sun-dried olives, a dish I've never heard of until now: instead of the forty days in the salt-water based *salamoia* that you use to prepare olives fresh from the tree, these dried ones just need dressing with wine vinegar—and, naturally, a dash of garlic and chilli—and leaving for an hour or two while they absorb the flavours. They are chewy, almost chocolatey, and extremely addictive.

Our *pappaluni* return to us as a pasta sauce: melted with onion, garlic, parsley and, of course, plenty of olive oil and fresh chilli, then mixed with *maniche di giacca*, 'jacket sleeves', a kind of gigantic macaroni. I was having trouble imagining how butter beans could possibly become a pasta sauce: but they really do melt, delicious, their texture complementing the pasta perfectly. I shovel away as fast as I can, hoping to finish the plateful before I'm beaten by the accumulation of ferocious chilli on the tastebuds. Nearly manage, but not quite. Still, I'm making progress: and the *pasta e fagioli* has certainly cheered Ciccio up, fortified him against the prospect of having to eat a *milanese* for his meat course. Francesca, meanwhile, is positively carried away by the pasta—she hasn't tasted this dish in twenty-five years! Hard to find *maniche di giacca* up North, and she's only had dried *pappaluni*—nothing like the real thing. Salvatore tried planting some, several years in a row, but they didn't do well at all. How has she managed without real *pasta e fagioli* all this time?

With their lifetime's chilli training behind them, my fellow travellers are dolloping spoonfuls of *'nduia* on to their pasta—the *'nduia* being the item that was advertised to me by the elder sisters back

179

in Liguria, made with minced pork and minced chilli peppers in more or less equal quantities. It turns out to be an extraordinary thing like a great rotund squashy salami, a sort of Calabrian version of the haggis, which stays in the centre of the table all the way through the meal and gets added, by the spoonful, to anything you fancy. The huge proportion of chilli acts as a preservative, explains Ciccio, who has naturally made a study of the stuff. I bet it does, too—I can't imagine a poor microbe surviving for long in that, when just a taste of it seems to have stripped the skin off my lips and tongue. As with so much of the food in this part of the world, it tastes lovely for a second or two, then explodes—as far as a weakling like myself is concerned—into a violent agony of hotness in the mouth.

The TV in the corner is on as we eat, of course—we are, notionally, watching the news, which is what everyone in Italy seems to do over dinner—and as usual I am missing most of it because everyone is talking over the top of it. No different to Liguria in that respect, at least. Now, as we move on to the *milanesi* course, the local news is announced—the bit I'm really looking forward to, hoping to get a taste of the goings-on in this new land. Carmela comes in with the *contorno*, the vegetable dishes. Green beans and aubergines from Graziella, she says, and *patate ullutte*. *Ullutte*? I repeat, intrigued, as this unknown Calabrian potato dish is set on the table—craning my neck to get a look, and raising a big laugh from Marisa, Ciccio and Francesca as I do so. *Ullutto* is just Calabrese for *bollito*—boiled. The aubergines, though, really are intriguing—a new one on me, kind of garlicky aubergine chips, the flesh cut into cubes and fried to crunchiness.

Now, just as the local TV presenter opens his mouth to say *buona sera*, Zia Annunziata startles us all by leaping from her seat and switching channels. We find ourselves watching one of those awful Italian game shows full of semi-naked girls prancing around a repellently smarmy presenter. Odd—Annunziata doesn't seem at all the sort of woman who wouldn't want to know what was going on around her. Or who would like smarmily-hosted tits-and-bums game shows.

Marisa's obviously thinking the same thing. Who's the fan of this show, then? she asks. Nobody, says Zia Annunziata. It's just that Carmela can't take watching the local news.

No, says Carmela. It's always just full of different kinds of *poveracci*, of poor souls, trying to get into the country and being ambushed or arrested or shot at. Or being sent back again, on to planes in handcuffs. Or you have to watch bodies being dragged out of the sea, drowned trying to get here . . . or they start interviewing the survivors when those *malavitosi* have taken their fare-money and then thrown them all overboard as soon as they're out of sight of land . . . wives who've lost their husbands or their children, wailing and tearing at their hair . . . And you can' t do anything about any of it. Or anything to help them. It would give you nightmares. Calabria is the gateway for the whole world, nowadays, right in the middle of everything. The poor and hungry from everywhere.

Still, look on the bright side, says Zia Annunziata. Who ever thought they'd see the day that people were flocking to Calabria in their

181

thousands! We're importing people at last—when we've always grown them for export! That's what Enzo, God rest his soul, always used to say. We're a Region that produces flesh: human flesh. Calabria's only major export for the last hundred years!—and look, she adds, pinching playfully at Francesca's ample arm as she reaches across the table for a smidgen more *'nduia*, what fine-quality flesh it is, too! You never will fit into the cab of my *Ape*, girl, if you carry on eating *'nduia* like that!—but now, Annunziata goes on, it's the other way round, isn't it? People are pouring into Calabria from all over the place. From places you've never even heard of!

Yes, says Carmela, and what would we do without them? All those Poles looking after the old folk for us, just to start with . . . ?

She now tells us the story of how she bought a holy picture from a foreign child, an Albanian, she thinks, who came round begging one day when she was running the market stall, before they gave it up for good. The woman with the next door stall not only refused to buy one: she sent the poor little creature packing with a flea in his ear, saying all sorts of ugly things about foreigners coming here and expecting to be looked after—as if Calabrians had never gone to someone else's country hoping for a bit of help to get on their feet!—and do you know, all that morning, Carmela sold and sold like she'd never sold before? Your woman next door was green with envy. So, seeing what good fortune it had brought Carmela, she called the boy over when she saw him passing later, and bought one of his pictures too. And what happened? What do you think! Carmela went on selling hand-over-fist: and

182

the woman at the next stall still sold nothing at all.

Now, she says, fixing me with a missionary stare, why do you think that was?

Annunziata saves us, in the nick of time, from the Moral of the Story. What did you all make of our own Lottery lawyer, then? she asks. Did Francesca tell you the story? How he ended up a lawyer, even though he came from an ordinary family with no hope of ever being able to afford to get their children an education?

No, she didn't. Lottery lawyer? Marisa and I abandon our table-setting, all ears.

Well, says Zia Annunziata, it happened like this. Anselmo's daddy, Vincenzo, had gone into a shop in Seminara one day, to get some cigarettes or what-have-you, and the man in the shop had no change for a thousand-*lire* note. He couldn't very well tell him to come back later for it—he wasn't from Seminara, was he? So instead of change, the man gave Anselmo's *papa* a lottery ticket. And what do you think happened?

No! we say, guessing the next bit.

Yes! It was a winning ticket—for hundreds of *miliardi* of *lire*! And there Vincenzo was, with two sons and a daughter in the house, none of them expecting anything out of life but the usual one-way ticket to the North, if they wanted anything better than scraping a living from bits and pieces. But now Vincenzo had money galore—so he just turned the lot of them into *dottori*, people with degrees, overnight!

Overnight? says Francesca. They had to work at it, go and study at the University, didn't they? The money wouldn't have been much good without the brains to use it!

Annunziata gives her an old-fashioned look. How many idiot doctors and lawyers do you meet about the place? Nearly every last one of them, as far as Annunziata can see. You just need to grease the right palms once you're at the University, and that's you sorted for life. They don't need brains. Just a nice fat wallet.

I have a horrible feeling she may be right about that. Not long ago, out with our friend Ingrid, who is studying law back home in Liguria, and some of her fellow students, a couple of them began complaining about the new law-school exam rules: from now on, they said, if you wanted to take your exams at a Southern university, you were obliged not only to register down there, but to actually attend classes for a full year into the bargain. Ruining the traditional scam they'd been expecting to take advantage of, where you just enrol for the exams down South, and (by some means or other— we didn't go into in detail, but I suppose it involved money changing hands) you automatically passed. I am pleased to report that Ingrid was disgusted with her friends: how could Northerners sit about complaining about the corrupt South, she said, while they were happily benefiting from it—and keeping the corruption going, moreover, with their own cash?

Anyway, the thing was, Annunziata says, that once Vincenzo could afford to get them all educated, he could keep his family here with him after all. They still live here in Melipodio, all of them: didn't have to emigrate to earn a decent living. Not like most people down here in those days. Her own granddaughters included. Eh, Carmela? she shouts to her daughter, who has

184

vanished into the kitchen with Francesca.

Coffee's ready, have you got the plates out of the way? responds Carmela.

Still, Annunziata adds, in spite of all that education, Anselmo is a good boy. He's never turned his back on his own: always stuck by his old friends.

Are there really lots of jobs for people with degrees down here, then? I ask, surprised.

The Calabrians round the table all answer at once. The gist being, once they've all stopped talking over one another, that there are indeed—loads of them. Just to start with, there are twice as many town halls down here as up in the North: even the smallest village has a *Comune* of its own, complete with full array of town hall bureaucrats and technocrats. Then there is all the extra administration from the various Special Funds for the South, also requiring university-educated folk: not to mention the full-time job of gathering up statistics to see if the Special Funds are having any effect on the local economy. Which they never are, of course: creating a strange conundrum whereby the money allocated to create work for the masses ends up supporting an educated elite instead. The more schooling you've had, the less you need to leave Calabria to find work: and vice versa!

*　　*　　*

Can this really be true? Good job I didn't bin Volume Five of my history book, the Modern-Day and Post-Millennium section. I snuggle up in bed with it some hours later, and read the tale of the *Cassa per il Mezzogiorno*, the funds allocated in the

1950s, with the help of the World Bank, to what the Italian government fondly imagined was a short-term 'extraordinary intervention'—*intervento straordinario*—in the economy of the South. So extraordinary that, begun in 1952, it lasted until 1992. The remnants of feudalism in the South might have been swept away by the land-laws, eliminating one major motive for discontent; but the healthy capitalist economy expected to pop up in its place had not appeared. Why was this? Evidently, because no enterprising, capital-investing middle class had ever emerged in the South. How could it have done, when social mobility hardly existed? You were born into the tiny *latifundia*-land-magnate class; or else you were born into the landless-peasant class, where you had no hope of ever accumulating any wealth, never mind investing it. Between the two groups stood only an insignificant number of functionaries, employed by the State or the landowners: tax-collectors, bailiffs, lawyers. Certainly no dynamic middle class armed with risk-capital and raring to start investing. What was to be done? Capitalism had to be shown to work. Italy's American partners in post-war reconstruction were only too aware of Italy's geographical position right next door to the communist bloc; and of the strength of anti-capitalist feeling among ordinary Italians. An extraordinary intervention! The World Bank would step in and provide investment capital, alongside the Italian State: the problem should be solved within a decade.

Forty years later, the *Cassa per il Mezzogiorno* was finally abolished, amid huge graft-and-corruption scandals. Although nowadays there certainly was a middle class, it was nothing like the dynamic, investing, profit-making, job-creating force the *Cassa* had dreamed of. Filippo and friends, with an impressive array of graphs and statistics, outline the apparent mystery of a Calabrian economy that produces less than half of the EU average per head, yet manages to consume goods amounting to over three-quarters of the average. Public money is still making up the difference, above or below the counter, they conclude. That insignificant number of functionaries, tax-collectors, bailiffs and lawyers has simply reproduced itself exponentially, virtually all of it living on public money in one guise or another. The healthy capitalist economy has still not taken off.

24

Has the washing-machine broken down, then? I ask cheerfully. I have just opened the French windows for a morning stretch; only to find Zia Annunziata out here on the balcony again, scrubbing away at her washing-vat.

Zia Annunziata looks mystified. Perhaps she's forgotten she's got a washing-machine?

No, she says, I don't think it's broken, but you'll have to get Carmela to turn it on if you want to use it, it's very hard to understand . . . we've hardly used it since we bought it.

No, no, I say, it's not that I want to use it, I just saw you washing everything by hand so I thought . . . ?

But I thought wrong. Zia Annunziata is not impressed by the machine. Ah, *bella mia*, she says, there is nothing like laundry that's been washed by hand in nice spring water with proper soap you've made yourself. Is there?

No, I say, somewhat uncertainly, wondering whether the machine has some separate supply of Nasty Water with which to perform its evil works. The Proper Soap You've Made Yourself looks good, though. It's kind of pearly-gold with coloured streaks in it, not at all like the only other example of its genre I've met, a grey, gritty, sludgy-looking item made by an extremely ancient lady in Liguria from the sediment left at the bottom of her olive-oil vat, mixed with the ashes out of her wood-stove. Didn't look like a tradition you'd be too sorry to lose.

Bah! says Zia Annunziata scornfully, when I describe the stuff to her. That's because Ligurians are tight-fisted penny-pinchers! Thrift is a good thing, but you mustn't carry it to extremes! Zia Annunziata makes her soap out of nice, new oil, certainly not from last year's old dregs. And you only have to strain the water from the ashes properly through a cloth and you'll have no grit in it. Oh, and the coloured streaks are leftover bits of bought toilet soap she saves to perfume it with . . . Some people say a bit of grit helps clean the clothes better, of course; but Zia A. reckons it just wears them out faster. Elbow-grease is all you really need.

Right. I think I'm getting the message. I won't be trying to use the nasty, complicated thing in the bathroom then. I'll just learn how to use the concrete vat instead. Hopefully it won't be too nasty and complicated.

A ghastly groan and a set of loud creaking noises comes from the bedroom. Ciccio is getting out of bed. The womenfolk on the balcony go into panic mode. Coffee! He must be served his coffee immediately! Zia A. calls to Carmela, who is down at the far end of the balcony, along with Francesca, to go down and make him some. But Francesca, proud of her son's simple Englishwoman, tells them not to worry; Anna is perfectly capable of making coffee. She's a very handy girl!

Zia A. and daughter both look dubiously at me. A woman who stays in bed this late, and who seems never to have eaten any normal food in her life? Could she be capable of making a decent cup of coffee?

Aha! Little do they know that I am already au fait with their coffee arrangements, made some yesterday while they were at Graziella.

She'll need to grind some beans, though, says Carmela.

I begin to feel slightly dubious myself. Will there be some thrifty medieval coffee-grinding device down below, that I won't know how to work?

Everything's out on the table downstairs, Anna! says Francesca brightly. You'll have no trouble at all!

Oh Lord. Mustn't let her down. I set briskly off for the staircase, while Zia A. and Carmela shout instructions after me: how to turn on the gas (why have they turned it off, I wonder?), how to find the breakfast biscuits, unless I want bread in which case it's in the other cupboard . . . and the whereabouts of the cups, the plates, the smaller espresso pot and so forth. I trip gaily down the

189

stairs, calling out agreement to everything, though I can't really hear what they're saying with them both talking at once. I won't be needing the smaller espresso pot, at any rate. I shall use the big one. Up North, Italians always become severely agitated if you drink more than a couple of their tiny cups of coffee at this time of the morning: they are convinced that it will make you *nervoso*. And to judge by that small-pot recommendation, they feel the same way down South. So, while anxious Italian eyes are fixed upon their laundry, I shall have a huge enormous secret cup of coffee all to myself, down here in the kitchen, and then take a pair of acceptably minuscule ones upstairs.

As I'm hunting for the gas tap, a car starts hooting away over and over again, just outside in the piazza. Our big fat jeep must be getting in the way of somebody trying to get down the alley. I stick my head out of the door to ask if I should move it.

No, no! says its driver, a large lady with a five o'clock shadow who has already got out of her car and is now opening its boot and pulling numerous suitcases out of it, which she is placing carefully in the middle of the road, spaced out at two-foot intervals.

Her vehicle is actually a travelling household linen shop, she explains, and she was just hooting to let us know she was here, in case we need a towel or a dishcloth or a hand-crocheted net curtain . . . Would I like to have a look? Before I have time to say no, she has opened the cases, each of which turns out to have a laundry-rack ingeniously concealed within it, and begun spreading her wares all over the piazza with gay abandon.

No! I don't want to be responsible for this . . . ! What if a car wants to get past? I don't want any household linen, thank you, honestly, I say, to no avail. But look at this set of hand-crocheted doilies . . . ! Or here is a whole bedspread, a traditional Calabrian one, all done in *filo scozzese!*

Scottish thread? What on earth can that be? Doesn't sound very traditionally Calabrian. The bedspread is enormous, snow white, and beautifully crocheted, it is true—but I can't see how it would fit into my life back in Liguria.

Francesca comes downstairs now, praise the Lord, and joins me in the piazza. I leave her to deal with the linen-and-traffic-jam situation, and scuttle off back to my nice easy coffee-making task instead—only to find that Carmela has made the coffee already, while I was engaged in frivolous household-linen inspection. Oh well. And she's taken one up to Ciccio, too.

Francesca now spends half an hour standing in the middle of the road at the improvised linen shop, completely unfazed by the town's traffic having to detour round an ever-growing assortment of curtains, sheets and tablecloths: eventually, after all the woman's trouble, she buys nothing at all. And shows not the slightest sign of embarrassment about it.

*   *   *

Antonio's daughter, Cousin Concetta, has been up to the North visiting quite a few times, and she knows Ciccio and Marisa well, though she's new to me. She bounces in amid lots of hugging, telling me that her name is really Maria Concetta, but nobody

191

bothers with the Maria part. A very Southern name: or a very Spanish name, more likely, left over from those several centuries of Spanish rule. Down here in the Hispanified South there is a long tradition of naming girls for the various phases of the Virgin Mary's life. You can be Maria Assunta, Mary Assumed (into heaven) just as you can be Maria Concetta, which would mean 'Mary Conceived'—in the sense of post-conception. Our Aunt Annunziata, of course, is 'Mary of the Annunciation'—Mary Announced. Most people just leave off the 'Maria' part, because there are so many of them about.

So, Sconsolata, says Marisa. Have you caught yourself a husband yet?

Sorry, what? I interrupt. I'm sure I was just introduced to this cousin as Concetta, but now she seems to be called 'Sconsolata'—Mary Disconsolate. Did I mishear?

Marisa, once she's finished giggling, tells me that Sconsolata is just the nickname they gave Concetta when she was up in Liguria—people really were called that once, down here in Calabria, you know! she says, laughing some more, as if being called Disconsolate was plainly much more absurd and hilarious than being called Conceived. Or Announced. They gave her that name because she never did manage to find herself a man up North, even though her family was desperate for her to bring one home, Marisa explains.

Too busy enjoying myself, says Concetta. And is your brother still available? she asks Marisa, with a grin at me and a roguish bat of the eyelashes at Ciccio. What you need, she tells him, is a good Calabrian girl. A proper hard-working woman. I

192

hear that this one hardly even bothers to make you your coffee of a morning: just leaves it to the rest of the womenfolk, she adds, giving me a broad wink. Terrible way to carry on. Give her the sack and take me instead . . . !

So you're still single? says Marisa.

Concetta's had three proposals since she last saw Marisa. But they were all *deficenti*—idiots. Anyone worth having is either married already or left town years ago.

Well, says Marisa, we'll have to take you out on the town for the Friday night *passeggiata*. See if we can give you a hand . . .

The *passeggiata?* And what on earth makes you think we would have a *passeggiata* here in Melipodio? says Concetta/Sconsolata. This is the serious small-town South.

What? says Marisa. Seriously? No *passeggiata*?

I am amazed too. I've always imagined that the evening *passeggiata* was the most traditional of Italian traditions—the dressing up in your best of an evening, parading around the main piazza, the opposite sexes checking one another out, chatting one another up. In fact I'm sure I've heard somewhere, can't remember where, that down here in the South the girls would have to walk in one direction round the piazza, and the boys go the opposite way, so the parents could easily spot any hanky panky and nip it in the bud.

Really? There's no *passeggiata* here? I chime in.

In Palmi, yes, or Locri, says Concetta; but that's degenerate big-town behaviour as far as we're concerned. Here the only time we're allowed to get all dressed up and check one another out is at Sunday Mass. Any man who fancied you would have to go and talk to your father before he dared say a word to you, anyway. He certainly wouldn't just start chatting you up and inviting you out, not without the parental blessing! Or—*poum!* she says, imitating a shotgun.

So did these three *deficenti* of hers really approach Zio Antonio first?

Two of them did, says Concetta—but only because they knew she would have spat in their eye if they'd spoken to her! They just hoped her father would see them as such good catches that he'd lay down the law on her.

You're all mad down here, says Marisa with conviction. Come back up to the North—get yourself a job—move in with us! I don't know how you can stand it!

No, no, says Concetta, she couldn't do that, she would never leave her father, he's getting on now, and her mother's very frail too—who would look after him?

A series of long hoots from a car horn outside in the piazza drowns our conversation. It must be another travelling shop. I nip to the front door in case it's a kind of shop I don't want to miss. I'm not sure if I could handle this haphazard shopping technique in the long term, but for now it's quite exciting to have no idea what kind of retail therapy will be coming up next. Francesca and Carmela are sitting chatting on the chairs by the door, though, and the car is already on its way out of the piazza. Was that another shop? I ask.

No, no, they both say, laughing. That was just the Avvocato Pipperi-pipperi.

The Lawyer what? I say. How could anyone be called that? Is it Spanish?

Certainly not. *Pipperi-pipperi* means 'toot-toot' in Calabrese. And he's called that because he always hoots his horn wherever he goes.

25

Vincenza takes her bottle of water in one hand, and my arm in the other. Come on! she says. The Madonna! And she frogmarches me out into the piazza, where she stops to say something to Giuseppa, who is at her laundry-vat again today. Wait here with Giuseppa! she tells me now, and disappears into her house, to return with an impressively large, ornamental and ancient-looking key. Giuseppa winks at me.

We're off to the sacristy, then, says Vincenza. And we head off towards a small chapel just past the end of the piazza, less than fifty yards away. A plain stone chapel, very austere and gloomy-looking compared to the twirly wedding-cake-style plaster façades I'm used to seeing on churches in our part of Italy. In we go through a side door, to find ourselves in a musty corridor-storeroom, piles of old spare benches, sheaves of those tall crosses you use for saints' processions leaning in a corner, rows of shelves covered in cobwebs and candle-ends, the paintwork yellowed and cracking on the wood panelled walls . . . I head for the ladder-like staircase at the end of the corridor . . . No, not that way! We turn left into the body of the chapel and find ourselves on the raised platform at the back of the church, behind a marble altar covered in faded crochetwork. Between the altar and the pews,

195

ranged to the right, stands a gigantic bulging sculpture of what looks, from this rear view, like a pile of twice-life-size Rubens buttocks, all pink and white with a hint of sky-blue shading here and there. Or perhaps a pile of monster profiteroles? A domed triangular object in solid Wedgwood blue surmounts the pile. Edging round towards the front, past the altar rail, to obtain the view the sculptor intended, I find that the blue object is in fact the blue veil covering the head of the Virgin Mary; it is the Madonna in the process of being Assumed up into Heaven, nestling comfortably amongst the celestial profiteroles as she ascends. Candy-floss colours and Shirley Temple looks.

No way, I say to myself, was this Madonna, who is built all of a piece with the bulging clouds that surround her, mystically borne here on a flooding river—unless it was one as broad as the Ganges. And even then, she looks as if she's made of plaster or papier-mâché or something equally friable; certainly nothing that could withstand a good dousing. Maybe it's another of Vincenza's peculiar jokes? No, but Zio Antonio confirmed the story, didn't he . . .

Now, though, I see that Vincenza, rather than standing next to me as I admire (or otherwise) this Madonna, is shifting impatiently from one foot to the other over at the far side of the church.

Take no notice of that Disney rubbish, she says scornfully. Come over here and see the real Virgin!

And yes, she is standing next to a most restrained and peaceful three-quarter life-size carved statue of the Madonna, no lurid colours at all, just the natural pale beige of the stone. She looks early Renaissance, her expression calm and contemplative, and she's balanced on a plinth with medieval bas-reliefs that can't be the original one.

The plinth was already here, Vincenza confirms: it had been standing here empty all that time, waiting to receive her when she was born. Born out of the mud and the filth . . . ! she adds in most vehement tones. What strange ways she has about her, I think, trying hard not to stare at her. Did she really say that? But then, all sorts of words that would be odd or poetic in Italian might be perfectly ordinary in dialect.

Vincenza is gazing intently at the statue, totally involved, mirroring the Madonna's contemplative look. After a while she speaks again, mostly to herself, it seems. She wasn't like this before, she says . . . she looked better. Her expression is changing . . . since she was shut away in here. She isn't so pretty, these days. Could it be the air? So dry and dead. Or the light? Just these few gloomy rays . . . She was so beautiful when she first came . . . now some days she looks almost ugly. Sad . . . and ugly.

I'm having a bit of trouble with the time-scale on this Madonna story. I must have misunderstood how long ago the flood occurred—I was imagining an event some centuries back, but if Vincenza saw her when she was first found, it must have been much more recent, mustn't it? Unless maybe she means that they moved the statue from one church to another? I'm lost. And I'm worn out with linguistic difficulties, anyway. I can't be bothered asking when exactly all this happened. I'm sure I'll be told soon enough.

I wander over to the wall a few feet behind the Virgin, just inside the door, where there is a big,

197

almost life-size cross carved from some dark wood
. . . the cross itself looks very primitive, though I
don't know if that tells you a lot about the age of an
artefact down here. And coming closer I see that
there are mystical objects pinned all over it,
talismans and amulets, charms and symbols,
cabbala-things dotted about on the wood like a
very untidy insect collection.

On the crosspiece hang tiny models that must, I
think, be meant as the insignia of every trade in the
town—a miniature sickle, a pair of tongs, a two-
handed saw, a hammer, something that looks like a
leather bottle; and various other implements I can't
identify. Lower down, though, there is a haphazard
chaos of unlikely items. Wax replicas of arms and
legs and feet, of long thin chilli peppers and fishes
and hearts. Bits of gold chain, little bunches of
what look to be dried berries and corn stalks; even
individual beans pinned through the heart. Right at
the bottom a distinctly pagan-looking pair of
objects, a tiny raw clay mask that looks a bit like a
bearded Bacchus, vine-leaves in his hair—except
that he has his mouth wide open in some kind of
roar, and his tongue is sticking right out, curling
down on to his chin in a most obscene manner:
below him, a model of a severed hand with its two
middle fingers curled into the palm, the index and
little fingers stretched out straight. The tips of the
outstretched fingers are painted, even more oddly,
bright red: as if the owner had varnished not just
their nails but their whole fingertip.

I prod at it, trying to see the other side. Is it
actually meant to be nail varnish? Can't be, it goes
right the way round.

Vincenza slaps my hand away. Ah, don't touch

that! she says. It's to keep off curses, ward off the evil eye! And she does the sign with her own hand—jabbing the two straight fingers forwards, as if trying to poke an invisible assailant's eyes out. You'll have to do this too, now that you've interfered with it, she adds, agitatedly. Go on!

I do my best, feeling remarkably silly. Not towards the Cross! says Vincenza, even more agitated. Point the horns at the door! That's where evil would come from, evidently, isn't it?

Well, sorry to be so stupid! I try again. Got it right this time, apparently.

And why are the fingertips red like that, then? I ask. As if they'd been dipped in a pot of paint?

Vincenza just looks at me as if I was potty.

They're always done in red, she says.

26

Ciccio can't wait to see Paolo's face, he says, when he catches him behind that jewellery stall. We're off to Palmi market, where he should be today: with Francesca and Zio Antonio, who can't be bothered finishing his olive-tree planting, and says he fancies a ride. We settle down in the car, munching our way through a bag of a fruit called *giuggiule* in dialect, which doesn't have a name in Italian because you can only get them here. *Giuggiule*— pronounced joo-joo-leh—look like dark pinkish-brown olives but are sweet like a fruity kind of date, and have turned out to be seriously addictive. They grow wild, says Zio Antonio, on a sort of evergreen bush that looks a bit like a scrubby olive.

He'll show me if we pass one on the way.

Ciccio continues his jewellery saga as we drive: the bit where he and Dario got arrested. He never ever told his mother about it, he says, because she would have been too worried by it.

Maybe you shouldn't tell her it now, then? says Zio Antonio.

Nonsense! says Francesca. I can't possibly not hear it now.

They'd been selling so well, Ciccio says, that after only a couple of weeks their stock was running low. And although they'd already made more money than they'd hoped for in their wildest dreams, it seemed a pity to give up the jewellery-selling when they were on a roll; not only that, but it was a brilliant way of getting to chat to local girls—no mean feat for a stranger in Calabria! Anyhow, they had arranged with Daniele, the friend who'd sold them the wares in the first place, and with some relative or other who worked in the train station in Diano Marina, that if they needed any more, Daniele would get another couple of boxes to this relation, who would use his railway connections to get it sent down for free, in the guard's compartment of a southbound train.

So, from the market café, Ciccio rang up Liguria and asked if he could get some more stuff to sell, as arranged. Of course, said the mate: as soon as he could. He would call them back on this number— there was a severe shortage of telephones in Calabria in those days, and the mobile phone had not yet been invented. Next day, he rang the bar and asked for Ciccio. The stuff will be in the station at Palmi on the last train tomorrow evening, he said.

OK, said Ciccio to Dario, who was waiting at his side. We're on, the stuff'll be here tomorrow evening, at Palmi station . . .

So now Dario and Ciccio sat there at their bar table sipping their *aperitivi* and trying to remember the layout of Palmi station. Can you just walk straight on to the platforms, or has it got those gates that stop you getting on if you don't have a ticket? If so how will they get to the train? Which they'll have to do, because, first, they don't know what the guard's name is, or even what he looks like: and second, he probably won't want to be seen carrying inexplicable boxes off his compartment and down the platform, will he?

What are you doing, trying to collect a parcel? says an interested eavesdropper at a nearby table, giving them a knowing wink. And he offers, just like that, to help them get to the train. No problem, he says, just mention my name. Go to the girl at the left-hand ticket window and say '*Mi manda Morgante*'—Morgante sent me. She'll see you right.

A Norman name! I interrupt, irrelevantly. Was Morgante tall and blond and blue-eyed?

Ciccio ignores me pointedly, and gets on with the story.

Amazing, this Calabria, he and Dario agreed, once their new friend had left. How cool everyone is, the way they would never sink so low as to ask questions, they just assume you're probably up to something dodgy; and, whether you are or not, they're ready to give you a hand. Marvellous.

So Ciccio and Dario presented themselves at the ticket window next evening and claimed to have been sent by Morgante; little knowing that the other half-dozen innocent-looking passengers

201

around the place—the woman arguing about her season ticket at the other ticket window, the respectable middle-aged couple sitting on the bench, the two youths hanging about the entrance hall, even the pair of tramps sitting on the steps outside the station, apparently stone drunk—every last one of them was a police officer. They had actually cleared the public out of the station in his and Dario's honour! And as soon as the train pulled in, the whole lot of them suddenly leapt to their feet, shouting at the top of their voices, pulling out their guns and pointing them at him and Dario, roaring *'Fermi!'*—'Halt!' and jumping on them mob-handed, flailing handcuffs at them, shouting into their radios . . . they were expecting a shoot-out with a pair of big-time drug-dealers . . . ! And how disappointed they were to find that the Stuff they were waiting for was nothing but cheap junk jewellery!

Francesca is horrified. Thank goodness he never told her any of this at the time! She would never have let him go anywhere ever again!

Best of all, the forces of law and order had pulled their guns out so ridiculously early that their Diano connection, the guard, had been thoroughly alarmed: he just jumped out, left the two parcels on a bench, and nipped back on the train: so nobody knew who exactly had dropped them off. By the time the officers realized that the only charge they were likely to be able to bring was for evading payment on a railway parcel, there was no way they could work out who on the train was to blame. So there were no repercussions, back home in Diano Marina, on the kind bloke who had done them a favour.

We're in Palmi's city centre now—a big wide arcaded central square, all stone flags, pavement cafés and designer shops, that would put small scruffy Melipodio to shame. But this place must have been earthquaked too, you realize as soon as you leave the centre and find yourself driving through tedious seventies apartment blocks and dingy cement. The town is right by the sea, and from the centre, where we have stopped for a quick coffee and a *ricotta* pastry or two, you can see the fringe of palms you'd expect to find along the shoreline of a town with such a name. But when I propose going for a walk down to the sea, Zio Antonio tells me that it'll take me a good hour—it's several kilometres away. But I can see it from here, I say—it's just over there, at the end of the road!

The sea certainly is just at the end of the road, yes: but you can't get down to it. Not without doing a very long detour. Palmi was built by the survivors of a Saracen attack on the city of Tauriana, some time in the tenth century. Tauriana was looted, pillaged and razed to the ground. And its citizens— those who had made it out of there alive—had no intention whatsoever of going through that sort of thing again. If you walk to the end of that road, you'll find yourself perched on top of a great, high, inaccessible cliff. There's no way down to the sea here: and, more importantly to the original inhabitants, there's no way up from it, either.

*　　　*　　　*

Francesca and Ciccio have thought up a way of making the encounter with Paolo even more entertaining. He's never set eyes on Francesca, has

203

he: so if Ciccio can manage to spot him without his spotting Ciccio back, we can point her in the right direction, and she'll go up to him and start telling him what a disgrace he is, going around selling women's jewellery like a limp-wristed Northerner . . . !

Brilliant. The pair of them cackle evilly at the thought of the poor man's discomfiture. We set off through the market, looking for a jewellery stall. Easier said than done, though, there are so many stalls—and it's hard not to stop and look at everything, the stalls are laid out so fantastically. We pass through the fruits-and-vegetables zone first, the wares all scrubbed and shining and piled up into impossible forms like static firework displays, or carefully arranged into columns, domes, pyramids, pyramids-with-a-swirl . . . Look, *giuggiule*! Quick, let's buy another bag! Now the *salumeria* area, whole salamis of every shape and size, long and thin, short and fat, laid out in complex whorls and zigzags and cornucopias . . . Further on, stall after stall of fresh fish: then of dried and pickled and salted fish—*baccalà*, stockfish, sardines and anchovies, preserved by every possible method and in every possible format—whole, filleted, halved, heads on, heads off, rolled up in jars, with or without tomato, chilli, vinegar; or spread out in thin slivers, under oil and lemon and flat-leaf parsley, ready to be eaten as a quick snack by hungry market-goers . . . While I've been taking in the stalls, Francesca has, it seems, been concentrating on the stall-holders. There are hardly any Calabresi running the stalls here at all! she says, after ten minutes or so. They're all foreigners! Those people selling you the fruit
204

sounded like Albanians or something—most of them look like North Africans, Moroccans . . . what can have happened to all the local people?

Milan? Turin? I say.

Denmark! says Ciccio.

Too many supermarkets around these days, says the Zio. You can hardly make a decent living with a market stall any more . . . not as a full-time job. Annunziata and Carmela gave theirs up too, didn't they? They sell their stuff on through an Algerian boy with a *frutta secca* stall, a dried-fruit-and-nut stall, these days.

At last we've come into a clothes-and-jewellery type zone—and look, says Ciccio, that one there! That's Paolo! He's starting to pack up, look. See him? Go, *mamma*! he tells Francesca, and does his best to keep out of sight by squeezing round the side of a ladies-underwear stall, whose owner looks at him askance.

We can't actually hear the exchange from over here, but we can see it's working a treat. The utter consternation on Paolo's face when this unknown respectable old lady starts, unprovoked, to cry shame on him for his unmanly wares and call his virility into question, is perfect. Ciccio is creased up with laughter within seconds, and hardly lets the drama run on at all—he can't contain himself, and rushes straight over to throw his arms around the sort-of-cousin, who is overwhelmed with confusion at this new development, and takes several long seconds to grasp that the two unexpected events are interconnected. Zio Antonio and I arrive at the stall just as he's got it, been told who Francesca is—No! Ciccio's mother! Really?—and is giving her a big hug too, more in relief than merriment.

Inside this snack bar—a kind of Calabrian fast-food bar, recommended by Paolo, who is coming to have lunch with us as soon as he's finished packing up and got his van out of the road—you choose a plateful from a glass display cabinet full of interesting-looking things I have mostly never seen before. Making it a bit difficult to choose anything. The only items in the whole cabinet that I recognize from my North Italian sojourn are the plate of roasted red peppers and the Parma ham. There are things that look a bit like Scotch eggs, which Francesca tells me are rice, not sausagemeat: there are other things that look a lot like meatballs; then there are triangular pastry things that look like Indian samosas . . . there are cheeses that look a bit like mozzarellas, various types of salami, all of a threateningly deep orange colour . . .

Try one of these, says Ciccio, pointing at something on the plateful of dainties he has just chosen. A vaguely triangular brown meaty-looking thing . . . Francesca took one of them, too. What is it?

Half a goat's head, says he with glee, waiting for my reaction.

And it is, too—a head sliced vertically from top to bottom so that you can see the half-a-jawbone with all the little goaty teeth still in it. And the tongue, slit in half. And the brain, also neatly halved. I do my best to spoil his fun by remaining calm and collected.

Look, he goes on provocatively, how many tasty

titbits you get in a head! A nice bit of tongue, a couple of mouthfuls of delicious tender cheek meat; some people swear by the eyeball—and the brain is delicious, he says, poking it with his fork. Especially with a bit of olive oil and a drop of balsamic vinegar.

Maybe later, I say coldly, taking my turn to choose a more or less random plateful from the girl behind the bar. Which does not include any half-goat-heads. He knows perfectly well that I need time to think over an outlandish new foodstuff before I can try it.

The peppers I've chosen turn out to be stuffed with a spicy savoury rice (you would get a breadcrumb-egg-and-parmesan mixture at home in Liguria—this is definitely healthier Mediterranean-cuisine stuff) and taste powerfully oriental; while the little plaited-looking white cheese I've chosen, which I imagined would be something like the mild, rubbery mozzarella it reminded me vaguely of, turns out to be crumbly and sharp, like a mellowed-out version of Greek feta, and like nothing at all that I've ever come across up in the North . . . And the little pastry triangles are stuffed with a similar but softer kind of cheese mixed with very garlicky spinach . . . Lovely. Coriander in them, too. The meatball thing is wrapped neatly in a vine-leaf . . . and now it dawns on me. That's why this stuff seems somehow familiar. Shepherd's Bush, my old London stamping ground! The myriads of Middle Eastern, Greek and Turkish snack bars around the Goldhawk Road, to be precise. Even the tumbler of wine we're given with our snacks reminds me strongly of the powerful Algerian wine they give you in the all-night Turkish Cypriot place near my old home on the Uxbridge Road . . . It would be interesting to do a sort of food safari down through Italy, recording the minor shifts in ingredients that take you slowly from a kind of Nordic ham-and-egg-flavoured cuisine way up at the German border down to the almost fully-fledged Middle Eastern flavours that dominate here, so close to Greece, Turkey and North Africa.

Ciccio and Paolo have been busy reminiscing as they eat; now, as they pick their way through their goat-heads, they are on the aftermath of the gunpoint arrest at the station.

Remember how we had to come and get you and Dario out of prison? Paolo is saying gleefully. And the *carabinieri* were still so certain that they'd caught a couple of North Italian drug-dealers . . .

(Try this bit of tongue, Ciccio says to me. Go on, just this little bit! You've eaten tongue before, I know you have! Yes, I reply, but not while it was still lolling about inside the creature's mouth! Oh, all right then.)

. . . weren't they? They thought you were so clever that you'd somehow managed to pull the wool over their eyes, but they couldn't quite work out how!

(Yes, all right, it tastes fine, I say. I knew it would. But it's the thought that counts, not the taste.)

They had him and Dario locked up in that brand-new Mafia building, you know, Paolo is telling Francesca. *Il Palazzo di Giustizia con Aula Buncker*! The Palace of Justice with Bunker Courthouse. No lightweight, your son!

Did they? *O Signor!* Francesca thanks the Lord she knew nothing of it. Her only son shut inside that terrible place! She would have been worried out of her mind!

Why, what is it? I ask.

You will have seen it on the television, says Francesca, even if you didn't know what it was. They always have reporters with microphones standing outside it whenever there's a big Mafia trial on . . .

It's a gigantic concrete bunker, adds Ciccio— they've built it to resist rocket-propelled grenades, dynamite, nuclear explosions probably, you name it: the law-courts are down below, under tons of reinforced steel.

The government decided to build it, says Paolo, because every time they had a Mafia trial, they ended up looking like idiots—there were Mafiosi being rescued, or witnesses being shot dead, or even worse, the State Prosecutors being shot dead . . .

Why don't we drive down and have a look at it, says Ciccio. It really is amazing. They do all the trials with the *pentiti* in there: the Mafiosi who've turned coat and are ready to grass everyone else up.

So we all bundle into the jeep, and set off to inspect the historic site of Ciccio's incarceration. Six-thirty, and the *passeggiata*—that shameless invention of modern immorality—has already started up in Palmi's main square. Where a mere hour ago there was nothing but wide stone flags and spaciousness, promenading bodies are now packed chock-a-block, all primped and perfumed and aftershaved, the sexes mingling with not more than a foot or two of space to spare between them. Drawing closer to our goal, though, reaching the top of the Palace-of-Justice-with-Bunker-Courthouse road, we hear wailing sirens nearby: and find a set of armoured cars moving slowly towards us, three abreast, blocking the road completely. A disembodied *carabiniere* voice shouts at us with great urgency through a megaphone: we are to do a U-turn, now, immediately, right where we are, and be on our way.

Some sort of high alert going on in there, by the looks of things. All we can see from here is a high fence, made out of what look like vertical strips of steel fifteen feet high: and, facing outward from it, a ring of armoured cars with machine-gun things mounted on their roofs, which (to make matters worse) are pointing right at us. An eerie greenish light below, a set of blinding spotlights above. Quick! says Francesca urgently. Do what they say! Some confusion ensues as we and the other three cars alongside us all try to follow these instructions at the same time, causing the U-turns we are attempting to execute to resemble more of a W than a U. Eventually we get ourselves disentangled, and away we go.

Is it something about me, I wonder? Other people do pleasant, attractive things when they go touring. They get to visit fabulous, beautiful places, go to elegant restaurants to eat fabulous, beautiful food. Why is it that I am the sort of person who gets taken, by people who claim to wish me well, to be force-fed goats' heads, and threatened by armoured cars outside state-of-the-art Mafia-resistant jail-and-courthouse complexes?

I mention this to my companions, in a horrible whingeing tone of voice, and they repent. They will make up for it all. It is not too late. We will go for a drive along the coast, they say, before it gets properly dark. Soon we are at the edge of Palmi's perch on its high cliff. Those would-be marauding Saracens must have been thoroughly frustrated: there really is no way up to the city from the sea, none at all. We stand a while and watch the waves crashing way down below, at the bottom of the vertical rock-face. The coast faces westwards here, into the setting sun; and there, in the distance, are the tiny Aeolian Islands, where the wind-harps come from. You can see the volcanoes of Stromboli and Etna perfectly, outlined against the sunset. Thank you. Much better.

28

A warm sultry afternoon back in Melipodio, and we're off to visit the house with the orange grove at last. Zio Antonio and Annunziata have convinced Francesca, between them, that there is nothing disrespectful to her brother Enzo-God-rest-his-soul about visiting the place before his month-mind wake. He would have laughed to see you sitting there fretting about what people would think, not daring to go and see what sort of state it was in! You know he would, Francescella!

So here we are, walking on down an alley towards the river, the cobbles slowly getting muddier and muddier, until now we're right at the end of the row, and the vista opens out on to gently undulating land, all put to rows and rows of vegetables. Beyond the vegetables are vineyards; beyond the vineyards flows the river. We can't be far along from the stepping-stone place I visited with Vincenza, at the end of the alley where our milk-sheep lives. Alberto is tootling along beside us on the old Vespa the Zio has dug out for him, happy and helmet-free. (Marisa has given up on the helmet business, after Antonello told her the terrible tale of a boy who, riding into Seminara wearing a helmet, was knocked off his bike with a big knobbly stick by an old man who was set on protecting the handbags of his fellow citizens from evil be-helmeted snatchers-on-bikes. Perhaps, she decided, it is more dangerous to wear one round here than not to wear one?)

The inheritance is not, of course, the detached farmhouse standing in the middle of its orange grove that I've been imagining. Why would it be? My English heritage has led me astray again. In Calabria, as in Liguria, people have no tradition of living alone and isolated on their land. But it is, at least, right next to its orange grove, on the very edge of the town, at the very end of an alley, where the buildings stop dead, and you're all of a sudden in the countryside.

Zia Maria's house is the last in the terrace: a chunky two-storey-high stone building, its slatted shutters drooping sadly from neglect, pale green paint peeling. There must be a wonderful view from it, right out across the plain. Maybe even right down to the sea? A wrought-iron veranda with slightly wonky railings, painted pale green to match the shutters, runs the length of the end wall, the one that faces the river banks and the vegetable plots. There is a narrow strip of overgrown garden below the veranda, with three banana trees on it: with real bananas on them.

It doesn't look in too bad a way, considering that nobody's lived in it for a good fifteen years, says Zio Antonio.

The orange grove is on round the side, says Annunziata. If there's anything left of it, that is, she adds cheerily.

She and Antonio will get the doors unlocked. Why don't the rest of us go round the back way for a look, and they'll come through the house and meet us round there. They disappear off through an imposingly carved green-painted door with a strange little brass knocker on it, in the form of a pointing hand. Just the one finger, though: would just the one keep the evil eye off, I wonder?

We head on down towards the river and the back of the house. Alberto starts to shove his way through the mass of exuberant foliage that has taken over the pathway under the veranda.

No, no, says Francesca, I'm not going through all that prickly stuff, leave Alberto to it, we'll just walk down the river path and back round, instead of getting scratched to pieces.

As we head off along the narrow path that curves through the vegetable gardens by the river, who should we bump into, coming along it with his donkey, but the handsome old man with the brush-cut hair—the one who was appalled by Ciccio's ignorance of the cost of modern-day donkey-shoeing.

Buon giorno, he says as we pass by.

Buon giorno, Ciccio and I reply.

Buon giorno, says Francesca.

He takes a second look at Francesca—then does a double take and stops dead in his tracks.

Francescella? he says, staring.

213

Francesca stops and stares back at him.

Fiore? says she.

Francescella! he says again . . .

They gaze at one another for a long moment. Then Francesca drops her eyes and—I can hardly believe it—goes pink. Francesca blushing! I've never seen such a thing. And she just called him 'flower', too! Good job Salvatore's a thousand miles away, because there's no mistaking this for anything but an old flame.

Francesca pulls herself together and introduces the gentleman. This is an old neighbour of hers, she says: Fiore.

What, his actual name is Fiore? I ask Ciccio once I've done my part of the hand-shaking ritual. Flower?

Yes, says Ciccio.

You don't mean his surname? I say, never having met a man called Flower, not in Italy, nor in England either for that matter. Seems most unlikely, in a macho-hard-man type place like Calabria.

Yes, of course it's his Christian name! hisses Ciccio. Will you stop embarrassing people!

Me embarrass people! Look at Ciccio, so insensitive about the price of donkey-shoes that Fiore took him for a dyed-in-the-wool Northerner! Not to mention the way his mother's carrying on, flirting away aged nearly seventy!

She is introducing Ciccio now.

Ah! says Fiore. The Northerner! Francescella's son, are you? Maybe not so much of a Northerner as you seem, then!

Our party proceeds on its way along the path, but the Man Called Flower seems to have been so

214

moved by the encounter with Francesca that he just stands rooted to the spot till we're round the corner and out of sight.

Ciccio surges on towards the house, whence Alberto's voice can be heard calling us. Was that a childhood sweetheart, then? I ask Francesca, giving her a conspiratorial nudge. From before you started going out with Salvatore?

But the response isn't what I expected at all.

Going out with Salvatore? she says in a strange, hard tone. She wouldn't call it going out! Her father just arrived back at the house with him one day, she was eighteen, and introduced him to the household. She'd never seen him before in her life. Then a week later he brought him round again, and said, here, Salvatore wants to marry you, meet your fiancé. And that was that. Her goose was cooked, and nothing to be done about it. Because once her father had done that, well, it made no difference that there were a couple of boys she was interested in here in town, one she thought was keen on her, too—there was nothing to be done now, was there?

I don't know—wasn't there? I say limply, alarmed by the turn this conversation has taken— and even more alarmed by the anger and bitterness in Francesca's voice, something I don't think I've ever heard before.

Not in those days there wasn't, says Francesca. Once your father had brought a man to the house, the whole town would know about it by next day, and that was that! You were an engaged woman, and if you tried to back out of it, you were second-hand goods. Even if some other man was keen enough to take you in spite of that, his family would probably be dead set against it. What family

215

would want their son to marry the sort of girl who disobeyed her father?

Is she talking about Fiore? But why, I ask, would he have to have his family's blessing? Could he not just marry you anyway?

Francesca just looks pityingly at me. He certainly couldn't, of course not, because in those days there was hardly such a thing as paid work down here. You worked the land, with your family—and if your family disowned you, what land were you going to work? Even if you managed to rent yourself a field, not too likely with everyone against you, you'd have to work it all alone, just the two of you, with no help. No, it couldn't be done.

What made her father choose Salvatore, then?

Ah, who knows! She was never told . . . Men's affairs, no doubt! They probably had some kind of business deal to seal, didn't they?

So what happened next? I ask nervously. How did you get to know one another? What would have happened if you didn't like him?

Well, he just started coming round to dinner once a week—which meant that he sat out with the rest of the menfolk while she and her mother and the sisters cooked and served them dinner . . . Francesca had never spent so much as a minute on her own with him before their wedding day. Salvatore got on with the rest of them, and in those days that was enough.

One thing is certain—Francesca is still angry, fifty-odd years later, about these unromantic beginnings. But then, why wouldn't you be? Does she just not allow herself to be angry back home in Liguria? How has she managed all this time?

Ah, *cara mia*, she says, once upon a time it was

216

normal, and you just had to put up with it, make the sacrifice, do your duty. That's the worst of it; living to see the day when nobody would put up with such stuff—wouldn't even dream of it. It makes you think you could have stood up against it. Should have done. But the truth is, you couldn't. Not in those days.

So . . . I say, fearful of what can of worms I may be opening, and not at all sure I want to know the answer . . . So . . . Do you mean you didn't want to marry Salvatore at all, then?

No, as I've begun to suspect, she didn't.

This is awful. I'm very fond of Salvatore, and it seems that now I'm going to have to view him as some sort of bogeyman. But Francesca has seen the tormented look on my face, and she gives my arm an affectionate squeeze. Salvatore didn't treat me badly, not at all, she says . . . it was just normal. *Normale*. And maybe she did better for herself and her children by marrying him than if she'd followed her heart . . . He's been a good father, always provided for her and the children, worked all the hours God sent and handed over every *lira* he's ever made, straight into the family purse . . . Look at Fiore, now, tramping around after that old donkey just the way his father did before him, off to the fields at dawn, home at dusk, fields and home, fields and home, year in year out. And even the donkey's an achievement, because Fiore was a poor *benzinaio* then, couldn't even afford a donkey, breaking his back three times a week walking all the way to Palmi, loaded down like an ass himself . . .

A moment's confusion here: a *benzinaio* is a petrol-man, a petrol-pump attendant . . . what on

217

earth does a *benzinaio* have to carry to work that's so heavy?

As usual, Francesca collapses into peals of laughter at my simplicity. Oh well, at least I've cheered her up.

Fiore was taking great loads of hay around on his back, wasn't he, because hay was the *benzina*, the petrol of the times. What do horses and mules and donkeys run on? Hay, of course! Hardly anyone had a motor down here in those days, only the landlord's agents and the odd lawyer or what-have-you, so us *poveracci*, us poor folks, called the hay *benzina*—just for a laugh.

Anyway, there it is. What would have become of her if she'd stayed down here and married the likes of him?

Phew. How glad am I that Francesca has decided to make light of the arranged-marriage business?

Selfish of me, though, I start to think a minute or two later, as we turn into the path that leads to the rear of the inheritance-house. I've practically shut her up, haven't I, just because I would hate to have to think badly of Salvatore? She must have had to shut up about it for fifty-odd years, ever since the day her father made his announcement. She certainly couldn't talk to her children, who are Salvatore's children too, about it. Imagine how they would react, if I can't handle it! And even if she did end up loving Salvatore—which I hope to heaven she did—that's still no reason why she shouldn't go on being enraged at the thought of such a beginning.

*   *   *

218

Ciccio and Alberto have come down the path looking for us. Where on earth did we get to? Annunziata and Zio Antonio are waiting to show us round.

Wait till you see! says Alberto. Does any of you remember a science fiction film, a black and white one, really old, with aliens who are kind of vegetables, and they get inside humans and slowly turn them into giant shambling cauliflowers? Alberto can't remember the name of it, but this orange grove, it looks just like a scene from it! The house is nice, though, he adds reassuringly.

We find ourselves entering a cobbled courtyard, half overgrown with grass, three almond trees standing at its centre. The house, we now see, is L-shaped, its second wing, invisible from the alley, forming the back of the yard. It looks older, or maybe just more countrified, from in here: instead of iron railings, it has a veranda made of wood, a ladder leading up to it; and its shutters are of solid wood, old-style, instead of slats. Through the courtyard and round to our right we go, to inspect this supposedly alien orange grove. Alberto is right: it is a most strange sight. There must be a hundred-odd trees there, but each one of them is so thoroughly veiled over in green trailing creepers drooping right down to the ground, old man's beard by the look of it, that the trees are mere blurred outlines of their former selves, as if a giant hand had drawn them and then roughly rubbed them out. The occasional orange that has managed to push its way out through the undergrowth, or rather overgrowth, into the sunshine looks surreal, much too sharp-focused against the blurred shape that bears it. Watch this, says Alberto, prancing into the middle of the grove. He grabs a handful of creepers and yanks; backs off, pulling yards and yards of the stuff away with him, till eventually the dark trunk of the orange tree beneath begins to be revealed, the old graft half-way up it clearly visible. Hours of fun! he says. Come on!

Are the trees still alive, though? asks Francesca in a whisper.

Of course they are, says Zio Antonio. Look at the oranges on them.

We've got some job to do, though, says Ciccio, before we can gather in our first harvest . . . Shall we get started right away, let Alberto loose on it while he's on form?

What about the house? I say. Can't we go and have a look at that first?

Francesca doesn't want to go in, she says. She was in and out of there visiting Zia Maria all the time in her childhood. She and Enzo together. If it's in as bad a state as the orange trees, it will just give her *angoscia*. She's feeling quite tired. Maybe she'll just go home and have a little siesta.

No! *Mamma!* Come and show us round the place, says Marisa.

Pick up your weapons and help us destroy the alien orange-invaders! says Alberto.

Are you not feeling well, Francesca? asks Zio Antonio.

Francesca agrees that she's maybe feeling a bit under the weather. She'll go back to Annunziata's and rest.

I'll walk you home, then, I say.

She takes my arm and sets off towards the river path again—yes, she knows it would be quicker to go through the house, but she really doesn't want to go that way, no, no!

Ah, *cara mia*, she says at last, as we walk slowly back up the alley. We who have left this place should not come back. *Non ci troviamo bene*, and that's that.

I take a big swallow and go back to where the censorship cut in last time.

So, I say, you really didn't want to marry Salvatore at all?

No, she didn't, she says, stopping in her tracks. Why would she have done? She was nineteen and romantic, and he didn't bring her a single present in the whole year they were engaged, not so much as a bunch of wild flowers . . . or ever say a loving word, never mind try for a bit of a kiss and cuddle. All the girls here knew that if you got hitched up with a man like that, a man who hadn't even had a childhood himself, you could hardly expect anything from him. Salvatore didn't know what closeness and affection were. How could he, when he'd had no family life since he was seven, away up in the high Aspromonte herding the sheep and the goats, brought up—if you could call it that—in some old hovel way up among rocks and mists and wilderness, by strangers who were only interested in getting their money's worth out of him, men who had bought him by the year, for a couple of cheeses and fifty litres of olive oil . . . He never saw his parents, his brothers and sisters, from one month's end to the next . . .

Well. I give up. Can't find a moral footing anywhere in all this. Francesca was forced, at nineteen, to marry a man she hardly knew and didn't want to marry: but then, in case you were thinking of blaming him, he was forced to give up

221

school and go and live in a shack up a mountain with brutish employers when he was seven. And apparently you can't even blame her father, either, because he was behaving perfectly normally for the times. How vile people were to one another in the Good Old Days.

29

Concetta leads us up past the-wrong-Zia-Maria's house, and into a sunny side-alley of low two-storey cottages. Half-way up the street we spy the long-lost Alberto—we've hardly caught sight of him for the last two days—lounging with his cousin Antonello and a few of the other boys on a long stone step outside a house half-way up the street. They are half-hidden behind their beloved bikes, set in a defensive screen around them like some circled wagon-train in a Western, so you can't make out what they're up to behind them.

Our place, says Concetta. The boys are always there, they seem to have made their headquarters outside the house. Alberto and company manage to tear themselves away from whatever it is they're doing for just long enough to say a distracted hello to us, as we turn into the doorway.

Look at that! says Marisa joyfully, dropping her voice so Alberto won't hear. Back home in Diano, she would never normally have got past her son like that, without him stopping her to complain about being bored, or tapping her for money for something-or-other to keep himself entertained. Look at him now, though, so busy that he hardly notices his *mamma* go by; and he hasn't mentioned money for days!

The street door opens, on a step down, straight into a tiny living-room whose décor is seriously hallucinogenic. Concetta, obviously used to newcomers doing a bit of a double-take when they first walk into her home, explains it right away. Her grandmother was from Naples, she says. That's why the house is like this.

Is it? I find it hard to believe that the inhabitants of Naples all decorate their homes in quite this style. The walls are entirely covered in trinkets and knick-knacks, shell sculptures with mini-Madonnas inside, tiny shelves of little glass ornaments, dangling mother-of pearl rosaries, good-luck tokens including many chilli-pepper horns, pairs of fluffy dice, brightly coloured postcards, religious images lit up by tiny light-bulbs, a collection of golden crosses of every size, backed by lacy silver doilies, plasticized 3D images of shepherds and saints . . . It is hard to make out where the walls begin or end: they seem to float backwards or forwards a foot or two, depending on which of these small shiny multicoloured objects, some two-dimensional and some three, your eye happens to focus on. The general effect is of a cross between Dr Caligari's cabinet and a gipsy caravan. Still, I've never spent more than a few hours in Naples. What do I know?

Once you've got the hang of the walls and found your equilibrium again, you notice a large oval table that takes up most of the centre of the room, and a pair of sofas set round it at right-angles. And there is Zio Antonio, sitting on the farther one. The other is occupied by an unknown couple dressed in those kind of synthetic fabrics that look startlingly synthetic, and are only worn by people from the United States of America. These, I deduce, are the cousins from Noo Joysey.

Hi! How are you? It's great to meet you! they say, in a mad parody of a New Jersey accent. Luckily, I am forewarned and forearmed by my earlier encounter with Zio Antonio's version of the Calabro-Noo-Joysian accent, and the conspiratorial giggle is thoroughly quelled before it gets anywhere near my lips.

Disappointingly, although they have the accent off to perfection, Joe and Annunziata, as they turn out to be called (another Annunziata: people certainly do stick to the old family favourites in these parts) don't speak much English at all. They've been living in the States for fifteen years, they tell us: they run an Italian-style bar in Noo Joysey. But it's too easy, round their way, to meet nobody but other Italians; where they live, almost everyone is Italian; and then, at work, the same thing. All their employees at the Nancy Bar are, naturally, Italian.

The Nancy Bar? Why, I ask, my imagination running wild, is it called the Nancy Bar? Now that I come to look at Cousin Joe more closely, he does have an unusually bouffant hairstyle for a straight man. I picture a New Jersey Italian-immigrant gay bar, a place where they serve walnuts and pumpkin seeds instead of peanuts with the beer, a red-hot chilli cocktail with a sun-dried olive-on-a-stick; maybe even keep a cold cabinet with a secret stash of goat's-head snacks and explosive 'nduia, strictly for the cognoscenti . . . ?

No. Scrub all of the above. Nancy, it seems, is

what you get called in Noo Joysey if your name is Annunziata. That, I am disappointed to say, is why the place is called the Nancy Bar.

A tiny, birdlike woman appears at the doorway that must lead to the kitchen, carrying a giant colander and trailing a hessian sack. Maria Angela, Carmela's mother, Zio Antonio's wife, Ciccio announces. A round of kisses, and without more ado Zia Maria Angela puts the colander down in the middle of the table and, lifting up her sack, tips the contents out next to it. Three guesses. Yes, it's a huge pile of bean-pods. Long-lost family members you haven't seen for a decade or so? Quick, find them a pile of beans.

Nancy/Annunziata starts shelling them without comment, throwing the beans into the colander: Marisa, Ciccio and I follow suit, doing our best to look as if we think this is a perfectly normal way of entertaining guests.

Stop playing the fool! says Zio Antonio, letting out a roar of laughter. Put those beans down!

A moment's confusion: but it is only Ciccio who is being foolish. Men don't shell beans. Us females can carry on. They're not butter beans tonight, at any rate, but cannellini beans. A change is as good as a rest, eh? says Ciccio smugly, in English.

Not necessarily, I reply.

What a lot of beans you do grow down here, muses Marisa.

Beans with everything, here in Calabria! says Concetta. They used to grind them into bean-flour and make their bread from them, even, once upon a time. Ask *papa*.

Yes indeed, says Zio Antonio. And the worse times were, the more bean-flour would go into it and the less grain-flour—once you were down to just rye and beans, it would hardly rise at all, and you'd be chewing your way through a solid block. If you could. Barley and bean-flour wasn't so bad though—especially if you could season it with a drop of oil.

Eni a pane iancu, I say in perfect Calabrese, causing everyone round the table to look up in shock. I smile proudly. I learned that all on my own, from the Alimentary Culture section of my history book. It means 'He's on the white bread'— as opposed to the black, bean-based stuff Zio Antonio's talking about. Calabrians might spend their working lives growing wheat for the landlords, the book said, but they would hardly ever get to taste the bread made from it; and hence the saying *'Eni a pane iancu.'* Eating wheaten bread was such an unlikely event in an ordinary Calabrian's life that it ended up meaning 'He's at death's door.' Ah, yes. Silly of me to forget that part. No wonder they're looking surprised. I apologize profusely to Zio Antonio, who says that he doesn't care, and I'm probably right, anyway. Causing Concetta to rush over to her *papa* and sit on his lap, where she smothers him in don't-you-dare hugs and kisses.

The beans we're shelling now, at any rate, are not going to be made into bread. They're going into a wild boar stew for us all to eat the night of Enzo's Mass, says Maria Angela.

Cinghiale with beans? Ciccio is gripped. He has never come across a boar-and-beans recipe before.

It's a recipe Nancy picked up in America, says Maria Angela.

An American wild boar recipe? That explains it then, says Ciccio.

226

But the recipe, it turns out, was originally from Runci, a village only forty or fifty kilometres from here. It travelled from Runci to the States, via immigrant ship, two generations ago; where it was eventually passed on to Joe and Annunziata at the Nancy Bar, Noo Joysey, by the granddaughter of its original bearer, who is a regular of theirs; and now it's made its way back home at last, by jumbo jet, to roost in Melipodio.

What did I say? says Concetta. Beans! Of course it's a Calabrian recipe.

*   *   *

As we leave, off for a drive around the Old Country with the American cousins, we see that behind their bikes the boys are not, as we'd imagined, playing at some computer game. Not at all. They, too, are shelling beans: they have three big sacks of them, corralled inside the Vespa-and-Piaggio wagon-train. Much more exciting-looking beans than ours, too, gleaming pink-and-black mottled ones, which they are throwing into a tall, slim Aladdin-style willow basket. These ones are to be dried for winter, Antonello explains. The basket lets the air in. It has to be tall and thin like this so they'll dry right through to the middle without going mouldy. You just have to make sure not to fill it too full, so you can give it a good big shake every few days.

Good. It's cheering to know, *pace* Francesca, that not every traditional container can be simply replaced by a plastic bag. Or even by three plastic bags.

Strange, though, it strikes me now, that Zio

227

Antonio felt it was beneath Ciccio's dignity to shell beans; and yet here is his son doing the job perfectly happily. Is there some specific age, I wonder, at which young males have to give up shelling beans? Some sort of rite of passage? *No, son, put those pods down! You're a man now!!*

I suppose I'd better not ask, though, in case it makes Antonello, who is just sprouting the first wispy hairs of a beard on his chin, go all self-conscious about his youth.

*　　*　　*

We drive to the south of Palmi, towards Reggio, today—and see our first bergamot trees, the only kind of orange you can still make a profit from. Their fruits are pear-shaped and irregular, greeny-yellow. Precious oranges, though, even if ugly: not used for eating, but for perfumery. The essential oil pressed from their skins is worth a fortune: it's the fixing base for some of the world's most famous scents, says Nancy/Annunziata. And you add it to high-class tea: that's what Earl Grey tea is. Tea perfumed with bergamot.

Joe tells us that once upon a time the bergamot tree grew nowhere but here. It is very fussy about its growing conditions. That's why its essence is worth so much. But in spite of being so thoroughly Calabrian, it ended up named for the city of Bergamo, way up in the North of Italy: the merchants of Bergamo were the first to exploit it commercially. A typically Calabrian tale. It's been established in a few other places now, though. He's heard there are even a few bergamot groves in the States these days.

Ciccio is inspired again. On the way back, we must stop and cut a small branch from one of the bergamot trees. He will try grafting it on to an ordinary orange tree back in Melipodio. If it takes, we could slowly substitute every branch in the inheritance grove, one by one! Make our fortunes! How much does Joe think you get for a kilo of bergamot oranges? Or would it be better to process them yourself, make the oil and sell that?

Joe doesn't know. But he thinks that if it was that easy, someone would have done it already.

We are going to be making our first stop at the town of Scilla, just along the coast. Its name was once spelt Scylla: opposite it, on the shores of Sicily, is a tiny place called Cariddi: once spelt Charybdis. Between Scylla and Charybdis! How many times have I heard that said, and had no notion that these were two real places, not just a pair of Odyssean legends. Probably we won't see a six-headed monster there, lurking on the beach, or even a whirlpool on the opposite shore. But we'll pass Etna and Stromboli again, and see Sicily from close up for the first time.

30

Have you found yourself a job yet, then? Rocco asks Marisa, spotting us sitting outside the Bar Z in the cool evening air with cousin Paolo, and with Aldo, who has wandered out to join us. How's the inheritance looking? he adds.

That was just some strange joke of Vincenza's. It wasn't the little town house at all, says Marisa.

Vincenza! says Paolo. That girl has a very peculiar sense of humour.

She certainly has, I say. What is her relationship to you two anyway? But Ciccio and Marisa have no idea. Paolo doesn't know either. He's a cousin from the other side of the family, he says. Well, second cousin, really.

Vincenza's always been around, though, Ciccio says; he knows that Zia Annunziata decided to support her through university when her mother died—she was sorry for her, because she was the youngest daughter and she'd been marked for years as the one who was never going to marry, she was supposed to stay at home and look after the parents in their old age. But then both the parents died young, and Annunziata convinced Enzo that she should be given a real chance, better than either of her big sisters had had, to make up for it. Ciccio thinks the same thing happened to Annunziata—she was the youngest daughter, too . . .

Didn't work out too well though, did it? says Paolo.

No, Vincenza only did a couple of years of study at Reggio, says Ciccio, and then something went wrong—he thinks maybe it was a man, but you know what people are like down here for being secretive . . .

Marisa is telling Rocco about the real house, a great big rambling thing down by the river, she says, with a massive orange grove next to it—or rather, something that once was an orange grove. No worries about us all fitting into it at once, anyway. You could practically make a hotel out of it.

A hotel! Just what Melipodio needs! says Rocco.

Really? says Ciccio, pricking up his ears. No. Not at all. A joke. Any tourists who make it this far south go to Tropea, on the coast: they hardly venture so much as ten kilometres inland, never mind twenty. This town does swell up to four or five times its normal size every summer—but not with tourists, only with people coming back to visit the relations, like us lot.

But has anyone actually tried setting up a place for tourists to stay? Ciccio wants to know. Up in Liguria, he adds, they're perfectly happy to stay inland; they like the hills as well as the sea.

What about campsites? Are there any campsites around? I ask, guessing that Ciccio is thinking of his as-yet-to-be-found goat pasture.

Campsites? Ah, you'd just be throwing money away, says Aldo. He is addressing Ciccio, not me, even though it was me that asked the question. I get a tiny flick of the eyes in my direction when I'm actually speaking—then I'm blanked again. I'm used to very old men in Liguria carrying on like this, not addressing their remarks to women if there's a man present, but Aldo wouldn't even qualify as old, never mind very old. And he's having no trouble talking to Marisa, who certainly couldn't be mistaken for anything but a woman. What is the matter with him? I am starting to get annoyed. Even more annoying is the sight of Ciccio watching how put-out I am at being so steadfastly ignored, and being greatly entertained by it.

At last, seeing that I'm about to reach boiling point, Ciccio kindly stops the smirking and leans over to explain in English. Aldo is being very careful, he says, having given us so much potential

231

for taking offence when we first arrived, not to do anything else that might be taken badly. Down here in Calabria, it is considered bad form to look at another man's woman for more than a second.

What? And what if I take offence at being totally ignored? I'm beginning to appreciate what a modern, enlightened place Liguria is.

A round or two later, though, everybody is getting good and merry—tonight we are trying out another local beverage, Amaro del Capo, a bittersweet *digestivo*, concocted from herbs and oranges, which is going down very nicely—and Aldo's amazingly rude form of politeness has begun to wear off, thank goodness; while the prospects for Ciccio and Marisa making a fortune out of their inheritance have begun to look a lot rosier.

Aldo, Rocco and company are now helping us design and build the classiest mountain-top campsite ever, with acres of balustraded terraces from which to view both seas, a café-bar (run by our host), the highest-tech shower-and-toilet blocks you have ever seen, guided tours of our own private Graeco-Roman temple, and cash registers that ring with gold day and night. Rocco will supply us with the building materials, earth-moving equipment, manpower, anything we want . . . And we won't have any trouble with planning permission, Rocco says, because one of his uncles is a Senator—sits in the Chamber of Deputies. So we're in luck.

He's a good boy, Rocco, you know, says Aldo, once the man in question has left the table to follow Marisa indoors, where he appears to think she may need his help to order more Amaro. He really will put in a word for you with the Senator, if

232

he says he will.

Well, all we need do now is find the place, and our financial futures are secure. And, of course, do our best not to worry about such matters as being caught up in webs of corruption. Because that's what was just offered there, wasn't it? People in this country may carry on all shocked about the Mafia; but as long as that actual word is left out of it, there's nothing wrong with a wee bit of corruption when you can get it. And what exactly might Rocco expect in exchange for tipping the word to the Senator? Probably just Marisa, by the look of things: and luckily she doesn't seem at all averse to the idea.

Ciccio, who is useless at spotting budding romance, now makes to join them at the bar; I have to forcibly restrain him. He just wants to order a slice of pizza: what's the matter with me?

You can go in a minute! I say sternly. Not now!

He's had a hard life, Rocco, but it hasn't made him bitter, Aldo is saying. Did you hear that his grandfather was shot dead right in front of his eyes when he was only fifteen? And his mother went to pieces because of it, she's hardly ever left the house since, not for years?

No, really? says Ciccio, fighting off my restraining hand.

And then his elder brother Pasquale was killed in that lorry accident last year, Paolo chips in.

Yes. So apart from him, there are only the two sisters left. But they went off to settle up North with their husbands not long after the grandfather died, says Aldo. Rocco's ended up looking after the business, the parents, everything. His father goes to the yard every day all right, and sits in the office

233

like he's still at the helm. But he's not well, not at all, hasn't been for years—it's really Rocco who runs the place single-handed . . .

Marisa and Rocco are heading back this way now, and the topic is abandoned.

You can go and get your pizza now, I tell Ciccio: but Paolo is calling over the latest arrival in the bar, a cheerful-looking bloke in his early fifties, to meet us. He will be a relative of yours, says Paolo. Wasn't Francescella's *mamma* a Versace? Well, here is another one!

Versace, Gianni, says the new arrival, announcing his name in the old-fashioned manner, surname first, as he puts out his hand.

Gianni Versace? we say in unison. No! Really?

Not the famous designer, as you can see, says he. Evidently, I myself am still very much alive. There are some advantages to being a simple postman. Nobody much wants you dead.

We go on marvelling. Fancy that! Gianni Versace!

I am only a distant cousin, though, says Gianni Versace the postman.

So does that mean the famous Versaces are from round here? I ask. They are: Gianni and Donatella were brought up in a small place not thirty kilometres from here.

You too, evidently, must be related through your mother's side, says Gianni.

If we are, it's so distant that you couldn't put a name to the relationship, unfortunately, says Marisa.

Unfortunately? Pah, says Gianni, it's fine to be related to the famous Versaces, but it's never put so much as a tile on my roof! But that day the

234

headlines were on all the front pages . . . 'GIANNI VERSACE SHOT DEAD' . . . Ah, that was a day! Wherever he went on his delivery round, people were throwing their arms round him, telling him what a shock they'd had when they saw the paper, and thanking the Lord that it was only that other one killed, and not their own homegrown Gianni Versace. There were people all over town tearing at their faces with their fingernails in grief and despair, he tells us, until they realized it wasn't him!! An honest postman is hard to come by in these parts. Ah, yes, people round here have a good sense of priorities!

(I check with Marisa that I have understood aright. Did he really say they were tearing at their faces with their fingernails? Yes, he did. This doesn't seem to strike anybody except me as an extremely odd, not to mention seriously melodramatic, way to demonstrate grief and despair. Marisa points out that the tearing of hair and the rending of flesh were perfectly normal mourning behaviour in ancient Greece. Then there was the wearing of sackcloth; the ashes on the forehead. And in Calabria, things change extremely slowly.)

And did you not worry that it might be your turn next, the start of a *faida* against all the Versaces, Gianni? asks Marisa.

What is a *faida*? I ask, since nobody seems in much of a rush to answer Marisa's question, and I've never heard the word before.

A family blood-feud, says Marisa, where people just keep on and on, an eye for an eye, a tooth for a tooth, until whole families are murdered . . . down to the last and most distant members. Like the business of the fourteen crosses in Seminara.

But is that not called a vendetta? I ask. Apparently not: a vendetta is a Sicilian thing. Here in Calabria you get a *faida* instead.

Lesson over, Marisa and I find that a deep silence has fallen around us. Eventually, Aldo speaks.

There are no *faide* these days, he says, not any more. It's all nonsense. That was in the bad old days.

But Marisa presses on regardless: the Amaro del Capo seems to have deadened her antennae. Have they really stopped? she asked brightly. Or have people just stopped talking about them to the authorities? A new *omertà*, maybe? Because one minute they were all over the national newspapers, a new outbreak every couple of months; and then all of a sudden you stopped hearing about them completely . . .

This time the response is so frigid that no amount of Amaro could make you miss it.

We prefer not to talk about such stuff these days, says Rocco. It only gives people the wrong impression. And he deftly flips the conversation back to genealogy. And thence, naturally, to property.

Not everybody in this bar is so close-mouthed, though.

It was a fishy business altogether, Pasquale's lorry accident, says Paolo some time later, when Aldo has left and Rocco is away chatting to Ciccio and the barman. The lorry plunged off a bridge and straight into the sea one evening, down on the coast road on its way home. But why was Pasquale driving it? And alone? He often got a lift back up to the yard in it at the end of the day's work, yes, but he never drove it . . . You can't help thinking the usual driver must have known something was afoot, he'd been told to make an excuse and get out of the way . . . So somehow or other Pasquale was left to take the lorry up by himself, at dusk, along that bad bit of road, no houses, no witnesses . . . And the police didn't turn up for a full week to do their job, all their measuring and photographing— and what use is that, a week later? How could you tell if it was a suspicious death or not? You couldn't even prove whose skid marks they were by then, could you? So nothing was ever said about it in the end . . .

The barman arrives now to set our drinks on the table.

So, there you are, accidents will happen! Paolo adds quickly.

Accidents? says the barman. You're not scaring our friends with your old terrifying tales, are you, Paolo?

Good job you don't have *faide* any more, says Marisa ironically, once the barman has left. But she has missed the point, says Paolo. A *faida* was about justice. Look in the Bible! he says.

According to Paolo, the *faida* was crude all right, in its eye-for-an-eye and tooth-for-a-tooth tradition. But, as he points out, that's how justice was always meted out, everywhere, once upon a time. And Pasquale's death was nothing to do with a *faida*, says Paolo. No honour in it. No justice. Just business.

Yes. Filippo has just been pointing out to me, in Volume Three, that people only ever gave up the do-it-yourself family version of justice, backed up

237

by a notion of family honour needing to be upheld, once there was some impartial public system they could trust. And down here, what idiot would have trusted the courts of the *latifundia* owners or the justice of their lawyer cronies? The law was theirs, and it had been for centuries. And when did they finally get booted out? Not till the fifties. That's why the *faida* lasted so long.

31

So, says Francesca, gathering up her coat and bag, it's high time I went and paid my mother a visit.

What? I do a double-take. Her mother?

In the cemetery, of course, she adds, in response to my look of bewilderment. Is anybody else coming? Not that I mind, she says disingenuously, I'm quite happy to go alone . . . Though you'll all be wanting to go and pay your respects to my brother Enzo at some point, I daresay . . .

Whoops. This means we'd all better go, now, or be deemed unfeeling wretches.

Right, I say, gathering up my own stuff. The others follow suit, and soon we're driving through the centre of town, stopping at a florist to get some flowers for the graves of our loved ones. Imagine that, a town with hardly a sensible, useful shop to its name, unless you happen to want stockfish and chicken: but managing to keep a florist's shop going. All the flowers go to the graveyard, too, I should think. I've seen no sign of flower-arrangements in anybody's homes, or even vases. Melipodio's not that sort of place, is it?

Soon we are at the gates of a high-walled burial ground set well outside the city walls, as is usual in this country. I am no longer perturbed, as I was when I first came across it, by the Italian habit of burying their loved ones in mid-air, in marble-built mausoleums that are often strangely reminiscent, when viewed from a distance—especially once their tiny lights come on in the evening—of a scale model of an English council estate circa 1970. The mini-blocks of flats are neatly set at right-angles to one another, the dwelling-spaces reduced to a mere six feet long by two wide, since the inhabitants no longer need room to move about. The departed are sealed, feet-first and airtight, into their own personal two-foot-square marble niches, each bearing an electric candle, a bronze plaque with name and dates, and often as not an enamelled photograph of the tenant in their prime.

We pay our sad respects to Zio Enzo, and leave him his flowers. We'll give him a good send-off before his Mass, we promise; then off we go hunting through the maze of blocks for an older, lower one, where Francesca's mother lies; hard to find, because they've built so many extra sections since Francesca last visited. But here she is at last. Serafina: 1905 to 1985. But there is no photograph. Francesca is mortified. Enzo was left in charge of getting the photograph organized, and of course she doesn't want to speak ill of the dead, but how could he not have got round to it in all these years? But then he never was much of a one for religion. What a good job we've come down at last. We will put that right, at least, before we leave.

Francesca surprises us now by extracting a small brown cushion from her handbag and placing it on

239

the ground. With some effort she kneels down on it in front of her mother's last resting-place.

Now clear off, the lot of you, she says, unceremoniously. None of you ever even met her, except Ciccio, and that doesn't count, he was only a tot, doesn't remember a thing of his granny, do you? Marisa, go away, and take Alberto with you, shoo! You were nothing but a babe-in-arms when she died. I need some time alone with her!

All right, *mamma*, calm down! say they. And we set off for a tour of the cemetery, hunting for any other relatives. We promised Grazia we'd do some research into the forebears, didn't we?

Unlike my Italian companions, who can't see anything unusual about it, I am startled to find that the cemetery is chock-a-block with Borgias.

Borgia! I keep saying. Maybe we'll find a Lucrezia, like the one that went around poisoning people. You know—the Borgias and the Medicis.

The who? they say.

The Medicis, I repeat. Blank looks all round. Surely they must have heard of the Medicis? Are they only famous in England, little known in their own land? Are the de Gilios a bunch of ignoramuses?

Ah, the Medicis! says Marisa. It's just that I'm pronouncing it all wrong. So wrong that it's incomprehensible. The stress is on the first syllable: not 'med-eee-chis', the way we say it in England, but 'medd-i-chees', like 'medicine'. And in fact, now that I'm pronouncing it right, I see that it just means 'doctors'. What a let-down. The Doctor Family. Doesn't have the same ring to it at all.

We find endless Tamburiellos, Francesca's side of the family, but not even one de Gilio/Giglio of either sex. Lending credence to the theory that the grandfather or great-grandfather was from somewhere much farther away than Santa Cristina. A family that had been established in the area for a few generations would be bound to have intermarried, have some relatives down here in the town, wouldn't it? Unless they all stayed up in tiny Santa Cristina and married among themselves? We will have to go up there soon.

I find several dozen Borgias; but the nearest I can get to Lucrezia is a certain Lucia. Still, the photos on the tombs easily make up for the lack of early-modern poisoners. Calabrians, it seems, like their photos bigger and more colourful than the Northern ones I'm used to: but it is the hairstyles portrayed in them that really grab the attention. Not the women's hairstyles: they are mostly just long hair put up in various ways, the period changes only rung in the fringe arrangements around the face. But the males of the species! You would believe you were looking at a gallery of cameo actors from a John Waters film. Hairspray is not the word. Clearly this was once a town of male fashion victims. Hair from the turn of the century is oiled and slicked down into wildly unlikely finger-waves: beards are coiled into Roman-statue-like ringlets. As history progresses, you get fewer beards, more and more exaggerated Marcel-type waves, and more sideburns. Very dramatic sideburns, sticking out a good couple of inches from the side of the head in some cases: a decade or two later, rather than being slicked down, the oiled hairstyles have begun to rise to quite amazing heights above the face: astoundingly tall quiffs that curl right around 360 degrees, bouffants as big as

1960s women's beehives, the side-hair defying gravity in a most unlikely manner, rigidly horizontal. Of course, the owners of the hairstyles did have the ideal material at their disposal: the dominant hair type down here being thick, curly and bushy. Ciccio is a good example of this: if he stops cutting his hair, it does not grow longer, but just upwards and outwards. Which is why he keeps it trimmed close to his skull. You can even do something very like topiary on it, if he leaves it to its own devices for a few months. I know: I have had a go. Great entertainment. I suppose this would explain Uncle Joe from Noo Joysey's bouffant, too.

Alberto is going round the cemetery in stitches, heartless youth, and has pulled out his disposable camera. He is going to make a hairstyle-portrait gallery for his mates back home, he says. What a laugh!

What about a bit of loyalty to his homeland? asks his uncle Ciccio. Does he really want to make a laughing-stock of Calabria? As if things weren't bad enough already!

But Alberto does not, it seems, identify with Calabria the way Marisa and Ciccio do: or at least, if he does, he certainly doesn't feel he needs to hide its defects from Northerners. Good on him.

The rest of us spend some time thinking up possible explanations for the extravagant hair traditions of the home town. Of course, there may only have been one barber in the place, a deeply eccentric one—and he could have had his own mad way with the population, couldn't he, because likely as not they would have had little idea of the prevailing fashions in coiffure elsewhere. No, it couldn't have been just one barber though: he'd have had to be impossibly long-lived. But, say, two or three generations of the same whimsical family? In fact, now that I come to think of it, living in a whole town full of seriously sculptable hair might be enough to turn even a perfectly sane person such as myself into a Mad Barber.

But enough of hairstyles. Francesca has finished communing with her mother, and we are now allowed to go and say our own few prayers for her soul. Then, says Francesca, we must go to the pottery shop in Seminara to buy some souvenirs of Calabria for the folk we left behind in Liguria.

On the road to Seminara, we find ourselves stuck in a long, long queue of stationary cars. Two cars have crashed head-on, various bystanders tell us: but it wasn't too bad an accident, nobody was much hurt, and only one of the cars is a write-off.

We wait nearly half an hour, and count six policemen on the scene, interviewing drivers and witnesses, taking photos, consulting with one another in agitated-looking huddles by the side of the road, going back and interviewing some more . . . Eventually, here we are in downtown Seminara. Into the pottery shop—where, down at the back, behind the everyday kitchenware, there lies a treasure trove of weird and wonderful Calabrian bits and pieces. All sorts of body-part amulets like the ones I saw pinned to the old cross in the chapel with Vincenza; a whole box full of those ceramic hands with the index and little fingers sticking up— and yes, she's right, the fingertips are always dipped in red. There are life-size ceramic masks, modern versions of the ones Francesca took with her for protection when she first left this place, and

243

which now hang over our doorways back home in Liguria—the same two varieties of pagan gods or benign spirits, one a Bacchus-like character, a god of crops and harvests, with his hair and beard full of ears of corn and bunches of grapes; the other an older, primeval-forest god, horned and wild-eyed, his tongue curling lasciviously out, glazed a plain dark green and twined in ivy. Sadly, they seem to have lost all their mythological past. I ask who they are, and I'm told that they're just for keeping off the evil eye. They're nobody in particular.

In a far corner we find many different versions of a small statue of a Virgin-Mary-like figure, with the veil and the babe-in-arms: except that, unlike the usual Mary, her flesh is glazed a deep, dark mahogany.

She is Seminara's treasure, says the woman who has popped out from somewhere at the back of the shop to serve us. She is the Black Madonna, the Virgin of the Poor: *la Madonna dei Poveri.* Her original lies in her shrine at the other end of town: she was made in Byzantine times, people say; and was even a goddess in her own right, perhaps, before Christianity came along. That's as may be. But for centuries she has been the hope of those who could expect nothing from the pink-and-white Virgin of the respectable and the well-heeled. This Mother of God would hear your prayers however little you were worth in the eyes of the world.

A sort of Calabrian apartheid, then. Two parallel justice systems, and two parallel Virgins: the white Madonna to protect the status quo, the rich and powerful: while the black Madonna gave hope to the hopeless, catered for the poor and the propertyless.

244

Francesca has come over to see what's going on: am I buying a *Madonna dei Poveri*? That's a good idea . . . What a pity we didn't make it down here for her *festa*! Did I know there was a whole week of feasting in her honour, every August, in the streets of Seminara? But she tells me no more: she and the shop lady have spotted one another. They let out a squeal, and fall into each other's arms. They went to primary school together! They were best friends! They finish the hugging and kissing and squeaking for joy—and now her friend steps back, holds Francesca at arm's length, and gives her a huge pinch on the cheek, shaking the flesh about the way you do when you're goo-goo-ing at a baby. What on earth is she doing that for? I wait for Francesca to slap her hand off. I certainly would. Is she mad? But Francesca goes on laughing away happily, and now does the exact same thing back to her old friend: pinches a great chunk of cheek between thumb and forefinger, and jiggles away at it. I gather that this is perfectly normal behaviour here, then: the thing to do when you're really pleased to see somebody. Seriously foreign body language.

A good half hour later we are on the road again, Francesca cock-a-hoop because we got our souvenirs cheap—there now, isn't it great to have friends, imagine how much money we've saved!

Now we go and do one of those smidgens of real tourism we occasionally manage to fit in—we drive along the coast to Bagnara, admire the state-of-the-art swordfishing fleet lined up along the harbour, making the old traditional fishing boats look like decrepit tubs—they must be raking it in. Inspired, we head off to a small restaurant on the port to try some fresh swordfish *al limone*—except for Ciccio, that is, who won't have lemon on it. If you want a hint of acidity with your fish, you should use a drop of white wine in the cooking, according to him. *Chi mangia u peixe cu limon, o e de Cuneo, o e un coglion,* he pronounces in deepest Ligurian dialect, to the great amazement of the waiter taking our order. 'He who eats his fish with lemon, is either from Cuneo, or he's an asshole' would be the rough translation of this saying: though it rhymes better in Ligurian. Naturally, we and the waiter now torment Ciccio for a while about where his real roots lie: but his Calabrian *figura* is thoroughly redeemed when we start on the sea-urchin pasta course, the *linguine ai ricci di mare*. He demands another half dozen live urchins on the side, and scrapes out with a teaspoon the tiny strips of bright-red innards clinging to the sides of their spiny shells—all a sea urchin possesses in the way of meat—which he swallows down, *au naturel*, with great relish. The rest of us are quite happy with the dish as presented by the restaurant: the flesh of the *ricci* a mere delicate sea-aroma, stirred into the pasta and colouring it a pale pink, along with plenty of olive oil, a sprinkling of freshly-chopped chilli, and a hint of garlic.

Lunch over, we drive on down to Reggio di Calabria, the capital of our Province, hoping we'll be lucky enough to see the famous mirage that occasionally appears as you look towards Sicily across the Straits of Messina: a shining city of marble towers and spires. The *Fata Morgana*, it's called. Morgan le Fay, in English. A strange fragment of Norman legacy. The Normans brought the old Arthurian legends down with them from the North; and their Arthurian name for the

246

mirage has stuck through all these centuries.

No sign of it today: the air and the sea have to be at their stillest, say the bunch of Reggino youths we get chatting to, who are sitting smoking a joint on the beach below the palm trees on the impressively refurbished Monte-Carlo-style esplanade. But we get to see Sicily at last, looking so close you'd think you could swim over. The huge red-and-white striped column on its nearest extremity once carried Sicily's electricity over from the mainland, the boys tell us. It is redundant now, but people grew so sentimentally attached to it over the decades it stood sentinel over the straits of Messina that it is now a Listed Building.

Hours later, and we're heading home for supper, when we get stuck behind some sort of tailback—in more or less exactly the same spot where the accident was this morning. Can there have been another crash here? It must be some sort of accident black spot, we decide, though it's hard to fathom why. Everyone else seems to have parked their cars and got out to go and have a look, so, there being, obviously, no chance of the traffic moving on while none of the drivers are in their seats, we do the same thing.

There are still six *polizia*, civilian police, stopping the traffic—can they be the same ones? No, the one with the beard certainly wasn't here this morning—but now two *carabinieri* of the military police force have joined them. And it is not another accident, but the same one. The same two mangled cars are still there, but they've been moved to the side of the road now, and the guardians of the law, both varieties, are taking turns at close inspection of the skid marks on the

247

tarmac. Two of the *polizia* are doing something intricate with a long yellow measuring-tape; now, it seems, it's up to the *carabinieri* to verify the results. Their tape is equally long, but brown. A case-conference now, first *carabinieri* with *carabinieri*, *polizia* with *polizia*: next, the interdisciplinary version, both forces in a huddle together. Away they go back to the skid marks, to do a few more very slow things with measuring-tapes and infinite patience; now they confer again . . .

Oh Lord. Have the police forces in this reputedly Mafia-riddled land really nothing better to do with their time than measure and re-measure the tarmac? Are we going to be stuck here all night?

32

The dreaded *milanesi* featured at lunch again today. Ciccio thinks the Aunt and Cousin are afraid to offend our delicate Northern-trained palates with their rough peasant food, so they have bought in plentiful supplies of frozen *milanesi*: the Italian equivalent of an oven-ready stuffed chicken breast, or some such simple and convenient food, bland and inoffensive—nobody would be likely to actually refuse to eat one—but utterly characterless. Probably, Ciccio says, the Aunt sees them as a sophisticated, classy food, something you'd give to special guests. Special guests who were not from Calabria, that is. Their Northern pedigree is guaranteed by their Milanese name—and they certainly cost a lot more than anything the relations would normally have on the table. We have been given them three times already. And either because they are so expensive, or because they are so boring, they have not been put on Annunziata's, Carmela's, or even Mamma Francesca's plates since that first night. Only on ours.

Annunziata, Carmela and Francesca, meanwhile, get the same vegetable dishes as us, but with interesting-looking bits of meat that have been cooked, Southern-style, in with the pasta sauce. A brilliant tradition: economy with style. The meat flavours the sauce that goes on your pasta course, the *primo piatto*; and the sauce has flavoured the meat that you eat next as your *secondo piatto*, your second course. This lunchtime Ciccio resorted to stealing mouthfuls off his mother's plate: earning him indulgent praise from the Aunt and Cousin— him being a big grown-up man and needing plenty of nourishment (although to look at the belly on him, I can't imagine how they'd think he went short of nourishment)—but the rest of us can't very well carry on like that, can we? We'd only create the impression that we were horribly greedy: terrible guests still famished after four courses.

We can't say we don't like the *milanesi*: that would not only be rude, but would also imply that we hadn't enjoyed our meals so far. We've tried saying we want to eat what they normally eat, real Calabrian food: but either they don't believe us, or they don't want to look as if they're stinting on the guests' board.

Tonight, though, Ciccio has managed, by dint of endless insistence that we are desperate for the stuff, to get us a stockfish dinner. Stockfish, *stoccafisso*, is dried cod: not to be confused with *baccalà*, salt cod. It looks like a piece of old flat driftwood when you pick it out of the basket in your chicken-and-stockfish shop, and it's as hard as wood, too, until you've soaked it for twenty-four hours—when it puffs up into something recognizably fish-like. Definitely an acquired taste, though. There is no denying that the first thing to strike the novice eater of either stockfish or salt cod is the strong whiff of crusty old socks about it. Luckily for me, I first came across the stuff at the home of West Indian neighbours in London, when I was young enough to be flexible about such matters as eating old-sock-flavoured foods. I enjoyed it again when I met its Ligurian incarnation, simmered into a sort of olive-oil-rich stew with plenty of potato and onion, ingredients which eliminate most of the more ferocious end of the old-sock spectrum. But Zia Annunziata told us, when we were discussing the stockfish-dinner request earlier, that there's nothing she hates more than overcooked stockfish that's gone all squashy. She likes it to still have some bite, she said. And the pungent flavour now wafting in from kitchen number two, as we start to set the table, tells me that the Calabrian version of stockfish may well be up at the high-note end of the scale. Still, an adventure: and infinitely better than being force-fed *milanesi*. Moreover, we have one of my favourite delicacies as a side-dish. Francesca came bouncing back from a walk by the river with a carrier full of wild greens she'd picked—which, instead of their usual name, *erbe selvatiche*, she is now calling '*erbi i margiu*' in Calabrese—something like 'herbs of the margins', I suppose. Whatever she may decide to call them, I love them. Wild greens by any other name taste just as . . . well, bitter, I suppose, is the right adjective. But an indescribably pleasing kind of bitter. Francesca is in there now cooking them herself: mostly wild chicory today, and a few *cime di rape* (turnip tips, not to be confused with turnip tops: these are the flower-heads before they open, something like a broccoli floret)—blanched in boiling water till soft, then reduced in a frying pan with olive oil, garlic and chilli: '*stranghiate*', you call greens cooked by this reduction-method in Calabria. Strangled greens. Doesn't sound so good, but just try them. And on top of this, to make my day, we're having my favourite Calabrian starter, one that I know from Francesca's table back home in Liguria, *insalata di friselle*: a salad of ultra-sweet oval tomatoes chopped small, plenty of garlic and olive oil, and the crunchy crouton-like roasted bread pieces, *friselle*, that give the salad its name—which stay deliciously crunchy even when inundated with tomato and olive oil and left to marinate. Carmela has got out a bottle of the Ligurian oil we brought to go on the salad—we'll try it raw first, she says, so we can really taste it.

Alberto and I have been left in the main kitchen to make the *insalata*—it's so simple that even infants and foreigners can be trusted not to ruin it—while Ciccio and Carmela commune over the stockfish and the potatoes that are an essential part of the dish we'll be having. As we chop and stir, the door to the Walnut Room opens and Annunziata appears, dressed in a voluminous apron. She's been in there all this time, unbeknownst to us, stuffing her figs. Tomorrow is the day she and Carmela

251

take them down to the Moroccan in the market, she says. No, she won't show us how you do it now, it's time to eat, and she's sick of the sight of the things. We can try after dinner, give her and Carmela a hand if we like. They'll be at it all evening. And no, we can't taste one now, either: we'll have to wait till the end of the meal, she has some ready for our dessert, fresh ones preserved in brandy. Come and sit down. She tries the salad, savouring the olive oil. Almost up to Calabrian standards, she says, deadpan.

Francesca bristles for a moment, then realizes it's a joke.

But why has Calabrian olive oil got such a bad reputation anyway? I ask. The stuff we've been eating here is lovely.

Too acid, says Francesca. It's the heat down here. Unless you beat the trees early, before the olives fall, and rush straight off down to the mill with them—that's what you do for your own stuff that you use at home, isn't it, Annunziata? But you couldn't really do that for big quantities.

Yes you could, says Annunziata. They do in Tuscany—she saw it on the television. And people could do it here, if they pulled themselves together. But, she says, in the old days when everyone was making a good living from olives round here, nobody needed to bother about acidity levels. The olive mills all had big export contracts to fill—and the oil was for industry, not the table. So people got into bad habits according to Annunziata—waited till the olives fell by themselves, left them lying on the nets for days, weeks even, till the whole harvest was ready to load up. There was no reason to give yourself extra work, was there?

I recognize this from the writings of Filippo, with whom I am communing regularly at bedtime, and eagerly tell Annunziata that it says in my history book that a huge proportion of Calabria's olive oil went to Britain, once upon a time, where it was used to oil the wheels of our Industrial Revolution.

Perhaps, says Annunziata, who doesn't seem too gripped by this information. The demand for it died, anyway, somehow or other. New, synthetic oils, she's been told. But people just went on working the groves the way they always had; ended up selling their oil cheaper and cheaper. There was no way it could compete as eating oil. It just got Calabria a bad reputation, says Annunziata. So people said to themselves, Oh, there's no money to be made from olives, and gave up. When what they really needed to do was get the quality up, look for new markets . . .

Mamma has always had a *mentalità di commerciante*, a business brain, says Carmela proudly. If only she'd been born a man!

Never mind being a man! says Annunziata. If only I was the right side of fifty again instead of getting horribly close to seventy, I'd know what to do—I'd set up a proper modern shop in this town. A supermarket-i, she adds, doing her best to use the businesslike, anglicized version of the word, but foiled by the inexplicable British habit of finishing words without a vowel.

Just supermarket, that's how you say it, says Francesca helpfully. No -i on the end. She knows: she went to them all the time in Australia.

Alberto waggles his eyebrows at her. Tuscan! he says.

But Annunziata is taking no notice. She used to

253

run the shop in the corner of the piazza, she goes on, heading for the other kitchen. Before she cut her losses and went for the market stall . . . But you need a big place these days, lots of turnover. A proper supermarket-i. Or people will just go to Palmi where it's cheaper.

Annunziata's bringing in the stockfish course now: and to my surprise, it arrives in an oven dish. Crispy roast potatoes, tons of sizzling golden onion, and the stockfish roasted in among them in bite-size pieces. Smells lovely. So much for my predictions. The fish certainly does have the bite Annunziata was after: which complements the other textures perfectly. As does the dark green bitterness of the strangled wild chicory. Ten out of ten to Calabria.

Carmela opens the jar of figs-with-walnuts and starts laying them out on a plate, plump and translucent.

Do you and Carmela make enough to live on by selling these, then? asks Marisa. Do you sell other stuff you grow down at Graziella as well?

Ah, we couldn't manage without Graziella, not at all, says Carmela.

No, says Annunziata, but we do all sorts of other things . . . You'd never make a living from just a few dry figs! Still, once you have a bit of land, you'll always manage somehow.

I cut into a fig to reveal the walnut nestling snugly at its heart. What is Zio Antonio up to, then, on his land? I ask. Why is he planting all those olive trees, if nobody can make any money out of the things? Is he going to try and go upmarket like you suggested, compete with the Tuscans?

Ciccio gives me a warning kick on the ankle just

254

as I bite into the fig. Fierce! Not bottled in syrup or juice, of course, but brandy. I'd forgotten, and, unprepared for the alcohol fumes, or for a brutal unprovoked attack on my ankle from beneath the table, I'm half-choking now. Why is he kicking me? What's the matter with asking that? Too late, I've said it anyway.

But Annunziata isn't bothered. Just a scam to get the unemployment benefit, she says.

Mamma! says Carmela. But Annunziata presses on regardless.

You just need enough work-hours, enough trees, to claim that one person has a full-time job on them for a couple of months of the year, she explains—doing the pruning, the harvesting, the clearing. Then a member of your family can claim benefits for the other ten months. Everyone does it. That's how Concetta lives. And Vincenza, too. Half the town, probably. What else are they supposed to do? If they have no job at all, they can't claim anything: that's the way the system works . . . and then what's left for them but to leave town and head North, and never see their homes and their families again, like as not? It's worth a few weeks of pointless work to keep your children around you, isn't it?

Disturbing. A whole town living on the dole, while pretending to work on profitless olives. Still, I suppose it's no more pointless than all the youth unemployment programmes and whatnot that you get in my own country. (I start on the next fig: they are lovely once you're expecting the alcohol, fruity and voluptuous, chewy and crunchy at the same time.) Italy doesn't actually admit to having a system of state support for the jobless: so people

255

here are constrained to be somewhat inventive. If they have no job, they have to think up some way to extract a bit of cash from the labyrinth of state subsidies for this, that and the other. It does say, in my Calabria Post-Millennium volume, that emigration from Calabria has more or less dried up in the last twenty years; no explanation is given for this phenomenon, except for a very abstract paragraph describing the mysteriously high turnover of goods, not far below EEC average, in a regional economy that produces less than two-thirds of the EEC average: the author concludes that the rest of the money must be being 'transferred from the centre'. Decoded, perhaps this means that jobless Calabrians have become very adept at working the system?

Dinner over, Annunziata soon has the lot of us wading through walnuts to take up our posts on the three-legged stools in her walnut zone, cracking nuts, slitting figs . . . Francesca is torn between being half-ashamed of Calabria's backwardness—fancy people still doing this by hand!—and the joy of being transported back to her youth. She amazes us all with her expertise, deftly stuffing a dozen walnuts into a dozen figs at the speed of light, then stringing the whole lot together, impaling them just below their stalks, one after the other, spiralling down their sliver of cane. She's nearly as fast as Annunziata and Carmela: looks as if she's done it every day of her life.

Ah, *cara mia*, she says, there is nothing so wonderful about that. There are some things that are better forgotten.

33

The landscape is full of tales of death and despair when you walk the hills with Zio Antonio: be they in the distant or in the recent past.

This spot, under this tree here, is where a certain Luca chopped his own son's arm off with a sickle, while trying to kill a viper in the grass . . . that was long ago, in Nonno Lira's heyday. And here is where another neighbour fell off his favourite tree while he was trying to prune it—that huge one there, look at the size of it, he never stopped telling you how it cropped better than ten of anybody else's trees, how it was a thousand years old. But pride comes before a fall, they say, and off he fell, right into a nest of red bees down there in the grass. (I've never heard of red bees—what can they be? Too dramatic a moment to ask, though.) Antonio himself and some of the other men— because in those days you always had plenty of company on the land, there were always people about, and it nearly makes you cry to look at it these days, lifetimes of work all gone for nothing, all silent and deserted and nothing looked after any more—anyway, they loaded him up on to his donkey like an old sack of olives and headed for the road, but he swelled up all over and died asphyxiated before they could even get him half-way home . . .

The Zio is taking us, at the moment, on a round tour through the olive groves to see the rest of the family lands—though it'll all be gone to rack and ruin, and quite a bit of it's been sold on, he says—

and then we'll head on down to the river at Graziella, where we are to help bring home yet more walnuts and *pappaluni* and various other kinds of bean, a whole string of unfamiliar dialect names. Whatever they may be, they are ready for picking.

Here we are now, paying our respects at the trees Nonno Lira finally ended up owning. He got twenty happy years' work out of them, day in and day out, at any rate, before he died, says Antonio . . . and see over there, hidden behind those clumps of wild canes, down by the ditch that carries away the water? That's where Nonno Lira and Zio Antonio's father made themselves a whole *orto* of vegetables, so the landlord's bailiffs wouldn't spot it.

Zio Antonio walks over to the ex-vegetable garden, now nothing but an overgrown patch of reeds; and stands silent for a moment, prodding sadly at it with his stick.

*   *   *

So, how did it come about that Nonno Lira and your father finally got their pieces of land? I ask Zio Antonio. I am hoping for at least a small glimmer of joyousness. You'd think, reading your *Storia della Calabria*, that people here would still be celebrating the day the land was finally handed over, after all those centuries of misery and yearning, of emigration and hunger, of failed revolts and land occupations. But nobody seems to have much to say about it at all.

Well, we got given some bits and pieces under Mussolini, says Zio Antonio grudgingly; and some

258

right after the war, too; then some more once the government had outlawed the *latifundia*.

And wasn't everyone over the moon, then? I ask, doing my best to liven up the tone. With a bit of land of their own at last, growing what they liked and not having to give any of it away to an invisible landlord? Not having to hide in ditches any more?

But no, apparently, they weren't. It all came in bits and pieces, anyhow, says the Zio: and it wasn't given as a present, are you mad? You got a debt along with it—you had to pay them back from what you made farming. And by that time, after the war, you could hardly make money from the land any more. The price of olive oil had collapsed; the Americans were growing their own oranges, and didn't need to buy Calabrian ones any more. And what could you make from a patch of beans or a couple of *quintali* of tomatoes? Did you ever hear of a smallholder farmer making a profit in these modern times? Once upon a time you would have kept your family on what you grew, and thought you were living in the lap of luxury, but those days were over by then. You needed cash, money in your pocket.

They might have done better, the Zio thinks, if the land hadn't been broken up into so many tiny parcels, if it had been kept together and they'd farmed it as a collective: you had a chance of making a profit if you were growing, say, a thousand hectares of beans. None at all with one hectare. But it was American money that was rebuilding Italy after the war, wasn't it, the Marshall plan—and anything that smacked of Communism was out. They didn't want collectives: they wanted a new Calabria of respectable small landowners. Pointless.

259

In no time at all, people were just selling up to pay off their debt, and moving away as penniless as before. Emigrating again. That's when Francesca and her husband went, isn't it?

I'm beginning to see why people don't talk about the death of the *latifundia* a lot. They snatched defeat from the jaws of victory. And I daresay felt that they had fulfilled the expectations of everyone who'd ever accused Calabrians of being hopeless and feckless.

At least Nonno Lira didn't live to see the day that his trees were sold on, says Zio Antonio consolingly.

Depressing, says Ciccio.

Who owns these trees now, then? asks Marisa, caressing the trunk of a nearby giant of an olive tree that might, but for fortune, have been hers.

Zio Antonio doesn't know any more. They were sold for a pittance to a neighbour a good thirty years ago—but the man passed away a while ago. He's heard that someone bought them up recently, some man who's not from round here.

And what would this man be planning to do with them? I ask. What use would they be to him, if there's no money to be made from olives?

Zio Antonio doesn't know: but nobody round here wanted them anyway, and the man's bought up quite a few plots of olives, he must have twenty or thirty by now, he's obviously a wild optimist. Probably planning to get finance to build a fish-packing plant here, or something. Unless he's got an awful lot of unemployed relations to support. Zio Antonio guffaws at the thought.

Wandering on our way, another path crosses this one: at the entrance to it a horned goat skull is

260

wired to an olive tree. Look at that! I say to Ciccio. Just like up at your *papa*'s! Salvatore has one fixed, just the same, to a tree at the entrance to his land in Liguria.

Marisa, our resident witchcraft expert, says that goat-horns protect your crops from the evil eye. Zio Antonio is very entertained to hear that Salvatore is keeping up the traditions of the Old Country in his Northern home. But Salvatore doesn't admit what they're really for, I say. When I asked him what the skull was doing on the olive tree, he said in a nonchalant way that he'd just found the thing lying about the place, and thought he might as well hang it up there . . .

Well, of course he did, in that benighted Northern land where the old ways have been well and truly lost, says Marisa, laughing. And he hasn't just got the one, either—there are four of them, nailed to the last olive tree at each corner of his land. Facing outwards, of course, to where the evil might come from. Which, she says, will be why I haven't noticed the other three.

Horns against the evil eye, I say, thoughtfully. Is that what the extended-fingers-sign that Vincenza made me do in the church is meant to be, then? She did use the word horns, come to think of it . . . I do the two-middle-fingers-down, two-end-ones-up sign at Marisa: and she and Zio Antonio laugh their heads off. What's so funny about that? I ask, peeved.

The answer is that I have just insulted Marisa. If you hold your finger-horns upwards the way I just did, as if you were doing the classic V-sign only with different fingers, it means '*cornuto*'—cuckold. (*Cornuto* literally means 'horned' anyhow: so we're

261

talking horns either way.) If you're aiming to chase away devils or evil-eyes with your horns, rather than to insult people, you do not raise them high, but jab downwards, hell-wards, with them.

See that bit of land there, over on the other side of the ditch? says the Zio cheerily. Well, that used to belong to old Giuseppe, a distant relation of ours. He hanged himself, at seventy-eight years of age, think of that now! Giuseppe's old horse had died, it seems, and his family had presented him with a nice new labour-saving *Ape* to make life easier. No more feeding and grooming and mucking out, no more long tiring trips to the blacksmith's. This was the last straw. Giuseppe, evidently a man after Nonno Lira's own heart, went off and tied a good strong rope round his oldest olive-tree, and that was that . . .

And that hairpin bend there, now (we are crossing a narrow asphalted road at the moment), that's where they found the body of a twenty-year-old—Zio Antonio pulls away at the grass on the verge, uncovering a tiny memorial stone with the boy's name on it. Gianni Baroccio, that's it. He was shot by the *malavita*, but Zio Antonio can't remember why, now, not for the life of him!

We have come to a small group of three detached houses standing way out here on the hillside—1930s bungalow-style farmhouses, all abandoned. Still, it's strange enough that anyone ever built them here in the first place, no village in sight, only farmland around them. An aberration, the Zio explains, caused by an ill-fated incentive scheme set up by Mussolini.

Mussolini too? I know from my Ligurian experience that Italian Ministers for Agriculture have been trying for a good century-and-a-half to persuade Italian farmers to abandon their nice sociable villages for isolated country living. Economically speaking, a good thing, of course: not needing to travel to and from your land would obviously give you rather a lot more actual farming time. But evidently Italian farmers are unusually alert to the fact that there is more to life than economics. It didn't work in Liguria in the 1870s: and by the look of things, it didn't work much better for Mussolini in the 1930s. Not even with the cunning three-houses-together ploy. Though you'd think there was more chance of it working in Calabria. Ligurians owned plenty of high, malaria-free land, and could easily have moved out of their defensive positions in their hilltop villages several centuries ago, once the Saracens had gone, if they felt like it. Clearly, they didn't. Whereas down here, not owning any land, people had never had the choice. They might have jumped at the chance.

Under Mussolini's scheme, the government would build your house for you, Zio Antonio tells us, if you went and lived on your land: the *coloni*, as the participants in this scheme were called (colonizers! that's how strange and fearful living on your land is here), were supposed to pay it off bit by bit, once they started making money. But when did they ever start making money? There were no proper roads: you couldn't even get a horse and cart down here. They had to use mule-trains. What kind of modern profitable agriculture is that, with mule-trains for transport?

Yes. I daresay not bothering to give them any decent roads was a bit of a clincher. Especially once they'd seen, as Zio Antonio is about to

263

explain, that to try to build one was to risk sudden death. He points out something that looks like a fallen concrete wall, badly cracked, lopsided and overgrown, half-buried in the side of the hill. That, he says, was to be the base for a driveable road down to all these parcels of land, right along to the head of the valley. A young lad was building it, a sub-contractor, only twenty-three and with two small children. The main contractors were on the fiddle, though; didn't care if it was built or not. They kept calling him in to work on it in fits and starts: probably whenever they thought an inspector might be about, or something. But you can't cast concrete in bits and pieces, a few yards one week, a few the next. He wanted to do a decent job, he told them, and this way the road would never hold. It would crack and fall down the mountain, somebody would get hurt . . . So that was the end of him, and the end of the road. A bullet to the head and two more orphans. He was right about it cracking, too, adds the Zio. Look at it now.

At long last, a cheerful story. Well, sort of. One day, Zio Antonio and his mate were baling hay on those slopes up there—it was a few days' work to get it all stooked up neatly, no baling machines in those days—and the handiest place to stack it was here at the bottom, on this field, nice and round and flat. They knew the *coloni* often used it to dance on of an evening; but they would be back next day with a set of mules to collect it. So off they went. But they couldn't get hold of the mules next day, or the day after. Back they came, though, on the third day: and they didn't notice as they loaded the mules, bale by bale, that there was anything unusual—till the poor creatures dug their hooves

264

in, stopped dead, and refused point-blank to go back up the hill. The *coloni* had untied every single bale, and stuffed a rock into the middle of it! Zio Antonio and friend had to unload the mules again, untie each bale, open it up, take out the stone, re-tie and re-load it. And there, inside one of the bales, they found a note saying *'cosi imparate a non imgombrare la pista da ballo'*—this will teach you not to encumber the dance floor!

What a relief to hear that people here did ever dance, or play music, or have a joke, or do anything at all apart from working themselves to death or getting shot. Or both.

34

So, after a long roundabout ramble, we arrive at the river and Graziella, whose entrance is protected against the evil eye by not one but two goat-skulls, flanking the path on either side. The tips of the skull-horns seem to have been dipped into shiny, dribbly red paint, and look horribly as if their skeletal owners have just gored some passer-by.

Bloodied horns, vanquished enemies. This is starting to get positively macabre. But wait! Blood! The incompetent nail varnish job, the strange red tips to the fingers on that ceramic sign-of-the-horns hand pinned to the wooden cross. That's what the red is meant to be. The pointing fingers are not just horns, but gory horns. There is layer upon layer of symbolism going on here, though: why not make ceramic bloodied horns, if that's what you really

265

mean? There must be some special mystical power to the hand as well. I once came across an old farmhouse in Portugal with its windows and doorways outlined in lapis lazuli blue, and handprints in the same paint dotted right round them like something a child had done in playschool. Lapis lazuli wards off evil spirits, I was told; and the handprint doubles the effectiveness. Most people just do the outlining though, these days, because the hands make the priests angry.

How would you ever get to the bottom of it all? I wonder if anybody still knows, even? Looks as if people are just carrying out the time-honoured rituals, but the source-book, the frame of reference, has been lost.

Annunziata, Carmela and Francesca are not picking *pappaluni*, as advertised, when we find them. They are standing in a sort of chorus line, legs akimbo, balancing on a set of stepping stones that cross a wide shallow stream, and passing carrier bags full of walnuts over from the far bank hand to hand, fireman style. A dash of Vaseline on the lens, and you could almost put their portrait on a tin of tomatoes.

Just in time! they shout when they see us arriving. Get over here! We need two more people for this to work properly!

Ciccio and Alberto go to help out, while Marisa and I create an impromptu bag-reception area, piling them up over this side of the stream.

The land still hasn't dried properly since the other day when we left the irrigation on, and what with the rain too, it's all turned to bog, says Carmela, who is nearest our side of the water. But we had to get the walnuts in, at least the windfalls,

266

can't leave them lying or they get maggots. We'll just get these ones stowed in the *Ape*, the rest into the *taverna*, and then we can get on with the beans.

Zio Antonio says that the *taverna* here—not a tavern, as you might think, but a cross between a storehouse and a workroom, the place where you keep the huge wooden wine-vats, the *botte*, for fermenting your wine—always reminds him of his mother. Before the *Ape*, with only a donkey for transport, you used to get the figs ready here at Graziella, stuff them and thread them up: there was no point taking them home to do it. You would stay the night in the *taverna*, and load the ass for market in the morning, leave direct from here. It was cooler here by the river anyway than in the house, and you slept better. He remembers one night, he and his mother were sleeping down here, and something made him wake up in the middle of the night . . . he opened his eyes, and there was the moon shining bright as day; and his mother still wide awake, sitting there beside him, apron spread, threading away at the figs by moonlight.

Under the impression that this is simply a beautiful memory of a long-lost mother by moonlight, I respond in what seems an appropriate aaah-isn't-that-lovely way. The look I now get from Antonio tells me that this is certainly not the response the story was expected to elicit. In spite of all that history-book-reading, I've completely missed the point of the tale. No pretty moonlit mother-and-son tableau, as far as Zio Antonio is concerned, but a terrible memory of how close utter destitution was in his childhood days: of his mother working her fingers to the bone to earn a few extra *lire* to keep the family. Times so

267

desperate that as long as there was any light at all to work by, be it sunlight or moonlight, she could not allow herself to sleep.

*   *   *

Back towards the *Ape*-parking place, where a cobbled road forks off from the river path towards the town, stands a semi-derelict water-driven olive-mill; an amazingly ornate stone mill, the likes of which I've never seen in Liguria. There are plenty of solid stone mills up there, certainly—the river beds have been dotted with them since the early Middle Ages—but they are plain and simple, workmanlike, never all carved and curlicued like this. The mills down here belonged to the *latifundia* owners, though; whereas up in Liguria there was no call for aristocratic showing off. Our Diano villages began breaking away from their feudal lords in the early 1300s—easy to accomplish up there, where they could simply go behind the aristocrat's back and offer to ally themselves with the Republic of Genoa, in exchange for Genoese protection. No tinpot lord could withstand the might of Genoa in its prime; and all our villages had escaped the feudal yoke by the mid-1400s and set up their own *comuni* under its wing. Except for my own Diano San Pietro, down on its shameful river plain, which for some reason didn't get round to doing the deed for another two centuries: the Sack of Ignorance must have been weighing heavy.

This beautifully carved mill is disused, anyway. There must be a good dozen of them dead along this stretch of river, says Zio Antonio. Where would they get the custom these days? And anyhow, a brand-new state-of-the-art electricity-powered one opened a way up the hill just last year.

What? A brand-new mill? Doesn't Zio Antonio think that's a bit suspicious—he's just told us there's a man going round buying up everybody's olive trees, and now there's a brand-new mill built, too? Wouldn't that make you think that somebody had a very good notion that you could really make money from the olives?

No, apparently it wouldn't. Zio Antonio thinks the new mill was probably just some scam to get money from the EEC or the government or something. They'll probably never even open it. Or if they do, it'll go bankrupt within the year.

I don't think I'm ever going to make head or tail of this place. People's brains seem to have got addled with all the reading-between-the-lines they have to do, with constantly having to suspect the evidence of their own eyes. Whatever something seems to be, it's probably really something else. But then it could be a double-bluff . . . Have they got to the point where they can't see their own noses in front of their faces? All that energy spent on suspecting their near neighbours of planning to put the evil eye on them, when it looks to me as though they'd do a lot better suspecting the mysterious outsiders who are buying up all their supposedly worthless groves. Would you not think that in a few years' time we'll be hearing that somebody has followed Zia Annunziata's advice and brought Calabrian olive-farming techniques up to modern scratch—and you can make a fine living from olives once more? Except that by now all the land will be concentrated in the hands of just a few men again—or massive olive-farming consortia, at any rate—while local people gain nothing from it? Watch this space . . .

35

The *taverna* is a most bizarre building. It is built into a hollow at the side of a steep hill, mostly of narrow Roman-style bricks, with a few runs of stones mixed in here and there. And it is clearly part of what was once a much larger structure, most of which fell down a very, very long time ago. So long ago, that the broken-off bits have been smoothed by weather and time, while whatever rubble was left has either sunk below ground level, or been carried off to be used to build something else. Two imposingly high arches rise to the side of it: they look as if they're what's left of an aqueduct that once carried water to the building in its earlier incarnation: but nowadays, the far end just breaks off dead, while the near end leads nowhere: just buries itself into the grassy hillside above. I can't even begin to imagine what it might once have been: or how old it is. A couple of centuries? Five? Ten? All are possible round here.

So do you know what it was, this place, before it was your storehouse? I ask.

Ah, who could tell? It's always been like that, ever since they've known it.

So much round here is unspeakably ancient, has gone through so many uses, I suppose you'd get used to it, and hardly bother your head wondering.

We are sitting outside the *taverna* on the grass, eating a mixed-race picnic of Ligurian bread and

270

Calabrian salami, with a jar of Francesca's Calabro-Ligurian anchovy chilli-peppers on the side. Francesca, I could tell from her expression, was not at all happy to see the jar of peppers appear out of the lunch-bag. She has already mentioned, twice, that we are getting through them too fast. She particularly wants them to be put out for the guests at Enzo's month-memorial wake. He always loved her chillies. It's all very well to say that there are plenty of them: but plenty for how many people? There has to be a generous portion for every single person, because it's better not to put a dish out at all than to look as if you're stinting . . . when it's your own brother you're waking, too . . . !

Gazing idly up at the many inexplicable features of the *taverna* as we eat—yes, I'm afraid I've taken one of the precious peppers, too: it seemed pointless to hold back when nobody else was showing any sign of doing so—I notice another unexpected echo of Salvatore's Ligurian lands. There has always been a large mirror hanging high on the side of Salvatore's *taverna*, pointlessly as it seems, twelve feet up in the air, where it could never reflect anything but sea, sky, and the other side of the valley. I've always imagined that it got left up there by accident, after some bit of horseplay or other. But here at Graziella, too, there is a pointless mirror wired high on the side of the building, reflecting nothing. My suspicions aroused, I consult the oracles again. And yes, of course, these mirrors do indeed have a function: their job is to reflect their own evil back on any ill-wisher who might turn his jealous gaze upon you and your crops. The exact same principle as those mirrored bags and garments that people bring back

271

from India: must be part of some ancient Aryan belief-system still not uprooted by newer ones.

Francesca has got over the unauthorized commandeering of her pepper supplies, and pottered off towards the river, where she is checking out the mysteries of Graziella's irrigation system. It hasn't changed at all since she used to come here as a little girl, she says. It's still just the same! Come and look!

Hearing talk of irrigation, I have imagined some high-tech computerized affair, tubes laid under the ground, sprays that rise up out of the ground on a timer system—something you see a lot of up in Liguria these days, ever since our summers began to turn more or less entirely rainless. (Due to global warming, many say; but then there seems to be no shortage of water down here, so much further South. Maybe Liguria has been drought-struck by the evil eye, now that nobody there remembers the ancient art of keeping it off?)

This Calabrian system, in any case, simply involves shifting a large log which is half-damming the stream: you move it a foot to the side, allowing the water to flow out of the stream and on to the land . . . then, with one of those pointy hoes called a *zappa*, you dig out a shallow channel towards whatever crop you're wanting to water. The stream does the rest. It's a pretty nifty system, too, because after a few hours the channel's nearly clogged itself back up again with mud from the stream, and you can shift the log back, leaving hardly a channel to trip over, no need to get the *zappa* out again to fill it back up.

Look how many pods on every plant! How well the beans have done this year! Francesca says, waving over to our right, towards an orchard of what I would, until I met Zia Maria's orange grove, have thought were rather overgrown-looking fruit trees. The beans must be over beyond them, I suppose. Or does the butter bean grow low to the ground, maybe? Francesca leads the way off into the trees, which turn out to be mostly pear and peach trees, mixed in with a few apricots and apples; we walk through them, Francesca plucking the odd bit of overgrowth from their branches, until a large white bean pod actually hits me between the eyes. I get it now. We are in the *pappaluni* field already. The butter bean likes to clamber up something, so why not let it clamber up something that's already there? Annunziata and daughter, rather than waste time and resources putting up cane frames for their beans, have simply planted them under these handy trees. And a few marrows too, I notice, when I spot a three-foot-long curly yellow *zucca* dangling before my eyes. Over to my right is a clump of apple trees with canes propped in them, leading tomato plants up into their foliage, where the tomatoes hang as if from their branches, looking strangely out of place. Mixing up your crops is recommended to smallholders these days, isn't it, as a way of providing protection against disease and pests without the need for chemicals? They have probably always known that here. But although the actual crops, the trees and the plants, seem very well cared for, this place seems oddly out-of-control, half-unplanned, as if temporary improvisations had everywhere fossilized into permanence. It is certainly very reminiscent of Salvatore's style of gardening. In fact, it makes his

273

place, very casual and chaotic compared to the neatness of its Ligurian counterparts, seem a positive haven of order and organization.

Is Francesca going to tell us later that this shows they can't manage the place without a man? Or is it just normal Calabrian-style agriculture? Salvatore, who is very methodical and careful in all sorts of other ways—planting and transplanting seedlings, watering and weeding religiously, doing each job at exactly the right phase of the moon—also manages to be serenely unperturbed by the piles of rusting bedsteads, rotting planks, spare floor tiles that have been lying about all over the place for years; and has gone on for decades nailing extra layers of old wooden blinds, broken chair-legs, bits of trellis, scraps of driftwood and old tin on to something that was once a shed, but is nowadays hardly identifiable as such. Would it not be easier to just start again from scratch? you ask him. Shall we come up and give you a hand?

Bah! Why bother . . . ? he says.

You need to know—as I now do, thanks to my bedtime reading—about the unusual style of land tenure that persisted in Calabria for centuries before you can understand. It's ridiculously simple. Calabrian landowners feared, rightly, that the labourers on their *latifundia* coveted their land. They knew that anyone who plants, harvests, and cares for a piece of land will quickly start to feel proprietorial over it: may even become convinced that they have rights over it—more rights, indeed, than some absentee landowner who's never been anywhere near it, or done a stroke of work upon it. Dangerous stuff. How to nip this sort of thinking in the bud? The *latifundia* owners, some time in the

Middle Ages, developed an ingenious strategy: the answer was never to rent the same parcel of land to the same family for more than a year. They certainly wouldn't feel proprietorial about a bit of land that wasn't going to be theirs by next spring. Good plan: except that in one stroke they had created a mindset, among their labourers, in which there was no point in making any kind of permanent improvement to the land. Who would do extra work on land that they had no control over; work that their family would get no definite benefit from? You would concentrate on the shorter term: put all that energy, instead, into the things you did have some control over—especially your own year's planting—and let the rest go hang. And *voilà*. You get Salvatore and Annunziata. All is explained. Or not quite all. Living in a land prone to violent earthquakes every few years doesn't encourage you to feel that there's a lot of point in taking the long-term view. Floods, landslides, and the malaria that might strike you down inexplicably at any moment, wouldn't help either. But only the earthquakes are truly natural phenomena. The rest is down to the *latifundia*. With nobody taking the long-term view, the quality of the land got worse and worse, and production per hectare dwindled. Now, if the landowner wanted to maintain his standard of living, keep the creditors from his door, he would have to plant more land, just to grow the same amount of corn . . . Perhaps, he would say to himself, I'd better clear another few acres of my hunting grounds . . . ? Plough up another bit of my pastureland? I could just get the flocks moved higher up into the hills . . .

The Eldorado of the coastal cities and their

fertile plains was already nothing but a distant memory: a few centuries of this *latifundia* farming, and there was more soil erosion, more streams and rivers blocking, more floods and landslides, more once-arable plains below turning to marsh. The anopheles mosquito was having a whale of a time. And in the rest of Italy, Calabrians were getting a bad reputation for fecklessness and improvidence.

36

Francesca is all of a tizz. She has made Marisa take off her jeans and put on a skirt; while I have had to remove my black crocheted cardigan because— although it was doubtless fashionable in other places, Francesca generously allowed—here in Calabria it looked like an old lady's mourning gear. At last we are well-dressed enough to walk across the piazza and round the corner to the Great Man's house. We're off to dinner at Anselmo's.

Once we are in through the ancient carved doorway, the house is strangely neutral: we could just as easily be walking into a dinner party in Islington as in Calabria. The huge kitchen-dining area is divided by a sparkly black granite work counter and paved in pale cream marble; a jug of apéritifs sits ready on the table, our hostess beautifully made-up and ready to pour; while her mother stands on the kitchen side of the counter, overseeing the olives in the cut-glass bowls, a choice between the bought kind of olive, all neatly stoned and stuffed with bits of pimento, and local ones in garlic and chilli—prepared by the lady in the kitchen, my mother-in-law, says Anselmo proudly. There are little cheesy biscuits in more glass bowls, and pizza cut into tiny elegant squares, and—can it be?—cocktail sausages on sticks. And the kitchen has been cleared of any sign of food preparation.

Before we eat, though, we must pick up our apéritifs and come for a tour round the house, says Anselmo. Good job they're nice long apéritifs in big tall glasses, because Anselmo has knocked together not one, not two, but three old houses to make this one: it has balconies on every floor to check out, with views down to the sea to admire on one side, mountains on the other (and, somewhat closer than the mountains, one of those ubiquitous unfinished-building-ruins, but everyone round here is so used to those that they hardly register as eyesores, I gather). We stop to appreciate, in depth, every painting on Anselmo's walls—all done by Calabrian artists, naturally—and spend a lot of time on the marble staircase with the wrought-iron banisters, where there is a work of art for almost every step. Once we've finished with the house, we still have the garden to do—including a state-of-the-art wine-making area, buried under a greener-than-life lawn. Computerized irrigation system, naturally.

Finally, seated at the table, we can relax. Anselmo's wife and mother-in-law begin to serve dinner: a kind of tour around the Italian peninsula, national savoir-faire. We start with local chilli sausage and slices of a *polpettone*, a meat loaf, from a Neapolitan recipe. Now there are mini-*saltimbocche*, fine slices of beef rolled around a sage-leaf and a lovely dollop of garlicky butter, based on a dish from Rome. The pasta course is *cannelloni alla Nizzarda*: theoretically, cannelloni as prepared in Nice, but not, as Anselmo points out, a French dish, because of course Nice was Italian for many centuries. The *cannelloni* are not pasta in the usual sense of the word, but tiny home-made pancakes rolled up around a stuffing of spinach, garlic, egg and *ricotta*, a combination as typical of Liguria as of next-door Nice; and I suddenly feel quite homesick. What joy to be certain that there will be no unexpected outbreak of chilli-burn on the tongue. Now, for the *secondo piatto*, we have—no! Can it be?— *milanesi*. Not frozen ones, this time, though: and gently cooked in butter and marsala—fine by me, especially once I discover that for *contorno* we have delicious home-made chips fried in olive oil. How it gladdens the heart of an Englishwoman to get meat and potatoes on the same plate at once; and how rarely it occurs in this land.

Meal over, though, I am on the spot right away. Anselmo wants my impressions of his house, of his town, of Calabria.

I certainly don't want to hear, or say, another word about the house: and my head is too full of tragic and disturbing tales—and of a deep suspicion that everybody would be much happier if I didn't talk about such things—to make talking about Calabria in general at all appealing. So I go for the town—how pretty it is, how lovely its old streets, how beautiful the old half-wood, half-stone houses are, how absurd that tourists all go to Tropea and hardly anywhere else, when there are so many other lovely towns around.

But Anselmo shakes his head. I am wrong. His

town is ugly. It could never attract anybody but the usual emigrants returning for their yearly visit. No, there's no comparison with Tropea. Melipodio is too ugly: and it's too far from the sea . . . No tourist would ever bother coming here.

Too far from the sea! It only takes twenty minutes to get there. Any tourist with a hired car would think that was fine, I say. And the basic structure of the town is just as pretty as Tropea. The only difference is that in Tropea, in the centre at any rate, they've re-cobbled the streets instead of concreting and asphalting them over haphazardly, the way the *Comune* seems to be doing here. And of course they've restored all the old houses and painted them up nicely; but, above all, they've finished off the building work. Tropea must be the only town we've visited since we got here that has eliminated all its half-built building sites. That's what gives it a more cheerful atmosphere. Just give this place the same treatment, I add, warming to my theme. Look, I say, at the piazza where we live: it's lovely, the old houses are beautiful (I pass lightly over the awful seventies façade perpetrated by our own relations), the original cobblestones in that lovely swirly design haven't been uprooted—not yet, at any rate, I add pointedly, since Anselmo is a Big Man in the Town Hall—and it has that wonderful fountain in the middle. But what is that ghastly eyesore of a concrete-and-bare-brick building site, stuffed full of old washing-machines, doing on the corner of it? And there must be a couple of dozen of them dotted about the town. Do they all belong to people who've moved away and abandoned them? Zia Annunziata says the one in the piazza has been like that for a good fifteen

279

years. Why doesn't the owner finish it? Can't the *Comune* make them? And there's another one just like it, only minus the washing-machines, outside your back windows, right in the middle of your view of the mountains! Doesn't it drive you mad, after everything you've done to make your house beautiful, to see that mess every time you look out of the window?

Well done, Annie. Both these ghastly eyesores just happen to belong to Anselmo's best mate, the architect who designed this house.

Fifteen years? says Anselmo. Surely not! Can it be that long since he started work on the place?

Of course, Anselmo's friend won't be paying rates or taxes on either of them as long as they remain building sites. I suppose they must be investments: he can't be planning to move into two houses at once, can he? He's finished the basic structure, they're saleable as they are—all they need is a bit of rendering and the windows putting in. Good job Ciccio and Marisa explained the no-tax business to me already—because Anselmo certainly isn't mentioning any of it. In fact, Anselmo is changing the subject completely. In his opinion, although unfinished building sites may be unattractive—and indeed, there is a by-law against their being left like that for more than a certain number of years, if anyone has complained, he says—a far worse problem is the rusting corrugated iron sheets that so many people in the older houses are using to repair their roofs. He and his architect friend, who is also on the *Comune*, are trying to get something done about that. But the dead weight of ignorance in this place is so depressing. Tiles cost more. The labour has to be paid. The corrugated iron remains.

Well! I hardly know where to start. And of course I'd better not, at a dinner party with Francesca's blue-eyed boy. But how could a few sheets of corrugated iron on the tops of roofs where you hardly notice them anyway—and which will presumably have been put up by people trying to stop a leak, rather than make money—how could that possibly be as bad as the mouldering building sites that spoil half the streets in the town? Something tells me that the tasteless corrugated-iron offenders will be persons of little influence. People who can't even afford a couple of dozen roof-tiles. While the building sites belong, no doubt, to well-heeled persons connected with the town hall bureaucracy, like Anselmo and his mate. Persons who, being in the know, will have made sure to grab every grant available—government money for restoring city centres, EEC money for underdeveloped regions, and all the rest of it. I shall be at this man's jugular if someone doesn't get me out of here soon.

(Odd, though, that Annunziata described Anselmo as a man who hadn't abandoned his roots . . . but no, here in Italy I suppose that just means still being prepared to do a favour for old neighbours. I recall the strange day, back in Diano Marina, when I found myself sitting in a bar full of depressed people whose preferred candidate, standing on an anti-corruption platform, hadn't been elected. What was the matter with him? He would have won for sure, all his supporters kept saying, if only he'd done a few more favours for people.)

I do my best to remain calm and stick to frivolity,

as befits a foreign guest at a polite dinner party. Oh, I don't know, I say: you hardly notice the odd bit of corrugated iron dotted here and there—once it's gone rusty, it's the same colour as the terracotta tiles around it, anyhow, isn't it?

So far so good—but I can't keep my tongue to myself after all that wine.

How come, I find myself adding, if there are all these laws against desecrating the old centres of towns with long-term building sites and bits of corrugated iron, nobody actually uses them to do something about it? (This is completely disingenuous of me: I know perfectly well that all Italy is bursting at the seams with laws nobody does anything about. But why not play the innocent foreigner, who has never known anything but honesty and probity in local government, when you get the chance?)

Anselmo's answer is quite flabbergasting.

It is, he tells me, all the fault of the *vigili*, the local town police force (well, a kind of sub-police-force really, with nothing like the powers of the *carabinieri* or the *polizia*: the *vigili* are more kind of traffic wardens cum local watchmen than anything else). The *vigili* in this town, he informs me, are all *vagabondi*—vagabonds. Nothing but *vagabondi*! They can't be bothered doing their jobs at all. They know it's almost impossible to sack them, and, one imagines, they just become lazy. They are supposed to make official denunciations, on paper, of all building work that is not being carried out according to the legal norms; also of building sites that are obviously being left as such for the purposes of tax evasion. But he never sees a single *denuncia* arrive at the town hall. Not one! Ever!

This is absurd. Two of the things within sight of his house, him a big shot in the *Comune*, and he is claiming that he has to wait for some little traffic warden to speak up before he makes a move. And of course they never will. Presumably these vagabond *vigili* would never dare denounce anything that belonged to an influential local person. Which would by definition cover every eyesore site in the town. Even up in the relatively transparent North, *vigili* are known for not sticking their necks out. They don't even give parking tickets to the rich and influential, never mind think of sticking them for loads of money to finish off building work against their will. Once you've managed to get yourself one of these precious State-paid *vigile* jobs, you have job security, paid holidays, sick leave and all the trimmings: luxuries in this insecure land that you certainly wouldn't risk losing by annoying powerful people who might take their revenge by getting you the sack.

That's terrible, I say. Strange, I add, that so many other towns in the region seem to be suffering from the same problem. Can it be that all the *vigili*, for hundreds of miles around, are also *vagabondi*?

Certainly, says Anselmo, smooth as you like. All *vagabondi*, he adds blandly. That is obviously the explanation.

How dare he! A cigarette. I must have a cigarette. They don't smoke in here, not in the house: this is Islington after all. So I step out into the piazza and slump at the table outside the door. No, I take that back. Not Islington at all. A place where people look you in the eye and lie blatantly and you have to pretend that you haven't noticed.

Calabria, in fact.

Ciccio follows me out for a smoke, laughs at me—why am I getting so agitated?—and tells me not to go back in until I've finished the whole packet. That was very entertaining, he says, but I must calm down now, and not row openly with Anselmo, because it will upset Francesca.

It's all very well for you, I say, but although I've been in this country for years, and got used to the notion of there being corruption everywhere, this is the first time I've ever actually had to sit down to dinner and make polite conversation with an exponent of it.

Marisa appears now, and lights up too. Amazing! she says. The man is so barefaced!

And it doesn't make sense anyway. Not if he really wants to bring some tourist prosperity to this town. His friends might lose a few bob on the swings, but they'd gain it back on the roundabouts. But I suppose that's what's happening all over Calabria. Nobody wants to rock the boat.

Of course it is, says Ciccio. Still, when you hear Zio Antonio's tales of the good old days, you realize that things have improved a lot.

But before we can get any further, Anselmo, who gave up smoking some years ago, joins us anyway. For some fresh air, he says. Smoking, he adds, is bad for the health—and it is also an unattractive thing in a woman. You will find eventually, he adds, addressing me alone for some reason, that if you go on smoking, it will darken your skin.

Good. Hopefully, Anselmo does not invite dark-skinned folk round to dinner at his house. That will definitely improve the quality of the rest of my life.

37

We're off to check out St Elias's grotto, just for the hell of it. Concetta, who claims to enjoy looking at us looking at her homeland, is coming too. She has never been there either, the way you don't when you actually live near a tourist attraction. But what is it exactly? A hermit's cave, that's all she knows. A holy hermit.

As we climb into the car, Giuseppa pops out to warn us not to take the usual road to Seminara. They've set up a road block now, she tells us, on the main road where the accident was yesterday. The *carabinieri* have been stopping cars since dawn this morning. They're checking everybody's documents, and we might be held up for hours . . .

Anselmo, arriving with a bottle of his home-made *limoncello* for Francesca, agrees that we'd be much better off taking the Castellace road. Unusual advice for these parts.

We set off on the Castellace detour, past the pile of boulders and through the millennial olive trees and the creeping mists—I see what Francesca meant, even by day you certainly wouldn't have any trouble concealing yourself here—and wind our way up into the hills. Driving through high woodland up towards Melicuccà, we're well above Palmi now, the sea a deep violet way down below, Etna looking just like a child's drawing of a volcano from this angle. Which oddly makes it look more, not less, threatening.

Slowing to round a sharp uphill bend, we come across a most unexpected sight: in a small clearing among the trees stands what appears to be a small but perfect train station, complete with a stationmaster's house. Ciccio stalls the car in amazement, and we sit and stare. Why would there be a station here, perched on the edge of a mountain and surrounded by incipient forest, in a place where there is no other habitation of any kind, and no sign that there's ever been any? Nothing but this phantom station-house, in such a fine state of repair that it looks as if it just fell from a model train set, its outdoor wooden staircase gleaming with fresh paint, three pots of wildly healthy aspidistras standing on its upstairs landing. But is there a railway in these parts? I thought the nearest the trains came was Palmi?

Of course. Once upon a time, there definitely was a railway up here—Ciccio remembers going on the train when he was a child, on his first ever visit, brilliantly scary; the train wandered along precipices and across gorges and through forests and all the way down to the sea . . . and it was always full of old ladies in black shawls with huge bundles of stuff at their feet. He thinks this higher section of it was already closed down by the time he came back on his teenage visit, though. Not that any of that explains why there would be a station here in the middle of nowhere, without a village.

Wait a minute! says Marisa excitedly. The railway! I remember the railway!

We wait indulgently. Yes, she has it. Another memory!

A tiny whitewashed waiting-room, she says, with the windows all thrown open and the sun blazing in, and a row of old ladies all dressed in black sitting on a bench, and I could hardly see them for the sun in my eyes, they were all sitting on the shady side and there was no room there for us, we had to sit in the sun . . . they were all in black, sitting in the black shadows, and I thought they were nuns and called one of them sister when she spoke to me, and it made *la mamma* laugh a lot. And then they made a space for me in the shade too, and one of them sat me on her lap, and I could see them properly now, and they all had identical silver hair tied back into identical buns . . . like extra-terrestrials . . . and when the train came, we couldn't get on it because one of them had a bundle that was so big she couldn't get it through the door, and everyone got off the train and helped her make it into smaller bundles, and then we all got on . . . and then . . . I can't remember anything else.

Still, that's enough for Marisa. She is looking positively dazed with the joy of it. And, speaking of extra-terrestrials, here is one coming out of the upstairs door of the station-house. Long black flowing robes and a very oddly-shaped head, sort of square-looking under the veil-like cloth draped over it. Or is he just wearing a mortar-board underneath the cloth? Seems only marginally more likely than my first theory.

He turns this way now, and heads on down the station staircase. A waist-length white beard. More Old Testament prophet, from this angle, than extra-terrestrial. But if this is a religious vision, it's an oddly prosaic one. He seems to be carrying a tray. A tray with four mugs on it.

Look! . . . I say. But the others already are looking. Gaping, you might say. The prophet, if that's what he is, reaches the bottom of the stairs, turns the corner of the house, and disappears. Was that a silver ponytail peeping out below the headdress? Was it some kind of priest, maybe? Was it an aged hippy? Do you get aged hippies down here? Four cups on the tray. There must be more of them in there, whatever they are.

As we sit staring, the side door of the house opens and another flowing-beard-and-ponytail man, no headgear this time, steps out with some kind of large basket in his arms. Across the garden he goes, places the basket carefully down on the grass . . . and starts to hang the washing on the line. Socks. An awful lot of socks.

And now his get-up is starting to look familiar. My old flat in Shepherd's Bush used to be right next to a church that nobody ever went to—until, one fine day, it transmuted into a Greek Orthodox cathedral, whereupon it was packed every Sunday, and became a lot more entertaining. Now we got processions with people carrying holy statues on their shoulders, bedecked with flowers; and real eggs dyed orange at their Easter, which wasn't the same date as ours; and occasionally—a bit alarming, this, when you weren't expecting it— you'd step out of your front door at dusk to find your street filled with a crowd of completely, utterly silent people, all dressed in black, all holding a candle, and all facing the same way. It was this all-facing-the-same-way part, for some reason, that was especially unnerving. Anyway, one of the interesting features of life near a Greek Orthodox cathedral is the way you often bump into what appear to be Old Testament prophets, sunk deep in theological debate, on the street corner, when you're on your way to the shop for a pint of milk. Prophets in long flowing robes and long curly beards, sporting ponytails and square headdresses.

Still, we are up in the foothills of the Calabrian Aspromonte, and a very long way from the Shepherd's Bush Greek community. Could there be a Greek Orthodox church round here? Or do they take over empty Calabrian station-houses as well as empty Church of England churches? But why would they bother? Where is the flock?

The laundry-hanging priest has finished his chore now, and is standing looking at us looking at him. Shamefacedly, we start the car up again and drive off.

We find our first signs to the Grotto of St Elias the Hermit only half a mile further on. Was it a special station just for visitors to St Elias, then? Another small hand-drawn sign points us to a winding path that leads off a hairpin bend. A quarter of a mile's walk uphill, in the shade of pine and beech trees, the path single-file width, a stream running along beside it, total silence all around us apart from the trickling water, no sign of any human presence; and Ciccio suddenly gives a cry of triumph and falls to his knees on the grassy bank at the side of the path. Liquorice! he says: and starts pulling and digging with his fingertips around a small fern-like plant. So it is! says Concetta. The plant eventually comes up, with a root and two or three runners attached. Try that! says Ciccio, cleaning the earth off his booty and starting to chew, passing us an inch-long piece each. Concetta takes hers with a will: so Marisa and I follow suit. It really does taste of liquorice, we say.

Taste of liquorice! It doesn't just taste of liquorice, says Ciccio. It *is* liquorice! This is what

289

you boil up, for hours and hours, and once you've evaporated all the water off, you're left with a dark brown paste—liquorice.

Concetta confirms this: people used to make a living gathering the stuff and cooking it up round here, once upon a time. And Annunziata still makes a pretty fine liquorice liqueur, especially good for the digestion. We must make sure to try it when we get back.

On up the hill we go, masticating and marvelling: and at last we find the Hermit's cave. It is huge and echoing, silent and empty apart from a rather makeshift-looking altar in the middle of the floor, covered in a white cloth. There is still not a sound around us. We came here knowing nothing of this saint: and it looks as though we shall leave in the same case. It's a good cave, though, and you can see why St Elias chose it. As well as being big enough to fit a double-decker bus inside, no problem, it is surprisingly dry and warm for a cave, with a clean sandy floor: and it has its own water supply. A single drip of water falls every few seconds from the centre of the arch of its roof, and must have done so for centuries, to judge by the depth of the cup-shape it has carved into the rock below. Along the far side of the cave wall stands a row of Russian-icon-looking paintings, just propped casually against the rock. Was St Elias an especially Orthodox saint, then? Come to think of it, the altar is in the middle, Orthodox style, too. The priests in the station must be connected with this place, for sure.

Luckily for us, just as we are beginning to feel extremely frustrated at our own ignorance, we hear a faint chatter of voices among the trees. Half-a-dozen brown-habited nuns soon appear, escorted by a priestly guide. Ordinary Catholics, though, not Orthodox, by the look of them.

Eavesdropping the nuns' lesson, we get the lowdown at last on Elias's life and times. He lived in the ninth century, and retreated up here to live as a hermit after a major disappointment involving the translating of the Gospels from their original languages. I seem to remember being told a tale in which one of these early Bible translators got stoned by the congregation for his pains. Apparently, he told them that Jonah's bower of gourds—the shady spot he rested in after his travails inside the whale—was not really a bower of gourds, but of ivy. The gourds were a mistranslation. His listeners, who for reasons of their own clearly felt a strong attachment to the gourds, went mad and hurled anything they could find to hand, mostly rocks, at the bringer of the bad tidings. Was that St Elias? It definitely seems the sort of experience that might make you take to hermit-hood.

Legend says, we hear from the priest, that Elias lived on nothing but green barley: and that the drip from the roof wasn't there before he moved in: it is a miraculous one, sent by God. Miraculous, too, was the way you could use the water he had washed his body in to cure your toothache. Unappealing, on the face of it, but then a toothache can be a desperate thing. Elias died aged ninety-four; and some time later the Saracens, looking for something to desecrate, got hold of his body and did their best to burn it. But it wouldn't catch fire.

The priest spots us, and as soon as he hears that I am English, insists on hearing my opinion on

291

Calabria. What do I think about it? Is there any hope for the place? What do I make of all the corruption, the crime, the Mafia?

Well, I say—I've been thinking a lot about this since the dinner with Anselmo—I'm sure there's plenty of corruption, but when people talk about its all being 'the Mafia' I'm not so sure: Mafia is just a catch-all word, as far as I can see. I don't think I really believe that the exponents of corruption and crime are all in some big organization together: or would need to be. Why would politicians on the make and bent builders and sticky-fingered bureaucrats and low-life drug-importers and people-traffickers all want to sit down to an annual meeting of law-breakers? What would they have in common? What advantage would it give them? I think the problem is more an attitude of mind than anything else.

The priest gives me the kind of benevolent smile you might give to a person you suspect of having suffered severe brain damage; or perhaps of being an incipient holy fool. So I ask for his opinion. Why did he ask? What does he think? Have I got it all wrong?

He thinks Calabria has many problems; but being Calabrese himself, he is obviously prejudiced. Any chance of his describing these prejudices? No: he's another *omertà* merchant. So we change the subject. St Elias and his cave: that's safe enough. Was he the bower-of-ivy man? The priest hasn't heard this story; but he is not an expert on St Elias. He and his charges just stopped here because they were passing.

Would he know whether the Orthodox priests at the station are something to do with this place?

They are bound to be. There has always been a call for Orthodox priests, he tells us, in this part of the world. This is where the two churches meet. Geographically speaking, of course, not theologically, he adds, smiling a thin smile. Wasted on us: none of us has any idea of the theological differences between the two churches. Apart from their disagreement over the calendar, which you wouldn't think would be quite enough to keep them apart for centuries. Though I don't suppose there was much love lost when the Normans snatched all the lands and property of the Byzantine church here in Calabria, and the Roman church happily accepted it as a gift. Or as a bribe, rather. But was the Byzantine Orthodox church the same as the Greek and Albanian one?

Yes indeed, says our priest, there have been Greek and Albanian populations in Calabria since well before Byzantium: they were already here at the time of the Romans, living side by side with them but in their own cities and villages. Their languages have become part of the local dialects. The Albanian communities have been the main Orthodox worshippers here for the last few centuries—but of course, since the fall of the iron curtain, many more have come to join them. Elias was probably of Greek origin himself: he was beatified in the tenth century, well before the schism between Catholic and Orthodox of 1054.

Ah, I say to myself: so there you have it. That's what the priests are doing in the station. Between the two events, who should arrive but the unscrupulous Robert Guiscard, going around expropriating the property of the Eastern church

293

left, right and centre. And no doubt leaving the poor Byzantine guardians of this shrine homeless, penniless and hungry, into the bargain. And it is a well-known fact, is it not, that the homeless and penniless will always gravitate towards a railway station? Which explains why they have ended up in a disused station-house.

*   *   *

On our return home, late afternoon by now, we take the normal Seminara road. The accident drama must surely have run its course by now?

But no. Though the smashed cars have finally been removed from the Accident Black Spot, the police are still here, though the investigation has, it seems, become more military than civilian. The proportions have been reversed: there are now six *carabinieri* to two *polizia*. The *carabinieri* have mounted their road block in camouflage gear with huge automatic weapons, patrolling the same spot.

They stop us, ask for all the car documents, start radioing our number-plate details through to their headquarters. They have an unconscionably slow computer system, it seems: fifteen minutes later we are still there, and Concetta the Disconsolate is making plenty of headway with the handsome black-haired one who looks a lot like a young Elvis. She insists on our digging out the camera from the depths of the glove compartment: she must have her photo taken with him. The young *carabiniere* loves it, and insists on posing for more photos with all three of us females, first singly and then all together. Will we send him copies? Of course we

294

will, we say. We would say anything to be allowed to go on our way. He is from Puglia, he tells us, and he wishes he was back home. That's the trouble with joining the forces of law and order; the job's secure, the money's all right: but you just have to accept that you'll never get posted back home till you're nearly ready to retire.

Why on earth not? asks the ignorant foreigner.

Isn't it obvious? Use your brain! mutters Ciccio, who often has trouble crediting how un-Machiavellian my thought processes still are, after all the time I've lived in his country.

So what is going on? we ask. Wasn't it just an ordinary road accident?

He has no idea, says the *carabiniere*. He was just sent here, told to check people's documents. Not for anything in particular, no, no, he says. Just the usual: is the car on the stolen list, have they got a driver's licence, insurance, certificate of roadworthiness . . .

How much mileage can you get out of a perfectly ordinary car accident? Two police forces have got two days' work each out of it. Imagine that, I say. How long would it take them to sort out an actual crime?

What, like a lorry inexplicably plunging off a bridge? says Ciccio, giving me an old-fashioned look, Calabrian-style.

38

The pale light of early morning, and from behind the bedroom shutters I witness sinister goings-on over on the far side of the empty piazza. A small group of men, all dressed in a vaguely military manner, in brown, khaki and camouflage, lots of straps and belts, silently moving to and fro around a pair of jeep-type vehicles, looking very businesslike as they check methodically through their gear, unpacking and repacking seriously professional-looking cases and boxes, all silver metal and matt black and nylon webbing. Now they start loading it into their off-road transport. The cars have Milan number-plates, but as we know that doesn't mean much in these parts. They could be from the next town. Or even the next piazza. But I don't think they're faces I've seen before around here. One of them has one of the long flat cases open on the bonnet now, is taking bits out of it and screwing them together. Can it be? I stare a bit harder. Yes, it really is a gun. A rifle or a shotgun, I'm not much of a firearms expert, but it's definitely something long and menacing-looking. And look, the man in the back seat of the other car, next to the one wearing the Fidel Castro-type cap and speaking into some kind of short stubby walkie-talkie, is holding a gun too, lying across his knees. Now, as they move slowly off, the gunman in the lead car lifts his weapon, points the barrel of the thing at the windscreen, and squints down its telescopic sight . . . Eek! Am I about to witness a Mafia slaying? Are they going to massacre some inhabitant of this square on their doorstep? And me too, probably, for witnessing the event? I edge out from behind the shutters to get a better view. Giuseppa's front door is open. Yes—there she is. Not cowering terrified in her doorway, though, but looking utterly unconcerned and raising a leisurely hand to the gunmen in farewell. The two jeeps disappear round the corner out of the piazza without firing a shot.

Buon giorno! Giuseppa calls up to me. Hunters already, did you see that? How fast the summer has flown by! The hunting season again so soon, and the Milanesi are already here! Would you believe it? We'll have to remember to smile nicely at them when they get back, and you never know, we might get a couple of nice wild boar steaks for our suppers!

Ah, hunters. Of course, that's what they were. You get a lot of them round our way in Liguria too, though not usually quite so well-heeled-looking as this lot. They must be heading up into the Aspromonte after wild boar. The walkie-talkies, I know from personal experience, are so they can keep in contact with one another as they try to close in on some poor boar family and encircle them. Ciccio and I once spent a most entertaining afternoon eavesdropping on a group of them. We had just got hold of a pair of walkie-talkies of our own at the time—this was in the days when mobile phones were still prohibitively expensive, and we hoped that they might help eliminate those awful moments when one of you has set off on the fifteen-minute drive down the twelve hairpin bends to the nearest shop, and the other one suddenly realizes there's no loo paper left . . . and, while we were trying them out, discovered that we were accidentally tuned in to a massive boar-hunt sweeping across our valley. A hilariously slapstick event, in which the only animals the twenty-odd daring huntsmen got anywhere near catching, a mother boar with three youngsters, got clean away from her stalkers—well done that boar!—and vanished out of the valley completely; while two of the hunters' dogs got lost in the chase, so that they actually spent more time hunting their own creatures than catching wild ones.

*   *   *

Zia Annunziata is busy in Palmi sorting out the accounts with the Moroccan this morning, she says. And Carmela is off on an outing to Pompeii for the day. So Vincenza will be taking charge of preparing the lunch.

Pompeii? I'm impressed. I hadn't thought of Carmela as the sort of woman who might dash off, as the fancy took her, to tour the odd archaeological site. I wish I was going too. I've only ever spent one afternoon in Pompeii: just long enough to realize I'd need a week to see it properly. Those fast-food stalls, two thousand years old! They were a surprise. Marble counters running right across the shopfronts, open to the streets; earthenware urns sunk into them, necks flush with the marble for easy serving and cleaning, a little fire burning below to keep the food hot. Three or four varieties of food, to judge by the number of urns. Some shops even had an extra couple at the back, with a kind of grill arrangement to the side of them. Impossible not to speculate. Did they,

298

perhaps, once sell little patties of ground meat, flame-grilled and wrapped in hot bread, across these counters?

It's a coach trip, says Carmela. With a whole bunch of women from the town. You're welcome to come if you like. Twenty-three of us, wasn't it, *mamma*?

Twenty-seven, says Annunziata. The Alberti girls changed their minds again. Don't worry, I told everyone when I booked to be prepared for up to thirty at a pinch. So they can't possibly end up short. Just keep a hold of the list of the people you have to ask for afterwards, and nothing can go wrong.

Annunziata is, she tells us, a travel agent today. I told you we turned our hand to anything, didn't I, she says, as long as we could make a few *lire* at it? She has the coach booked, and a hotel meal at lunchtime, because they like a bit of glamour; and a stop for coffee and brioches half-way there, and one for an afternoon *merendina* with a plate-glass sea view on the way back. And a guide to take them round and tell them what they're looking at—and help Carmela keep an eye on them so they don't get lost in the souvenir shops and miss the coach back. This is Carmela's first trip without Annunziata, she says, giving her daughter's hand a squeeze. And she's nervous, aren't you, Carmela? But there's nothing to worry about.

This is the first time I've seen Annunziata be motherly to her daughter since we arrived, I realize. They usually act as if it was the other way round. Carmela treats Annunziata like an exuberant child in need of constant calming down and shutting up; and Annunziata happily plays along.

It's the idea of sidling up to people with my hand out, Carmela is saying. They don't know I'm your daughter, I'll have to tell them that first, and I'll go so shy that I can barely whisper, or else I'll be so full of nerves that I'll suddenly find I'm shouting. And everyone from the coach will know.

Well, there's no shame to it, says Annunziata. It's normal. Everyone does it. Just drink a nice big glass of wine with your lunch, girl, and you won't even notice.

All three of us, Marisa, Francesca and me, are glued to this intriguing conversation, waiting for a clue. What can it be, this thing that Carmela needs to get drunk to do? Annunziata glances our way, and bursts out laughing at our rapt expressions.

We always get a few bob on the side, she explains: the restaurants, the souvenir shops, all of them give her a *pensierino*, a 'little thought', for delivering her twenty or thirty captive trippers into their hands. But Carmela will have to collect the tribute today.

Does it amount to a lot, then? asks Francesca, who goes on quite a few of these ladies' coach trips herself, and obviously feels she should dig the dirt.

Sometimes it does, says her sister-in-law. Especially the hotel restaurants. They'd be half-empty at this time of year, so they give her a percentage on what the group spends, to show their gratitude. Which, Annunziata says, is not necessary, because she would always tell her trippers to treat themselves—it's a day out, isn't it, and if they fancy an expensive wine or what-have-you, why not? But the percentage makes her feel like she has an ulterior motive! Anyway, the hotel's happy, and so are the trippers, happy as larry, because a hotel is a great luxury as far as Melipodio folk are concerned. The food isn't always that special, to tell the truth, but a few gilded mirrors and a grand stairway certainly stimulate the tastebuds! Not that there's anything wrong with the food. It's just the kind of food that—you know— *Non crepi, ma non campi!*

The pair of them fall about laughing for some time, now, repeating this phrase over and over. *Non crepi, ma non campi*: 'It won't kill you, but you couldn't call it living, either.'

Once they've got over it, Annunziata confesses that she sometimes feels guilty about the whole thing, making money out of these coach trips. It's not really work: anybody could do it. You just have to pick up the phone.

Nonsense! Francesca is very impressed with this new evidence of Annunziata's *mentalità di commerciante*, her well-known business brain.

Annunziata thinks she got a big advantage from there being no men around at all, most of the time she was growing up—all away in America, every last male in the family, and nobody to say you couldn't do this, that or the other because you were female. Good times! There were only females around—and they could do everything, of course. Because they had to.

All very well for Annunziata, says Francesca. But then the few men who were left behind, her own father for one, turned into worse and worse tyrants over their own womenfolk. Francesca got the other side of the same coin.

Carmela is almost ready to leave for Pompeii to collect her first-ever bribes—or to meet her doom.

301

She and Annunziata prepared most of the lunch earlier, she says from the doorway, as she waits for Annunziata to put on her coat; there are green peppers stuffed with anchovy rice for the first course, Vincenza just needs to put them in the oven for a bit, then for *secondo,* there's the rest of the stockfish to eat, she's made a salad with it, seasoned it with plenty of olives and red onion, and a nice big dollop of Calabrian oil, because the Ligurian stuff is too light for *stoccafisso.* And for our meat course, if we fancy one, there are plenty of *milanesi* in the fridge.

Porca miseria, says Ciccio as the door closes firmly behind our hostesses.

Fear not, I reply. There is hope yet. Go and talk to Giuseppa next door. I think she can put you on to a wild-boar-steak connection for tonight.

39

Archaeology? You thought they were going to Pompeii to admire the ruined city?

Vincenza laughs uproariously at the notion, as she struggles to light the oven.

Old Pompeii! Not at all! That would be the day! says Vincenza, chuckling some more. They're off to see some Very Important Bishop or other say Mass there today—in Pompeii the town of the living, though, not of the dead.

Lucky I didn't change my mind and go on the spur of the moment, I say.

Imagine that! she says, savouring the thought. You'd surely have been too far from home to turn back by the time you realized. What a holy day that would have been for you! And she does a very rude imitation of a devout lady mumbling her rosary . . .

Carmela's peppers are on the side, waiting to go in. I put the stockfish-and-olive salad next to a pile of lettuces on the table in the middle of the second kitchen. I have brought in a bag of *rostelle*, goat kebabs, too, that Ciccio bribed or blandished out of Giuseppa this morning. They only take a few minutes to grill, he said: any other cut of goat has to cook slowly for hours, or it's tough as old boots. Shall I put these in the fridge? I ask. Or should we add a few to the lunch now?

Imagine the scene, she says, ignoring my question completely, when you confessed to caring more for the Ancient Pompeiians than for the Bishop! They'd have had some praying to do then, all right, over the pagan in their midst! The fun they would have had! Perform an exorcism, that's what they would have done. Twenty-seven devout ladies of Melipodio, beating the devil out of you with their rosaries.

We both giggle at the image. Would she mind if Ciccio came in and cooked a few of these *rostelle*, if he won't be in the way? Is there any particular place I should put the rest? I ask. I still haven't gained any clear insight into the three-kitchen system here. Would it go out in that small fridge in the very back room?

No, worse! says Vincenza, ignoring me; still gripped by her imaginary scenario. They would have thrown you out of the bus for fear of contamination! Trailed you at the end of a rope until you recanted! Think of that! Your last sight ever—those twenty-seven saintly, rosy faces

303

pressed up against the back window agog, as you suffer your sinful pagan death!

As she dwells upon my martyrdom, Vincenza has begun working a bowl of home-made pasta dough. *A fileia*, it's called in dialect, she says—a kind of home-made *maccheroni*. She didn't want to just heat up somebody else's cooking. She's done the *impasto* already—just flour and water, no egg— which she's making into little balls, then rolling into foot-long worms. You leave the worms to rest for an hour, she says, then wrap them round and round this hazel-rod—it's a foot long, like the biggest size of knitting needle—now, a quick press-and-swirl on the floured wooden board, and she slips out the rod, leaving a perfect tube, with pretty spiral markings all the way down it. Wonderful! Can I have a go?

No, says Vincenza. You'll only make a mess of it.

She's probably right, alas. It took me months to master the press-and-flip you do with a fork to make *gnocchi*.

So, will I tell Ciccio he can do his *rostelle* when you're finished? Or what?

Certainly not! says Vincenza, emphatically.

OK, then I'll put them away . . . The meat fridge? I say again, hopefully.

Yes, out at the very back.

I head for the scullery. Vincenza, shutting the oven door on the peppers, comes after me. Did anyone tell you, she says, that the Madonna of the Waters came from back there? After the flood, that is?

What, she was found in the scullery? Is this one of Vincenza's strange jokes?

No indeed! Come on, she says, lowering her

304

voice as if somebody was trying to eavesdrop and heading off along the dark narrow space between the myriad sinks. I'll show you! Look, over there . . .

I do: she is pointing to the black corner between the senseless shower-base and the rock-face that forms the back wall. You can see the water dribbling down the surface of the stone, a fine film of pale limescale growing on it, veining it where the trickles run . . .

That's the place, she says, laying her index finger flat along the side of her nose—the sign for secret knowledge. That's where the lovely Virgin was found. Where she grew up. Now you know.

Grew up? She did say '*è cresciuta*', which usually means either 'grew' or 'grew up'—but it must be some Southern usage of the word. What, the statue was found in here? I say, hoping for clarification. It doesn't look possible; but then you can see that an awful lot of building work has been done on this house over the centuries, bits added and bits taken away. It must have changed dramatically since whenever this flood was; maybe the gulley thing was an open stream at the time? Up in the Ligurian hills I've seen a stream diverted to run past the backs of a whole street of houses—an early rubbish-and-sewage disposal system from the days before indoor plumbing. Would the gulley once have been something similar?

Did she float in down the underground river, then? I ask.

Of course, says Vincenza. And lay here a long, long time . . .

Maybe, then, Vincenza really did mean 'grew'? Perhaps the limescale would have accumulated on

305

the Virgin's stone face as she lay under the dripping rock-face walls in this corner, waiting to be discovered? And that's how her expression would have changed, then? Oh, this is ridiculous, why am I calling a statue 'her' ? I'm starting to sound like Vincenza myself.

Before I can check any of this out with my guide, Vincenza suddenly decides the visit is over. That's that, now! Out you come! she says loudly, as if to give anyone who might be about the impression that she's just caught me red-handed nosing about in the private recesses of the house. Let's get on with the lunch!

Really! The woman is definitely barking mad.

Will I chop up the lettuce for the salad, then? I say, picking up a chopping knife and heading for the lettuces.

No, it's too early to make the salad. Put that down! Vincenza snaps, plucking the knife from my grasp.

Well, is there something else I can do to help?

No! says Vincenza, even more emphatically. I said no. I said no twice! *Qua, non si può ragionare!* There's no reasoning in this place! Why does everybody always have to be sniffing at one another's armpits round here?

OK, got it, I'm off.

*   *   *

Lunchtime, and Vincenza has called us to the table, but there is no sign of her; and the door to the second kitchen is firmly shut. There is no sign of food yet, except for a basket of rolls. Marisa opens the door a crack; can she help? No, says Vincenza.

306

We sit and munch our way through the bread, listening to much banging and crashing from the back kitchen. Francesca, desperate, has begun foraging around the sideboards for food. She lets out a cry of triumph.

Pastori! she says, bringing a small bowl full of round brown deep-fried-looking objects, like tiny onion bhajis, over to the table. She puts one into her mouth and goes into a transport of delight. How many years since she's tasted one of these!

But what are *pastori*? we ask. 'Pastori' literally means 'shepherds'—and none of us has ever heard of such a foodstuff.

Wild garlic bulbs, dipped in chilli powder and deep-fried in olive oil! Francesca tells us excitedly. They're for medicinal purposes really—they will cure anything, from a cold in the head to a broken leg! She passes the bowl around. Eat one, she says, and all pain will pass!

Her children and grandson take one each. Keeping a close watch on Alberto's expression as he chews, I decide to take a rain check. Less dangerous just to wait for Vincenza's offering.

And here she comes in triumph at last, bearing a tray of peppers in an oven glove; she serves us one each, and Francesca, still starving, cuts into hers right away.

But Vincenza, she says as her knife crunches through raw pepper, this isn't cooked!

Isn't it? says Vincenza, cutting crunchily into her own, and taking a large mouthful. That's how I like them, though. They're much better for you short-cooked, you know, she adds. And she goes quietly on eating, making absolutely no move to solve the problem.

307

Alberto takes a fit of the giggles. This certainly is an unusual way to treat house guests in an Italian home. But then, I suppose Vincenza is a guest too. I try my own pepper: it is definitely undercooked from a traditional Italian standpoint, but fine from an English one. And as it's stuffed with a cooked rice mixture, with anchovies and tomato and garlic and olive oil, it's perfectly edible. Very tasty, in fact. I carry on eating it. Easy for me, with my peculiar English upbringing; but the Italian contingent is deeply disconcerted. Nobody has ever presented any of them with a pepper in this state.

Vincenza is showing no sign of pandering to the guests' whims, though: she's just munching her way steadily through her own pepper, oblivious.

Marisa decides to defuse the situation. I'll go and put yours and mine in the oven for a bit longer, will I, *mamma*? she says. How about you, Ciccio? Alberto?

No! No! says Vincenza, leaping from her seat as if she's only just noticed that something was wrong, and grabbing the dish from Marisa's hands. Let me! I'll take them in—you won't know how to work the oven, anyway!

Francesca, Marisa and Ciccio start on the salads to fill in time—and Vincenza disappears into the back kitchen again, whence she re-emerges some time later with the peppers, now blackened nearly to a crisp.

There! she says, presenting them to her victims.

You've burnt them now, says Ciccio. You need a bit more practice with that oven.

More practice? Why? says Vincenza. It wasn't an accident—isn't that how you wanted them?

And she picks up her knife and fork and goes

308

back to eating her pepper, crunchy version. I have finished mine already: Vincenza flashes a conspiratorial grin in my direction . . .

What on earth is Vincenza about? She seems to do these strange things in a spirit of scientific experiment, rather than in malice. You'd say she was conducting a sociological investigation into what happens, exactly, if you break all the unspoken rules of normal behaviour.

Francesca just sighs and picks at the edible bits of hers. Marisa starts laughing. So does Vincenza. So do I. I'll go and get the fish salad, then, I say to Vincenza. If that's all right by you.

Of course, she says airily. And there's a green salad ready on the side . . . But there's the pasta first.

All goes well for some time. Vincenza's *fileia* are delicious, in a simple home-made tomato *sugo*—or *sucu*, as you call it here: and Francesca goes off into transports of delight again over the dishes of her youth that she hasn't tasted for so long. We move on to the stockfish salad, exclaiming over the olives in it, which turn out to be the ones Francesca pinched from the tree outside the garage when we broke down: good as her word, she has cracked and roasted them, and they are every bit as pleasing an experience as advertised.

Some time later, I pile a second helping of the green salad on my plate, and ask if anyone can see the oil.

Here, says Vincenza, passing it. Don't you want the vinegar too?

No, I say. I'll just have oil and salt for now. So Vincenza picks up the vinegar bottle and sprinkles it liberally all over my plate . . .

40

We have an appointment with Anselmo at the town hall later on, to look at the Births, Marriages and Deaths register. There doesn't seem much point to it, though. We'll only find Francesca's side of the family in there, won't we? And Grazia isn't looking for the maternal ancestors. There weren't any de Gilios in the cemetery; and I don't suppose there'll be any in the town hall either.

I don't know if I can face being in an enclosed space with Anselmo again, anyway. I've only just managed, by the skin of my teeth, to be civil to him the last couple of times I've bumped into him. No, I won't come, I say. But I'm kind of torn between fascination and repulsion. And I'd like to see inside that lovely town hall building. Maybe I will?

Plenty of time yet to decide, says Ciccio: the most urgent thing now is to keep those frozen *milanesi* at bay. We must go and find a proper butcher's shop pronto, and buy some goat. We'll get a leg, maybe. Or a shoulder. Or both. That's the meat he was always given last time he was here, whenever he ate at people's houses: goat. They're brilliant with it, too.

But the nearest butcher to here is at Seminara. No butcher at all in this town. This seems to be par for the course round here: you get chicken-and-stockfish shops all over the place, practically every town we've been through has its chicken-and-stockfish shop, but butchers' shops are few and far between.

(I have tried investigating the stockfish mystery,

and got nowhere. What is dried cod doing embedded so deep in Calabrian tradition that you get stockfish shops instead of butchers' shops? How does a place so far from the Atlantic develop the habit of eating a kind of fish that not only does not exist in their own Mediterranean sea, but comes from far away in the northernmost tip of Europe? You can tell by the name it bears that it arrived in Italy from our northern end of Europe: *stoccafisso* is obviously just an Italianized pronunciation of 'stockfish'. And it was already being imported here in the Middle Ages, according to the Alimentary Culture section. Italy buys a large proportion of Norway's annual production of the stuff to this very day: of which, I'm told, tiny Calabria takes two-thirds.

I have not found the answer to the conundrum: perhaps its popularity is due to its keeping for ever? To its being very lightweight and nothing but pure protein? The Alimentary Culture has stockfish down, along with any kind of meat, as a luxury food, consumed only at the couple of great festive periods of the year: at Easter, before the fasting of Lent started: and at the town *festa* on the local saint's day. Otherwise, until recently, most Calabrians hardly ate first-class protein at all: which explains the major role of nuts and beans. Apparently the everyday diet here was, for centuries, mostly beans, nuts and grains: the human body can create its own first-class protein as long as you give it a combination of pulses and grains. Every culture in the world, the book tells me airily, has its traditional pulse-and-grain dish. Has it? Peas and rice, tortilla and beans, rice and dhal . . . Baked beans on toast! Maybe he's right, too.

311

But to return to the topic in hand, when they first appeared, chicken-and-stockfish shops must have been luxury shops. People may have spent much of their time looking after beasts, but they mostly belonged to the landlords; any four-footed animals the labouring folk owned themselves were to be sold off for desperately needed hard cash, not to be eaten. Thus we are left with the chickens. But whence the stockfish? There was no fishing in Calabria worth speaking of for centuries, not once the people of the coastal towns had all fled inland from the Saracens. Was stockfish just better than no fish at all?

*   *   *

So, here we are in Seminara, a place with an actual identifiable shopping street. And a butcher's shop in it. There, in front of us, is the Piazza of the Fourteen Crosses. Three families, according to Rocco, were exterminated down to the very last member while that last *faida* was going on. There are an awful lot of those ceramic anti-evil-eye amulets, the pointing-fingers-with-red-tips, hanging above people's doors here. Life, I suppose, must feel more precarious here in Seminara, with that bloodstained piazza in the middle of it. Unless it's just that the ceramics shop is so close by?

Who, I ask Ciccio and Marisa, do all these people suspect of being likely to try and put the evil eye on them? Does anyone ever say? Is it something just anybody can do? Or would you have to be some kind of adept at the Black Arts before you'd know how to go about it? Are there professionals you go to, people you pay to put the

312

evil eye on somebody for you?

Ciccio doesn't know. He doesn't think so. There are just people you pay to take it off. But of course, you don't exactly pay them. They can't ask for money, it wouldn't be right to suggest that one could simply buy the powers of good. They accept an offering from you all right, though.

So nobody knows where the evil eye might come from at all? Would it be something that just kind of emanated from other people's envy of you? They wouldn't know they'd done it, but they'd have put the evil eye on you with the power of their negative thoughts?

Marisa thinks that must be it. She's never considered the matter before now. How would you go about putting the evil eye on someone? Hmm.

Alberto thinks we are all mad. And how do we dare to laugh at his fantasy computer games when we go around talking such supernatural gibberish ourselves?

Nice to see Alberto in so sunny a mood. We drive on, looking for somewhere to leave the car. Parked at last, and somewhat lost by now, we head up a narrow alleyway that we hope leads towards the piazza.

But what on earth is that thing hanging outside the corner door at the far end of the road? Another anti-evil-eye thing by the look of it, but completely over the top—a huge pair of horns, a couple of feet long, with tufts of matted hair around them, dangling lopsidedly in mid-air amid an obscene tangle of bones. Long, knobble-ended bones, like human leg-bones. The whole contraption swings gently, horribly, in the back draught as a car passes by: a dozen flies buzz lazily up from their resting places, circle around it, and settle back down again.

And now we're closer, we see that the bones actually have shreds of bloody flesh still clinging to them. Now that, I say, appalled, is going too far. I should think it's a health hazard, too, apart from anything else. Revolting!

That, says Ciccio with a sly grin, is the butcher's shop.

What? Marisa is disgusted. They leave the meat hanging out in the street, in dirt and flies and exhaust fumes? We're certainly not buying anything in there! We'll just have to live on *milanesi*. But Alberto has worked it out. There is probably something similar in one of his fantasy games. That's not the meat, *mamma*, he says. That's just the carcass. The butcher must hang it outside so you'll know what animal he's slaughtered today. Isn't it, Zio Ciccio? Then you'll know what meat is available in the shop! Alberto thinks it's very sensible. It saves having to writ labels to put in your shop window; and people can see it from much further away, so it's like an advertisement, too. I bet they've been doing that for centuries, he says, since the times when hardly anyone could read and write.

Alberto gets a round of applause. But his mother is not mollified. Can't we just go to an ordinary, normal butcher's shop?

The rest of us just look at her. Where does she suggest we go? Liguria?

Anyhow, Ciccio's eyes have already lit up at the thought of communing with the butcher inside. Discussing the intricacies of meat production, breed, feed and pasture, with butchers, who also have many interesting opinions on the best techniques to be applied to its cooking, is one of his favourite pastimes. There's absolutely no hope of getting him to go anywhere else, even assuming that there was anywhere else to go.

He is now stoutly maintaining, to a most sceptical sister, that this is how things should be. The butcher slaughters an animal, he says, and you go in and buy bits cut off it, fresh from the chopping block. What could be more normal than that? Does Marisa prefer her animals killed hundreds of miles away from the shop, their carcasses loaded up, by porters in dirty overalls, into dirty lorries—and carted to and fro across the country for a week or two before she gets to buy it? Is it better to cut the flesh into bits, wrap it up in plastic, and freeze it for a few months, or years for that matter, before you eat it? He defies Marisa to produce a more normal butcher's shop than this one! And in he goes for some manly meat talk, Alberto following.

Marisa and I, on the other hand, go off, with only a slight frisson of trepidation, to the bar in the Piazza of the Fourteen Crosses to wait: where, just inside the door, neatly laid out in a glass cold-cabinet, sits a prominent display of those half-a-goat's-head snacks. We avert our eyes and order a cappuccino and a brioche. No brioches, *signorine*, just *zippoli*, says the barman. I look nervously at Marisa. *Zippoli?* Never heard of them. She looks reassuringly pleased at the notion. Yes, we'll have a couple of those, then.

We get a whole plateful, as it turns out, piping hot. Little oval balls of pizza-type dough, each with a tiny taste of anchovy or onion rolled up inside, and deep-fried. Crispy on the outside, voluptuous within. Lovely. We order a second helping.

Ciccio and Alberto appear, loaded down with bags of meat, just as the waiter is putting them on our table. *Zippoli!* says Ciccio. What? says Alberto.

They grab one each; *che buono!* they say, in stereo, and immediately go for a whole handful. They have the lot devoured in seconds, not a crumb left for us: and they haven't even sat down yet. The waiter, witnessing this scene of barefaced robbery, smiles benevolently on. Ciccio and Alberto are men, of course, and need plenty of nourishment.

Alas, he replies when Marisa and I beg piteously for another plateful, there are no more *zippoli*. The *aperitivo* hour is over, and they won't be making any more till tomorrow. Would we like a nice goat's head instead? With oil and vinegar, or with green sauce?

Perfect! says Ciccio. Oil and vinegar, please.

OK, why not? says Alberto. The boy has clearly been much hardened by his recent experience in the butcher's shop.

And the ladies? asks the waiter.

Silence falls.

41

Yes, this is where we keep all the documents—births, marriages, deaths, every important event in our inhabitants' lives, says Anselmo. All kept in here, preserved for posterity. As far as we can, at any rate. Until they get lost . . . ! he adds, laughing as if he'd made a comprehensible joke.

What on earth does he mean by that? What's funny about it? Is he playing a mock feckless-Calabrese?

He digs a tome out of the bottom drawer of the cabinet in the corner, puts it on his large mahogany desk, and starts to hunt through it. No record of de Gilios/Giglios here, he says: Salvatore seems to have been the first. We'll have to go up to Santa Cristina if we want any more. But plenty on Francesca's side of the family—would we like to look ourselves? He turns the volume round towards us. Not much use for discovering aristocratic connections, he says, but interesting anyway. Ciccio and Marisa start tracking back through the maternal side of the family: I take a look over their shoulders. Every entry is handwritten in a mad, curlicue-laden, antique Italian style. How on earth can they read it? I can't understand a word.

They work back conscientiously until the 1870s, taking down a list of parents, grandparents and great-grandparents. Then they ask for the tome before this one.

Ah, indeed, how fascinating is local history! says Anselmo, smiling urbanely. But alas, the *Comune* holds no records before 1871.

How come? asks Ciccio.

They were tragically destroyed in a fire, says Anselmo.

What, recently?

No, no, says he. At the time, as he understands it.

And he just leaves it at that, as if the thing required no further explanation. But in 1870,

317

Calabria was fiercely divided, there was almost a civil war going on, with some towns taking Garibaldi's side against the landlords whose high-handed behaviour he had promised to moderate, others fighting against him. It must have been in the midst of all this that this tragic fire took place. Surely there must be more to tell than just the bald fact that the records were destroyed? Especially from a man who has just been telling us how fascinating local history is?

Did the whole town hall get burnt, I ask, or just the records?

Ah, alas, that is all Anselmo knows.

Was it something to do with Garibaldi and all the turmoil over the Unification of Italy?

Ah, alas, Anselmo could not tell us.

Wasn't it around then that half Calabria was in revolt? Because the promises about redistributing the land once the country was united hadn't materialized?

Yes, indeed it was, says he.

So would it have been the locals who burnt their own records to stop them getting into the hands of the authorities? Or the authorities who burnt down the town hall because it was held by rebellious locals? Or what?

Unfortunately, I couldn't say, says Anselmo.

And that's all we get out of him. The mania for secrecy in this place is starting to get to me. They are all deranged. Well, no, I suppose not all. I can see why Zia Annunziata or the boys at the Bar Z might do their *omertà* number about recent events, local events, things that might tend to confirm outsiders' notion of Calabria as a land of bloodthirsty savages, or as inescapably corrupt, and

318

doomed to remain under the thumb of the Mafia for ever. But what is Anselmo's motive here for denying knowledge of events he couldn't possibly be ignorant of? The fighting didn't only go on down here: and it was over a century ago. We're talking major political events here, events that involved the whole Italian nation. Surely you can't simply deny whole chunks of national history that took place in Calabria just because you think they might reflect badly on Calabria? You might as well say that Calabria reflects badly on Calabria. And there you have it in a nutshell: I suppose that is exactly what Anselmo's problem is, underneath all the urbanity. Internalized racism.

Anyway, it seems you can deny history as much as you like in this town hall. Anselmo goes on stonewalling, keeping up the bland façade of politeness, until we give up and leave, with a very truncated family tree, and none the wiser about how the records we'd like to have seen were destroyed. Or even about local attitudes to joining the rest of Italy.

Never mind: maybe we'll have better luck up in the mountains at Santa Cristina, where folks are less refined? For now, though, back to the Bar Z.

*   *   *

Marisa, Alberto and I are finishing our digestive espressos outside the bar, and Ciccio is inside ordering another round, when Carmela's errant husband Pino finally arrives in town. A car with Sicilian number-plates, Catania, pulls up and parks in the middle of the road, and a small bouncing man jumps out bearing a bulging black briefcase.

319

He's just driven all the way from Naples, he says, planting a pair of kisses on Marisa's and Alberto's cheeks. He left Sicily yesterday, he says, but he had to go there first, for a meeting with some very important Azerbaijanis.

Azerbaijanis in Naples? I echo, foolishly. I don't know why I should be surprised. No more unlikely than Bulgarians and Poles in Melipodio. Or Senegalese women in the fields of Cosenza. I'm beginning to think that Liguria must be the least cosmopolitan place in the whole of Italy. All we get is Germans on family holidays, a few Moroccans who sell household goods door to door; and the occasional Albanian looking for labouring work. The Albanians are deeply disapproved of, poor things: the new Calabresi. Everyone who's learnt, over the last decade or two, to drop the stupid stereotype stuff about Calabrians seems to feel entirely free to say the exact same things about Albanians.

A business meeting, says Pino, smoothing a distracted hand through his hair. And he's worn out now after all that driving! But it was worth it.

Marisa and Alberto have become engrossed in a heated debate about pocket money. So Pino, leaning forward across the table, fixes me alone with an intense pair of bulbous dark eyes.

He was in Azerbaijan himself, only last month, he tells me. It's a great place, where capital and enterprise are really and truly given free rein—not like this mollycoddled bureaucracy-ridden part of the world where the words Free Market are bandied about all the time, but mean nothing in practice. No, if you want a really free market economy, where there's still room to wheel and deal, the place to go is the ex-communist countries. That's where the rich pickings are these days. And where the buccaneer spirit still survives!

Really? I say feebly, doing my best to humour the man. I am mystified. I'm sure I was told Pino ran a café-bar in Catania, wasn't I?

Yes, really! The Azerbaijanis he just met in Naples have won the contract to build a petrochemical factory (or did he say a gas processing plant?) and Pino thinks he's well on the way to cornering the sole contract to supply and build the pipelines for it.

And, um, have you done that sort of thing before? I ask.

But no, of course he hasn't. That's the point. A man like himself wouldn't get the chance over here. But there in the East, he can do anything. Nothing is impossible.

Something about my expression tells Pino that I'm not entirely convinced. He pulls the bulging briefcase out from under the table, rummages about in it, and is soon waving a great sheaf of legal-looking documents at me—here, he says, look at that, there are the contracts. They all have to be printed out in Russian, with copies in Arabic. I am indeed looking at page after page of documents divided into two columns, one in Cyrillic and the other in Arabic script, but being unable to read so much as the respective alphabets, never mind extract any meaning from the words, I am no further forward in gauging the level of lunacy, if any, involved here. Marisa is now smiling interestedly, Alberto having gone off inside with whatever booty he managed to extract from her, heading for the ice-cream cabinet. But Marisa missed all the introduction, so I can't really take this as proof that the man's not a penny short of a shilling.

Shuffling his great handful of paper together, Pino thrusts it back into the briefcase. Aha! he says, encountering something else at the bottom of the bag. With the air of a magician pulling off an amazing trick, he produces a most peculiar object, a thing like a large plastic drinking straw. A very hefty drinking straw indeed, of a rather sludgy blue.

Another of his business interests, he says, passing it to Marisa. He has sole distribution rights on this item, and it may make his fortune if only he can get some manufacturer interested in producing it. He's waiting for an answer from one factory in Milan and another in Turin, but he thinks the entrepreneurial spirit is dying in this land.

Marisa fiddles about with the blue plastic object. Which is indeed a drinking straw, Pino tells us; except that inside it is composed not of one, but two tubes. Hence its chunkiness. Try it, go on, he says to Marisa. Suck as hard as you like, it can never go flat and collapse in on itself . . . the air can go down one side as the drink comes up the other, you see? It could catch on and spread all over the continent like wildfire, if only he can get it launched, he says, no reason why it shouldn't. People have made fortunes, do we know that, from little insignificant things like this . . . from tin-openers, needle-threaders, nail-clippers, biros . . . And here (more rummaging in the briefcase, this time to produce a small transparent plastic bag full of tiny blue bobbles) is the plastic, recycled plastic, out of which the things are to be made—and on which, as it happens, Pino also has sole distribution rights.

Overwhelmed, I try to catch Marisa's eye. But she is busy playing with the straw.

Azerbaijan? Petrochemicals? Plastic knick-knacks? Recycling? Free Market Buccaneer? Perhaps he's a Method actor trying out a scene from a Bertolt Brecht play? I can't imagine what this extraordinary buzzing man can possibly have to do with the tranquil Carmela . . .

All the good business has gone out of the EEC, he tells us now. Anyone with any nous is heading east. Once upon a time you could have a field day here, if you knew how to play the subsidies, take advantage of Special Funds for this, that and the other, wheel and deal among the bureaucrats—but too many people are at that game now, it's all getting too tight, the funding is shrinking, the loopholes being closed at the speed of light.

Ciccio arrives back just as Pino is telling us how much he disagrees with anything that interrupts the freedom of the market economy—and he doesn't just mean the EEC, either, but the Mafia too! They're just the same!

Luckily, since I am having a bit of trouble making sense of this remark—sounded as if he agreed just fine with the EEC when he was on to an earner—Ciccio says he knows exactly what Pino means. Last time he was down here, he and Dario discovered by chance, chatting in some bar, that restaurant premises were absurdly cheap to rent in Calabria—less than half the prices up in the North. And Ciccio happened to have been saving to do just that: to open a restaurant. He had a way to go still before he could afford to get started back home in Liguria: but it sounded as though, if he decided to start the business down here, he could get going right away. Why not give Calabria a chance? If he was going to create a few jobs, why not show some loyalty to the Old Country? Create them here, where they were needed most? Full of fine and selfless thoughts, he and Dario went around looking at a couple of places. But, would you believe it, the very next day some local hard nut came offering to find local staff and local suppliers for them—to help them avoid making mistakes, as he put it. Result? They gave up on the plan right away, and Ciccio went and opened his restaurant back up North. What if he didn't like the staff they proposed? Or the suppliers? He didn't care how much cheaper it sounded—because there was no way of telling how much more it might cost you to keep the *malavita* happy.

Exactly! says Pino. People may say you wouldn't have the *'ndrangheta* if you didn't have poverty: but then, these days, you can equally argue that you wouldn't have poverty if you didn't have the Mafiosi. A businessman has to be able to work out his business plan, calculate his cash-flow, wages, outgoings, projected profits. And how can you do that with an imponderable *malavita* mixing itself up in your accounts? That is Pino's point. The Mafia and the EEC both destroy competition. They distort the free play of market forces. They are one and the same!

42

At last! Santa Cristina and the high Aspromonte! We are about to set off on the hunt for Zio Fantino, his wife Elisabetta, and the Lost Inheritance—not to mention the Lost Surname—when Francesca suddenly clutches at her head and claims to have come over all faint, and to be unable to face the trip. The roads are too scary, and the way we get lost all the time, anything could happen . . . she hates driving about with us, unless we take Zio Antonio or somebody sensible to guide us, because we always get lost. And spend hours trafficking about with that map of ours, though what use it is Francesca can't fathom, why can't we just work out the way before we leave? Because we always end up sitting poring over it in the worst possible places, places where nobody in their right mind would stop. And you wouldn't want to be hanging about the roadsides up near Santa Cristina, she says, there are still wolves up there . . .

Wolves! No there are not, *mamma*! says Marisa, exasperated. Don't be ridiculous! If you don't want to come, you don't have to. Just say so.

Fine. Francesca does not want to come, no.

I wish she would come. They're not even expecting us. There is no phone at Zio Fantino's house, so you're supposed to ring the bar in the village and get someone to go and fetch them. Except that Francesca couldn't remember the name of the bar, and in the phone book there were a good dozen bars under Santa Cristina. It's not that it's a big place; just that there are a lot of scattered hamlets around it that count as Santa Cristina too. So there's nothing for it: we'll just have to turn up out of the blue. And the only one of us who's ever met him before is Ciccio. Nobody except me thinks that this is a problem though. People bursting in on you unexpectedly out of the distant past is all part of everyday life in Calabria, where so many have left in their centuries-long diaspora, and where until quite recently hardly anybody had a phone—not even the bars. Imagine that, you don't see someone for a decade and then they just appear at your door. And stranger than that: people you've never met before and didn't even know existed may appear at your door; they are your relatives, they will say, born after the departure. I think I would find it seriously disturbing. But then, of course, as we know, I am not from Calabria.

And what about Zio Fantino? Francesca hasn't seen her brother-in-law for twenty years, not since he last came up to visit us! Doesn't she care what a *brutta figura* she'll be giving us, says Ciccio, looking like she can't be bothered to travel those last twenty kilometres, after she's managed sixteen hundred to get down here?

Nonsense, says Francesca; she'll see him at the month-memorial. Unless he doesn't come, in which case it's his own fault.

Alberto, who as usual is taking no interest in family politics, is keenly interested in the wolves. Are we sure there aren't any? Would there still be some higher up in the Aspromonte? Can we drive up and have a look? Will Uncle Fantino know?

Well, says Francesca, I'm sure I don't know. If the young folk say there aren't any left these days, maybe there aren't. But anyway, the very thought of Santa Cristina, of all those high mountains and hairpin bends, gives her *angoscia* . . .

So we give up, and set off without a guide, Marisa and Ciccio speculating wildly about what on earth Francesca's problem is with Santa Cristina and its environs. I don't join in, because I think I know the explanation, and they wouldn't want to hear it.

Does she really think there are wolves up there? says Marisa. Is she really afraid of brigands on its high mountain roads? Does she secretly dislike Zio Fantino, maybe?

Impossible, says Ciccio: he is a lovely friendly chatty outgoing man, and not at all the sort of person you could imagine his mother not liking. Did you know, he says, turning to me, that the word *fantino* actually means horseman, or jockey maybe . . . or at any rate, 'man on horseback'?

No, I didn't. How on earth can someone be called that? Is it a nickname?

No, it's just his Christian name. But it sounds odd even to an Italian. Or at any rate, to one like himself, brought up well to the North of Calabria. Ciccio thinks it must have sounded classy to the grandparents, something like the way Americans call their children Earl and Prince and stuff: because only the rich had horses once upon a time, didn't they? Nobles? Gentlemen?

Mulling this over for a kilometre or two, I realize that Ciccio must be right. You say 'chevalier', which means the same thing but in French, for a man of gentle birth in English, don't you? But then, the real upper classes here call themselves Cavaliere, too, not Fantino—like the mysterious Cavaliere

Spinella who owns everything round here. After a bit more mulling, I notice that we have the same word in English. Or rather, the opposite of it. Infantry! They are foot-soldiers, aren't they? The opposite of men on horseback. In-fant-ry. No-horsemen-ry. I check this out with Ciccio. Yes, they do have *'fanteria'*, horse regiments, in Italian. Wonder how we came to lose the Fantry, then, in our own language, and end up with only the Horseless Regiments? Seems absurd.

Here we are at last, in the real Aspromonte. In Italian *aspro* means harsh, rough; I've always thought what a brilliant name it was for a mountain range, the Harsh Mountains, whenever Salvatore's been telling us tales of his youth up here. Disappointing to discover that, according to the tourist leaflet Marisa has got hold of, the 'Aspro' part of the word is actually of Greek origin, and only means 'white': not even white with snow, either, but called that for its pale earth and rocks,

On we go and up we go, through tiny straggly villages that look poorer and poorer, getting lost several times. As Francesca knew we would. We overtake a very slow *Ape* at one seriously-lost point, and pull in alongside of it on a hairpin bend to ask the way to Santa Cristina.

You're on the right road, you're fine, says the driver. Straight on!

Thanks! we call out, accelerating off up the hill. Straight on!

But be careful, though! he calls after us, leaning out of his window. Watch out for forks in the road!

What?

So here we are, at Fantino's house at last. Ciccio couldn't remember the place, and we had to ask

328

quite a few neighbours, all of whom needed to be filled in on our exact relationship to Fantino before they would let slip any information on his whereabouts; but now that we're on the right street, not in Santa Cristina itself but in one of its outlying hamlets, he's recognized it straight away.

And there is Fantino, sitting at one side of the first-floor window, green shutters thrown wide, watching the world go by; and opposite him, sitting at the other side of the window, there is his wife, doing the same. They look just like one of those weathervane couples, the ones that pop in and out of the tiny doorway to their tiny house to let you know if it's going to rain or not. Startlingly, when he turns towards us, Fantino is wearing Salvatore's face. You'd think you were looking at his identical twin. His look of amazement is identical too: and his welcoming grin. When he stands up and leans out of the window, though, waving both his arms at once in greeting, you can see he's a much more heavily-built man than his brother.

The house is set into a steep hill, and Fantino signs to us to go on up round to the side door, where what is the first floor at the front becomes ground level at the back. He appears at the door, which opens straight into the kitchen, and leads us through to Zia Elisabetta, picking up a pair of kitchen chairs as he goes. We soon realize that Elisabetta is in a bad way. She shakes continuously, trying to hold trembling hands steady on a long knobbly walking stick as she half-rises to greet us.

Sit down! Don't be silly! says Fantino, pushing her gently back down into her seat. Stay put, they'll come over here to say hello! Won't you, he adds, turning to us. Over we go and kiss Zia Elisabetta on each cheek, tiny and thin and trembling like a bird. Fantino motions Ciccio and Alberto to sit on the two single beds, and sets the chairs in a semicircle between his and Elisabetta's. For you girls to sit on, he says. We join Elisabetta at the window, gazing out on the neighbours' to-ings and fro-ings, at the street and the deep valleys that sweep off just beyond it, as if we were watching a TV. I have never seen such a bare and simple house. The two of them live in just these two rooms, by the look of it: this one, with the window on to the street, doubles as their bedroom, and the other, the kitchen, must be where they sit in the evenings, a small sofa squeezed between the big round kitchen table that takes up most of the room, and the wood-burning cooker.

Apart from the beds and the chairs, the only furniture in this room is a long thin 1950s laminated sideboard against the far wall, with an exceedingly ancient-looking radio sitting on top of it, surrounded by medicine bottles and those little pictures of saints, the size of cigarette cards, that you get when you go to a shrine, each with the saint's own special prayer printed on the back of them—obviously all being invoked to intercede and cure Elisabetta, candles ready to light in front of them.

A big long plank is fixed to the back wall, running the whole length of the room and serving as a cross between a shelf and a wardrobe, their clothes hanging from hooks on its underside; two box-like items, also obviously home-made from the same planks, stand next to the beds, for bedside cabinets, two photos—wedding photographs, they look like—hanging above them.

As predicted, Fantino and his wife seem to take our unexpected appearance all in their stride. It's lovely to see us, they say, we'll have to stay for supper but it'll be pot luck.

No, no, we say, we couldn't do that to you with no warning!

Don't worry about that! says Fantino. The last lot to turn up unexpectedly, just a couple of months ago, were family they hadn't seen for over thirty years, not since they were newly wed, and left looking for work in Germany. The only news they'd had of them in all that time was the occasional letter to Elisabetta's mother, who would pass it on to all the family . . . They turned up along with their three children, all in their twenties, who'd never even been to Italy before—and it was a mad day, wasn't it, Fantino, says Elisabetta, because by chance they arrived on the very day we were making the *sugo* for the year, the whole house full of tomatoes piled up everywhere, on every kitchen surface and every chair and all over the table and the sofa too, boxes of them all over the floor so you could hardly move, and of course you can't just stop, can you, once you've started your *sugo*, but they didn't seem to understand that.

No, they didn't, says Fantino, they just kept saying: Stop work, drop everything and let us take you out to lunch! We haven't seen you for so long! Think of that! Just drop everything, when you've got a house full of tomatoes, and all your jars out ready and half of them just sterilized, and the cauldron on the stove with the first load coming to the boil! And the strange thing was that even the parents, born here in Santa Cristina, didn't seem to realize . . . But I suppose you forget a lot in thirty

331

years, don't you? And maybe they don't even have tomatoes all that way up there, so far to the north? Maybe they can't grow them? So, the upshot of it all was that, in the middle of the *sugo*, we had to stop everything and cook pasta for seven! That was all we could manage—and at least the sauce was already on, so that was all right!

But the best thing was, says Elisabetta, that once they'd eaten, we sent the old ones in here to lie down and digest, and they fell fast asleep; and once the young folk understood what we were doing, even though they could hardly speak the language at all, they joined in all right, and with so many extra hands we had it all bottled and boiled in no time, and we weren't that late finishing after all. Which just goes to show that you should never stint on hospitality! *Chi mangia sulu, schiatta!* she adds in Calabrese. 'He who eats alone, bursts.' A tiny bit obscure, but you get it once you think about it.

Well, if we're not eating, would we like to join them in a *caffè freddo*, a cold coffee, at least? They were just about to have one.

We'd love one, we say, a bit surprised at the offer. *Caffè freddo* isn't a thing you usually make at home, not in our experience anyhow. It's a drink you get in bars, where the barman makes a fresh espresso in the machine, froths it up in a cocktail shaker with sugar and a load of crushed ice, and pours it out into your glass looking like a tiny Guinness. All a bit sophisticated, you'd imagine, for these surroundings. But to our surprise, here in Santa Cristina a *caffè freddo* is something you buy in a shop, ready-made, in a little brown bottle with a beer-bottle cap to it, fizzy and ready-sweetened and slightly spicy, the coffee amazingly strong. We all exclaim over it—it's lovely—where do you get it? Just the ordinary village shop? So is there a factory round here making this stuff? We've never seen it before! Ciccio and Marisa immediately launch a plan to begin importing the stuff to the North. Our hosts are mystified. It's obviously so ordinary to them that they can't understand what the fuss is about.

Marisa has gone over to look at the wedding photos. Look at you two! she says. That's beautiful! Would we know anyone else in it? Fantino goes over to look—but yes! Of course we would! Francesca's mother, your granny, came to stand in for her and Salvatore, they were away in Australia. Look, that's her! Serafina! Fantino thinks he can see a resemblance, takes the photo down off the wall and holds it next to Marisa's face. He's right, too.

Inspiration strikes Alberto. Wasn't his granny looking for a photo to go on her mother's grave? Remember she was upset how Uncle Enzo never got round to doing it? We certainly do. Well remembered, Alberto. Zio Fantino will certainly lend it to us, he says, as long as we promise to guard it with our lives.

And the other family chore we have to do, while we're up here, says Marisa, is go and look up the ancestors. Grazia wants us to find out where the de Gilios came from, how we came to be called that, a bit of family history . . . Should we look in the church registers, do they think? Or go to the town hall?

The priest is the man to go to, says Elisabetta. That town hall is a terrible place, you'd never find anything out in there. They wouldn't even tell you their own names unless they had to. But Father Pierino is a lovely man, and he's very interested in local history.

Fantino can't see the point of it at all. Why on earth does Grazia want us to do that?

Elisabetta thinks it would be lovely to know all about the family, but she doesn't think we'll get anywhere much.

There are two stories about your great-grandfather, aren't there, Fantino? she says. One is that the original de Gilio, or de Giglio some people say he was, came from far away in Puglia: but the other is that it was just a made-up name, though she can't imagine why anybody would want to do that . . . but maybe, she says diplomatically, to conceal the circumstances of his birth?

Exactly! says Fantino, sounding just like Salvatore. A waste of time, and if you did find out, it would probably just upset people.

Well, anyway, if you want to, go and find Father Pierino in the chapel of San Rocco after evening Mass, says Elisabetta.

Ciccio doesn't care about the family tree business. But he does care about finding the bit of land Uncle Lino left him. Do they have any idea where it is?

Salvatore was right: his brother has no idea. But the temple story rings a bell: he's definitely heard the tale of the foreigner and his digging. What we should do is to go up into the town and find the Finanza. He'll take us up, if we like. They're bound to know.

What, the Finance Police? says Ciccio, alarmed. The Finanza have a nasty habit of sequestering your property unexpectedly—and he is imagining, like the rest of us newcomers, that the tax enforcement agencies must have sequestered his patrimony for lack of payment of some inheritance tax or other.

Zio Fantino roars with laughter at our horrified expressions.

Not the Finance Police! Does Ciccio not remember, he says, the two old men who always go around together like a pair of Siamese twins, everyone calls them the Finanza?

But no, Ciccio doesn't. And I still haven't got the joke, though Alberto and Marisa are laughing away merrily.

The Finanza, says Ciccio, helping me out, always go around in twos. Have I never noticed that?

No, I haven't. (Not too surprising, this, since the Finanza also go around in plain clothes most of the time, so that unless you happen to know their faces—unlikely, in my case—you wouldn't spot that they were Finance Police in the first place.)

Of course you remember the Finanza! says the uncle to Ciccio. You and me and some of your mates spent an evening drinking with them, years ago. It was that time Ciccio came down in his teens, he says, with the bunch of lads all on their Vespas. That must have been some trip! All the way from Liguria by scooter! It was the night that one of your gang was driving everybody mad—I think he was a bit *brillo* (brillo in Italian—'shiny'—is used to describe a person who has been drinking enough to make them noticeably cheery, but not so much that you'd say they were actually drunk)—he was a little runt of a fellow, he adds, only looked about fifteen, kept riding round and round the piazza on his orange Vespa, revving his motor—we were sitting outside the bar in the centre of town . . .

Ah! says Ciccio. Yes! It was Federico. He remembers now! An old man came out of a bar on the other side of the piazza in a raging temper!

Yes, says Fantino, and told us they were trying to concentrate on a game of poker in there, and who was the boy on the scooter driving them all to distraction, was he with us?

Yes, says Ciccio excitedly, and you said he was, and they said, Oh, that's all right then, lucky for him, because otherwise we were about to shoot him . . .

And were they really? asks Alberto, all agog.

Who knows? says the Zio.

43

Fantino will take us off up to the town for a bit, see what we can do about this bit of land, he says to Elisabetta, if she'll be OK on her own for a while?

Of course she will, she says, smiling the sweetest smile at him, for all the world as though they were a pair of young lovers.

She's not well, you see, says Fantino. She hasn't been for ages. Still, I've done my best to get everything mechanized, make life easier for the pair of us . . .

Elisabetta giggles. Wait till you see! she says, as her husband takes hold of a piece of twine which I had thought was just lying on the floor by chance: he pulls at it, and a door-sized section of the floor suddenly flips up, nearly catching on a wooden box, full of what seems to be their winter woollies, as it goes. Elisabetta, obviously used to this problem, whisks the obstacle out of the way with the tip of her stick.

Poised on a counterweight, Fantino explains proudly, so it's no effort to lift it. All his own work.

The stylish trapdoor squeals to a halt, vertical now; and reveals a staircase leading down to the lower storey. Just my workroom down there, says the Uncle, flipping it shut again. Show over, Elisabetta pushes the box back to position A again, with a dextrous flick of the stick. Now Fantino points out his latest addition, a switch by the bed, a wire across the ceiling, so that Elisabetta can turn the radio on and off without getting up when he's out. And here, come to the window—another of his own inventions, an electric motor for moving the washing-line along on castors or whatever you call them outside the window. So Elisabetta can take things in off the line without moving from her seat, if she wants to!

Off into the kitchen now; where the only obviously mechanized item I can see is a very rusty-looking washing-machine. But lo! here is a knife-grinder, all electric, fixed to the wall behind the front door; and there, an electric circular saw fixed to the wall by the stove, for the firewood, Fantino explains. By the sink, we have an electric tin-opener and a thing for pushing the stones out of olives; into the bathroom now, where a strimmer and a chainsaw lurk in the shower box.

Right! We'll go off now and see if we can find anyone to help track down Ciccio's inheritance. Silly to use that big car-thing of yours, though, he says. It'll hardly fit down the main street once we're inside the old town, cause no end of trouble, the

Lambretta is a much better idea.

So we walk on up the steep road to his parking place, the valley falling steeply away to our left, the view stretching away across broad low-lying plains—must be those once-malarial ones, I suppose—and on down to the sea twenty-odd miles away. To our right, fold after fold of dark, tree-clad mountain rolling away to distant peaks half-hidden in fierce grey snow-clouds, the nearer slopes looming over us, patched here and there with the beige-brown of rocky screes, the lighter green of pasture-land.

Would that be where Salvatore used to hang out in his youth, when he was herding goats? I ask his little brother. Well, says Fantino, it was mostly a lot further up than that. Any grass you can see from here would only be winter pasture: it would be all dried up in the height of summer. And there's not a lot of it, anyhow. It would be a good day's walk on up to the summer pastures, steep rocky paths, high, high up in the mountains. That's where they spent most of their time: they have stone roundhouses up there to camp in, that have been there since only the Lord knows when, thousands of years ago, since the Good Lord was no more than a twinkle in his father's eye. And that's why they only ever came down to join the rest of humanity for feast days and market days, from April till October. The family hardly ever saw Salvatore, not while Fantino was growing up. He was away up there among the rocks, alone walking the hills with his share of the herd by day, huddled up against the cold with two miserable old skinflints by night. Rather him than me. There are no flocks up there any more these days. And a good job too.

Now that I've actually seen the place, I realize that some part of me has secretly held a kind of romantic Heidi-style notion about the child goatherd. Wrong again.

We wind our way round a couple more hairpin bends, and we're entering the town, passing a most extraordinary building, an angular 1930s-looking thing with a manic frieze panel all the way round it, ceramic tiles of outsized fruits and vegetables, piled two foot deep and glazed in unlikely pastel shades. Used to be a health spa, apparently, a place to come and Take the Waters, and they're about to start restoring it. Must have been some Mussolini bring-work-to-the-South initiative, I guess, although the Uncle can't remember anything much about it. Wonder if it's being restored as yet another similar initiative, or is there actually a demand these days for Calabrian health spas? I hope so: it seems a very pleasing and rather dignified little town, narrow though its streets may be. Whatever Francesca may think about it. But still, as we pop in and out of the rather large number of bars in the place, hunting for the Finanza, of whom there is no sign so far, there's no getting away from the fact that they are much too well-frequented, at this time of a weekday, for you to believe there's much worthwhile paid work about.

Busy though the bars may be, nobody in them has any notion about the whereabouts of this particular ruined temple. They've all heard of it, or rather they've heard the stories about the millionaire Englishman and his eccentric ways, his mysterious disappearance. But as we'd already gathered, bits and pieces of Temples of Antiquity are ten a penny round here.

Was it the ruins up past what's-its-name? . . . there are still a few columns lying about there; or is it the one somewhere over that way, where Ardito keeps his sheep? they say, waving their arms towards it. Although it could be the one over the other side of that hill over there . . . or isn't there one up above something-or-other, by the side of somebody-else's cheese-making sheds?

These people, you can tell, roamed the hills checking out the remnants of Greek, Roman, Byzantine culture in their youth, in just the way I and my childhood friends would go poking about in the ruins of wartime gun emplacements that dotted the English countryside: and naturally, took as little interest in their place in Classical history as we did in the details of World War II.

*   *   *

Ciccio and I have nipped off to buy a few more of those very nice little bottles of sweet fizzy coffee, and have stopped by the probably-health-spa, where we are now sitting on a strange concrete-and-mosaic bench by a phone booth to cool down in a bit of shade while the Uncle pursues his investigations. Two aged gentlemen, somewhat the worse for drink, more than *brillo*, as you might say, come tottering up the hill towards us, stop to say hello, and ask us who we are and what we're doing there, as is the wont of local people. Leaning on the phone box, one of them starts pulling away at something in his full-to-bulging pockets. Walnuts. He manages to extract a few, and starts piling them up against his chest. Would we like a couple? He just picked them himself. He holds out the next handful to us. As it happens, there has been a bit of a surfeit of walnuts in my diet recently: but our new friend seems so delighted to be able to offer us them that it would be churlish to refuse. Luckily Ciccio has the local knack of cracking walnuts with his teeth, a skill that has so far eluded me. Must be genetic. He hands me mine, and I munch stoically away at it. Don't think it's going to go down, though. In the distance I see Zio Fantino and the others heading downhill towards us.

Meanwhile Ciccio, speaking his best almost-Calabrese, is filling the newcomers in on the search for his inheritance, in general, and for these two very old men his uncle knows, nicknamed the Finanza, in particular.

Well, even I could have told him not to say that. Naturally, these are the very two old men in question. And of course, nobody calls them the Finanza to their faces, as a rather red-faced uncle soon tells us.

The nickname is ruder than it sounds in translation, and might have been taken badly, since in this country all the police forces are held in such low esteem that they are the butt of constant jokes about their stupidity. But the Finanza are not bothered. No matter, say they, they know perfectly well that that's what everyone calls them. They know it's not meant badly: they re not at all offended. And of course they remember the Englishman who started digging up columns and then vanished. No, they certainly haven't forgotten where it was! What do we want to go up there for? Are the English going to start excavating again, then? they ask, cackling at me.

Ciccio, feverish with excitement, shakes their hands over and over again, explaining the history of his inheritance in his own version of Calabrese, and going into so much detail that they are soon quite bewildered. We arrange to meet them up here with Zio Fantino, the morning after the memorial wake: we will go up and find the inheritance at last.

44

As the bottle of Annunziata's liquorice-flavoured *amaro* goes round—it even has a couple of chunks of root lying in the bottom, and it's perfect for opening the stomach before a meal, everyone agrees—a certain Uncle Tommaso is reliving this very night a month ago, with Enzo's coffin standing over there in the corner, when he and Fiore slipped a bottle of wine and a loaf of bread and a bunch of the hottest chillis they could find in with Enzo, something to take with him and remember them by. And then, along came the priest to do the blessing! Leaning so far into the coffin you'd have thought he was going to jump right in along with Enzo! He and Fiore were petrified, Tommaso says, because you know what he's like about that sort of thing! Everyone agrees that this new priest—he who cannot grasp that 'Summertime' is a sacred melody—will give you his lecture about Christianity and paganism and the golden calf as soon as look at you.

We put a thousand *lire* note into the pocket of Enzo's burial suit, too, says Tommaso—one that Fiore had kept from before the euro. Because a thousand *lire* in Enzo's prime was something you'd only dream about. Even though by the end it wasn't even worth the price of a packet of cigarettes . . . Still, says Fiore, we couldn't give him euros, could we? Nobody, Fiore adds firmly, could make him believe that they've started accepting euros to get you across to the other side . . . !

There they go again, mixing and matching mythologies. Poor priest: they must drive him to despair. We're well away before Christ here, aren't we? Back in ancient Greece, with the boatman Charon waiting for payment to take us across the river Styx to the Underworld, if I'm not mistaken. We're all sitting in the second kitchen, and at last I see the use of having this many kitchens. The first one, with the fireplace, is filled mostly with women: this central one is mostly men, with the boar-and-bean stew bubbling gently upon the stove; and the end one, the Madonna-scullery, is full to bursting with all the supplies everyone has brought with them—bottles and bottles of wine, and a whole *salumeria* of various types of ham and salami, interspersed with pots, bowls and bags of olives in various dried-or-*salamoia*'d states. We are even going to have music: Zio Antonio has brought a fiddle, while Tommaso has a kind of lute-looking thing resting on his lap, ready to go.

Soon, the month-mourners of Enzo's own age are reliving the years of their youth and his—years when the desperate search to fill your belly seems to have been the driving force in Calabrian life. Especially poignant, I daresay, when you have a plate piled high with bread, salami and *'nduia* in front of you to take the edge off it, not to mention the bowls of olives and the plates laden with

Francesca's anchovy-stuffed chillis, come into their own at last. And the bottle after bottle set out all along the centre of the table, where Francesca's offering of Salvatore's wine alternates with Enzo's own *'nchiostro*, ink; Annunziata has saved what was left of his very last vintage for tonight. And the sisters were right: it is amazingly powerful stuff, must be well over fourteen degrees, and it stains your lips and tongue deepest purple. Ciccio did all the bottling this afternoon with Zio Antonio— Salvatore's from the canister it never quite made it out of, and Enzo's from the demijohns in the scullery—and the corking machine really did turn out to live in the bathroom, as predicted by Marisa. (Have I mentioned that there really is a proper main bathroom here? It nestles cosily under the landing of the big staircase.) Ciccio says that the staining is the sign of a good *'nchiostro*: it has to stain, of course, or it's not ink. He's relieved to see it out, too. He'd noticed those demijohns in the scullery—and he was beginning to think we were never going to be offered any of Zio Enzo's last brew.

How did Enzo get it this strong? Easily! The strength of a wine is just down to the amount of grape-sugar there is to turn to alcohol. With all the heat down here, and the grapes ripening so sweet, you'd be hard put to stop it coming out strong. Fourteen degrees is just normal, in Calabria.

I decide to stick with Salvatore's wine. I'll be on the floor in no time if I keep on with the ink. Better the devil you know . . .

So, on with the joyful tale of Uncle Beppe's first job in the rich North, aged thirteen: on a wonderful Piedmont farm, he says, working the vineyards. It was Enzo that got him in on it. Enzo had already been there three months, and sent word down with one of the boys, coming home to take some money to his mother, that they needed another hand, and if Beppe got up there quick he'd get the job. Beppe set off the very next day, walking, hitching rides on carts or vans or any old thing, he says, and what a performance it was, trying to make yourself understood at all once you'd got North of Rome! Nobody could understand Calabrese; he hardly spoke any Italian at all; and he was only half-way there! Still, three days later, there he was, language or no. And, he says, he knew he was on to a good thing as soon as he saw Enzo. Because you could hardly recognize him after three months of eating Piedmont-style. Not a skinny runt of a youth any more, but a proper man. You didn't actually get wages, money wages, at their age, Beppe says: just a hand-out once the harvest was in. But who cared? You got a cup of milk three times a day, and a whole roll of bread to go with it. And cheese on Saturdays. And Sunday mornings off. In Calabria he'd done the same job, from dawn till dusk, seven days a week, for half-a-roll and a beaker of watered wine three times a day . . .

Eating Piedmont style! I was expecting Beppe to talk of bacon and cabbage, of smoked sausage and rich, buttery polenta. Bread, milk, and cheese on Saturdays! Enzo must have been seriously malnourished to have filled out on that. No wonder Francesca goes all funny about a good harvest of butter beans, or a nice big sack of walnuts.

We move on, as Annunziata, Carmela and Vincenza dole out plates of the boar stew, to the tale of the day that three of them, now in their late

345

teens, Enzo, his big brother, and an uncle whose name escapes me, managed to get hold of a whole kilo of probably-stolen horsemeat steak, somewhere near San Remo, and just lit a fire right then and there by the side of the road, grilled it and guzzled the lot before anyone could turn up and take it off them . . . No doubt contributing something, in the process, to the Northern image of the Savage Calabrian.

Ah, the box of cigars, Zio Antonio is saying, over at the other side of the table. Now that was some story, he says, picking up the fiddle and doing a quick scrape of the bow on it to introduce the tale. You're half dead of starvation, and what do the Heavens send you? A box of cigars! *Justizzia e sanità—amaru cu 'ndi va circandu* he adds. That one again. 'Justice and health—bitterness to him who seeks them.' So here comes the story of the box of cigars: though whether it represents Justice or Health in this particular case, it is hard to tell.

There was this German soldier, Antonio tells us—he thinks it was after Italy had changed sides, and the Germans were digging themselves in and waiting to fight off the Americans and the British . . . but maybe it was before that, when they were on the same side? . . . Anyhow, the German started coming down through the vineyard to the river to do his laundry every couple of days, and taking a dip himself while he was at it. Antonio doesn't know why. Maybe they didn't let them wash their clothes at the camp? Maybe the water was rationed? Or the man just liked his stuff cleaned more often than the rest? He has no idea, because the German could only speak a dozen words of Italian. Still, there he would be, scrubbing away at

346

his socks and vests and his what-have-yous, or standing up to his neck in the river, splashing about . . . They would always say hello to one another, as best they could, because Antonio and Enzo and Beppe would be down there seeing to the vines. But then, one day, they arrived to find the German storming about the place in a terrible rage. Fully dressed, for once, says Zio Antonio, and swinging the butt of his rifle around him like a crazy man, battering at the vines, and doing them some serious damage.

Antonio and Enzo ran up and grabbed him, and only just managed to hold him down between the two of them. That's how mad he was. They had to sit on his chest to get the gun away from him, with him roaring and struggling, convinced they meant to harm him. So Enzo pulled the bottle of wine from their lunch-bag, took a swig himself, gave one to Antonio, then put the bottle to the German's lips, so he'd get the picture that they were all friends, having a drink together. It worked, too. All of a sudden he stopped struggling, lay back, and burst into tears!

So between sign-language and pidgin Italian, they worked out that someone official—it must have been the bailiff—had turned up, pointing a gun at your German, and told him to get off the property . . . *Via! Via!* says Zio Antonio, waving an invisible shotgun, doing an imitation of the German imitating the bailiff: Away! Away!

The German had mimed to the man that he was only having a bit of a wash, and the bailiff—it would be typical of him, it was Artallo, remember him?—he'd gone, this is private property, and if I see you here again, you'll be shot! Poum!! And he'd

347

frog-marched the German off the premises. So the German was disgusted—because he'd thought we were the owners, couldn't understand why we'd always been so friendly and then turned around and set a man with a gun on him.

And, says Beppe, if anybody was marching anyone about at gunpoint, it was meant to be the Germans, wasn't it, don't forget that, except that he was all alone and in his underwear!

Carmela is coming round now, putting out loaves of bread, big round ones—of course, they're our own Triora loaves. She hands me the one for our section of the table, and gives me a big serrated knife. Cut some slices for everybody, she asks me, there aren't enough sharp knives to go round, and then pass the knife on. So I lay the loaf on the table, stand up to get a good cutting angle, and prepare to slice—only to be stopped by a roar from everyone around me. No! No! Not like that!

An uncle, or is it a cousin, snatches the knife from me, grabs the loaf and holds it to his chest, sideways on, and begins sawing slices off it in mid-air, cutting towards his body with the serrated blade in a manner that would have given my mother kittens in the days when I was being taught how to use cutlery.

You must never cut a loaf from the top! everyone starts telling me at once. The top of the loaf is Jesus's face! Do they not teach you that, where you come from?

No, they don't, but I'm pleased to have learned it now. Alberto and Antonello seem to be getting a lot of entertainment out of the lesson, too. I sit back down and decide to abdicate all responsibility, for bread or for anything else, at this event. You

348

couldn't even begin to start guessing what you might be doing wrong, could you? Though come to think of it, that style of bread-cutting is not entirely new to me. I've seen a few seriously old-time mountain-folk back in Liguria, barbecuing their lunches in their olive-groves over the fresh-cut wood at pruning time, cut it that way too. No mention of Jesus's face: but then, I've never asked. I always imagined it was just an oddly risky way of dealing with the lack of tables in olive groves.

*   *   *

So anyway, Antonio continues, now that my table manners are under control, the German had crept back the next day, and once he'd made sure nobody was around, he set about getting his own back, mashing the place up in revenge for the pettiness . . .

Terrible, says Beppe, trying to get him to understand that we weren't anything to do with the bailiff, we weren't the owners at all, but we needed the vines just as much as the real owner, more, really, because we had to pay him in wine for the hire of the vineyard for the year, half the wine we would be making was already his, before the grapes had so much as shown their faces, and the other half was ours to sell, or to drink, that was how we would get paid, but if that German mashed up half the vines, we'd have done all that work, a whole year, just to pay your man, and get nothing back for it at all! Because the noble lord certainly wouldn't listen to some absurd excuse like Oh, sorry, sir, an angry German destroyed half the vineyard because your bailiff wouldn't let him have a wash in the

349

river! Would he? Not that Artallo would ever have told him that, in the first place. And we would never have got within a mile of his Lordship to say it ourselves.

No, says Antonio, chuckling, but just you try and explain all that in sign language! I don't think they had *latifundia* in Germany, people just owned their own land and that was that. We had to act it out for him, scene by scene! He was laughing his head off by the end of it, and he'd certainly understood something, because he went off quietly, never showed his face again, and a couple of months later, when the troops had left for the North, there was this box of cigars, Swiss cigars, with a German Army label on it, sitting in our *capanna*, the shed where we kept the tools! Imagine that, no food in the house, the olive oil all gone, broth with the same bones boiled up in it for a week, the family out combing the countryside after wild greens or snails or anything to put in it: and there the three of us were, half-famished, but smoking away at real Swiss cigars like people who didn't have a care in the world!

Germans weren't all bad, that's true—another uncle remembers, he was only eleven or something, and he had gone to the vegetable garden looking for a tomato or any old thing you could eat, but there was nothing, not so much as a leaf of *rucola* to be had—because, he explains for the younger listeners' benefit, they'd had a camp full of soldiers billeted on the town for months, who would just come into your vegetable garden and take whatever they fancied, Italian soldiers that is, never mind the Germans, they'd only just arrived then—and what were you going to say to a bunch of men with guns?

350

Nothing! So, no food in the *orto*—but there, lying on the ground, was a set of keys, car keys. The uncle realized in a flash that the soldiers must have dropped them last time they'd been there . . . nobody else round here had cars in those days . . . so he was overjoyed, and he said to himself, I'll take them up to the camp and give them back, just make sure I go at lunchtime, and they're practically bound to give me a plate of hot food as a reward, aren't they?

But you try getting into one of those camps! Sentries all round it, Italians, and the first one just snatched the keys off him and sent him packing! And when he wouldn't go, and stood there pleading for food, the soldier actually cocked his gun and pointed it at him, seriously looked as if he was about to shoot him—so the Uncle legged it, threw himself over the nearest wall and hid in the field behind it . . .

Meanwhile, though, one of the new German soldiers must have been watching all the carry-on, because five minutes later, while the Uncle was still trying to get his breath back behind his wall, the German appeared—he nearly died of panic, he thought it was the Italian come to get him—but it was a German, huge, with pale, pale hair, and pale eyes, and pale skin too—who crouched down next to him, with a slice of bread held in the flat of his hand, says the Uncle, still excited to this day at the thought of it, and he put it into mine and signed to me to keep it flat, and then he pulled two whole tins of corned beef out of his pocket, the ones with the little keys on them, and he just opened them there and tipped them out on to the slice of bread. Two whole tins! Then he waited and watched till

351

I'd eaten the lot, maybe he thought if he didn't I'd run home and share it out with the family—some chance, not when you're eleven and you're that hungry!—just crouched there by the wall watching me eat, and signed to me that he had a son my size back in Germany . . . Ah, that was a day!

I give up on the men. Too much hunger. I'll go and see what the women are up to.

Annunziata is wiping her eyes with a napkin, telling everyone how strange it is to think of living the rest of her life all alone. To think that she didn't really want to marry Enzo, all those years ago, and now she can't imagine going on without him.

All the assembled ladies agree that it was God's will, nothing to be done about it, you just have to content yourself with your lot, *che sarà, sarà*: whatever will be will be. Annunziata too! Didn't anybody round here manage to marry a man they actually wanted to marry in those days?

It wasn't just Enzo, she says: she didn't want to marry anybody. She was nearly thirty by then, nobody had ever expected her to marry, being the youngest daughter, and she thought she'd got away with it!

Ah, says Cousin Concetta, that's the thing, you get too independent if you wait that long. You go off the idea of promising to obey some man, for good or ill.

So when did it stop, all this arranged-marriage business, down here? I ask.

Still hasn't stopped, says Concetta, if you ask her. Look at her *deficenti* suitors, going to her father first!

Antonio wouldn't dream of saying yes for you,

though, would he? Marisa asks.

Of course he wouldn't! He wouldn't dare!

Annunziata, over the other side of the kitchen table, is telling us that by the end of the first week, she'd realized that her parents were right all along. She was glad she'd married Enzo: she'd fallen in love with him.

Ah, yes! say the other ladies of a certain age. That first week! How lovely that used to be! It would make anyone fall in love! That was your honeymoon in those days, they explain to us Northerners: you stayed in the house together the whole week, and friends and relations took over your share of the work in the fields, and there was nothing to be done in the kitchen either, because family and neighbours would drop in dishes of food for you: everybody who'd come to the wedding would bring something, the pair of you would be snuggled up all alone in the house by day. Ah, yes! says Carmela. She remembers she and Pino could hardly move for goodies and sweetmeats, honey cakes and sweet almond milk and marzipan and *vino cotto*: and in the evenings, the record player would come out, and everybody would visit, and you'd all sing and dance . . . wonderful! If you couldn't fall in love in the lap of such luxury, you never would fall in love.

Sounds like an odd way round to do things to my modern ears, getting married first and falling in love afterwards. But I'm glad to hear that it worked so well. As Carmela told that little story, Pino, about whose lack of commitment to her there have been so many hints, has come in and put an arm around her shoulder in a most affectionate way. Maybe she'll be joining him beside the oil-pipelines of Tadzhikistan yet, once his fortune is made—or do I mean beside the plastic-straw factories of Northern Italy?

Come through to the other room, he says: there is dancing afoot. Antonio and Tommaso are playing a *tarantella*, the dance of the spider-bitten: a couple of the men have got to their feet. Some of the ladies in here are disapproving—that's no way to carry on, disrespectful on an occasion like this! But Annunziata starts clapping along, and the muttering stops. I stick my head round the door; several of the men, and a couple of the younger women, are dancing a sort of wild cross between Zorba the Greek and English country dancing, with plenty of extra stamping and twirling, the fiddle squealing up and down the scale at the speed of light. It looks brilliant, but I don't think I'd dare try. Not yet, at any rate.

Back in the first kitchen, Cousin Concetta is telling a story, something I can't quite understand —it's hard work following them now they've had a few glasses of Enzo's *'nchiostro,* and the dialect is flying thick and fast—about somebody-the-baker getting married, and a baker's wife gets no honeymoon, of course, because if the baker's not up and the dough ready well before dawn, where will the town get its bread? And this bride got no rest at all, she was worn out by the end of the week, he had her wide awake all night, kneading that dough from dusk till dawn. Dough enough for the entire town!

Lots of giggling from the ladies here. A risqué story, Calabrian style.

The other side of the table seems to be on to hilarious wedding-day stories. Well, do you know, I was so scared I shut myself in the bedroom on my wedding morning, praying for a miracle to save me! . . . My mother and my sisters had to fight to get the dress on me, with me clinging to the furniture, begging them not to take me to the church! I'd just been sitting there for a good hour, staring at that wedding-gown, making no move to put it on, saying to myself, if I don't put that white dress on, they can't make me marry! You've taken leave of your senses, girl! they said. We'd better get you up to that altar and married off quick, before he notices, or we'll never get you off our hands! And off they dragged me, willy nilly . . . and home I came, a married woman!

That, believe it or not, was Francesca, sounding as if she thought the whole thing was a great laugh. The music is coming louder and faster from the other room—and somebody has started singing a Neapolitan ballad. We're on the coffee and digestive now. Nocino, naturally. Time to go through and join the men.

45

Lying in bed, I hear the sound of somebody pottering about the sofa-and-ironing room. Vincenza, of course, who seems to like sitting in there of a morning; uses it as an extra sitting-room, I gather, to judge by the bits of knitting, newspapers and half-read books lying about the place . . .

The trouble is, she doesn't seem to be able to last more than half an hour in there without needing to use the loo; and comes bursting in, either through the interconnecting door or through the French windows, as the fancy takes her, yelling *Permesso!*

Ciccio, delicate flower, is complaining that he has enough trouble getting back to sleep after the daily call-to-Mass extravaganza from the bell tower—Vincenza is the last straw. Still, I've seen her place, and he hasn't. She's welcome to invade our privacy, as far as I'm concerned, if that's what it takes for her to breathe. After all, we invaded hers first. Ciccio wouldn't even notice she was there, anyway, if only she'd give up on all that *permesso*'ing business. I'll go and tell her just to walk on through in future, not to bother asking . . .

By the time I've thrown on my bathrobe and put this thought into action, there's no sign of her next door. She must be coming back, though, the French windows are wide open.

I sit down on the sofa to wait, pick up Vincenza's magazine, move an uncomfortable bundle of crochet-work out from under my bum . . . but something else, something between the backrest and the seat-cushion, is still sticking into me. A couple of contortions, and I manage to get hold of it. A book. With a knitting-needle stuck between the pages as a bookmark. *La Gioia del Sesso*, I read. *The Joy of Sex*. Terrible! Poor Vincenza, reading a sex handbook and having to stuff it down the back of the sofa like a naughty teenager. Imagine that, she's had two children and still can't admit to being at all interested in Sex. Or worse, she still needs to find out about Sex. No, I suppose it's not necessarily a handbook, is it? She could be reading it just for titillatory purposes . . .

356

I look a little more closely at it. The knitting-needle marks a tasteful pencil drawing of a nude woman astride a nude man. The text is very restrained: husband-and-wife stuff. The gentleman in the illustrations sports a fine fluffy-mullet hairstyle and a set of drooping moustachios, very San Francisco summer-of-love.

Now it dawns on me: *La Gioia del Sesso!! The Joy of Sex!* I am looking at the 1960s original, Italian translation! Probably worth a fortune . . . Oh no! Does this explain the manic burstings into our bedroom? Is Vincenza hoping to catch us in The Act? Help. I quickly stuff the book back in its place behind the sofa cushions, and dash back into bed. Perhaps, in the light of this discovery, I won't bother telling her to use the bathroom without knocking, then. Will I tell Ciccio? I'm dying to— and to show him the vintage copy of *The Joy of Sex*. Perhaps not till we're leaving, though. His carrying on about the bells is bad enough, and about Vincenza's *permesso*'ing of a morning: imagine how restful it would be in this bedroom if he were to realize that she's doing her best to catch him with his knickers down.

After this morning's visitation from a high-speed Vincenza, I wait till I hear her leave, then nip into the ironing/sitting-room to check. Yes. *The Joy of Sex* is still in the same place—but the knitting-needle has moved. The moustachio'd lover is now going for it in the upright position, his missis leaning up against the wall, in transports of ecstasy.

What a terrible disappointment we must be.

*   *   *

357

Downstairs, Gianni Versace the postman has stopped by. Knowing the household's habit of switching off the local news on the TV, he makes sure to pass on any titbits that may interest them without depressing them, along with the post.

Those hunters who are staying next door to Giuseppa, he says, the Milanesi—their cars have been stolen!

Poveracci! says Zia Annunziata. The poor things!

They were flagged down at dusk last night, says Gianni, by *malavitosi* disguised as policemen—and robbed of everything they owned! Their guns and all the bits and pieces that went with them, hi-tech night-sights and such state-of-the-art stuff, even down to their cartridge-belts and ammunition, all worth thousands. Then they took their wallets, their credit cards, their watches . . . and the two cars as well for good measure.

Fancy that! All the way from Milan, too! Isn't that terrible? Zia Annunziata doesn't sound too distressed, though. And Gianni seems to be positively revelling in the story. And do you know what? They even took their shoes, too! Left them standing there in their socks to walk the five miles into town!

Five miles from where? Where did it happen? asks Francesca.

Where do you think? Castellace!

*   *   *

This is the day that Zia Annunziata takes her weekly consignment of figs to the Moroccan in the market, neatly packed into two large brown suitcases. She always goes on the bus, she says, you

358

can't park anywhere on market day. Vincenza, taking her coffee with us this morning, decided that she would go to the market too, and went off to change into something tidier.

She now reappears wearing the most peculiar outfit. It features, most noticeably, a bright-green satin jacket with a pattern of huge polka-dots woven into it, each dot a good three inches across, in two-tone black and lime green. And hugely padded power-shoulders. Very cunningly chosen as a boundary-tester. The effect may be weirdly clownlike, and it is glaringly obvious that this is no normal going-to-market jacket; but what, exactly, as a long-suffering relative, could you specify was wrong with it? Nothing.

Carmela sighs, but does not rise to the bait. Zia Annunziata, busy organizing the carrying of the suitcases—no, she'll carry the big one, she's done it every week of her life, why should she stop now?—appears oblivious to the strange looks Vincenza is getting as they head off up the road to the bus stop.

*   *   *

Alberto comes and sits next to me on the steps under the fountain. Antonello and company are riding over to Locri this afternoon, he tells me; and he wants to go with them. They will be wearing their helmets all right—they always do when they go out on the main roads. One of the boys is looking for a job over there. But do I think Marisa will kick up a fuss?

I can't see why she should, I say, somewhat mystified by the question.

The thing is, says Alberto, that when he

359

mentioned Locri to Carmela, she went into one about how the place is riddled with *malavitosi* and he shouldn't go there and what on earth sort of job could you possibly get at Locri that wasn't something dodgy . . . And maybe Marisa will have heard all that stuff about Locri too? Or at any rate, if she mentions to Carmela that he's going there, Carmela will probably scare the life out of her, won't she, and Marisa will end up saying he can't go? So anyway, he was hoping I'd look Locri up for him in one of those guidebooks we've got in the car, and find some other attraction, unconnected with the Mafia, that he can say is the thing they're really going to see.

Phew. Well, I'm glad we got there in the end. I dig the car keys out and send Alberto off for the guidebook.

There's definitely something odd about all this, though. Alberto seems strangely agitated. He doesn't usually carry on like this.

What is this job, anyway? I ask him when he returns.

Well, he says, I shouldn't really tell you . . . You won't want to know.

Well done, Alberto. I have to pursue it now, don't I?

Eventually, with a mere touch of the thumbscrews, he confesses all. A cousin of one of the boys, a cousin who ended up leaving town in haste a couple of days ago—he'd got into trouble with drugs, and the family thought he was best out of it and sent him off to an aunt in Turin—anyway, this boy was earning quite a bit of money doing the odd evening's work down at the harbour in Locri. All he had to do was sit up a hill well away from the

360

scene of activities—a boat delivering cigarettes from Albania—with a pair of binoculars and a mobile phone, and send a text every now and then to give the boys down on the beach the all clear. Or a different text if there was anything to worry about. He shouldn't really have told anyone, but when he was off his head he'd chat away about anything, Lino says. That's how he knows. And that, adds Alberto, fixing me with an earnest eye, is why the Mafia hate people who do drugs. So anyway, they've decided to go down to their bar in Locri, and Lino's hoping that he might get chatting to one of them and somehow let drop that he's the cousin of the vanished lookout . . . Which, Alberto says, he thought sounded a bit far-fetched, why would any of these Mafiosi talk to him, anyway? But Lino says they're always on the look-out for likely lads, and that bar's where you go if you want to get talent-spotted . . . So Lino thinks, because they'll be realizing they're a hand short by now, he might get offered the job . . . and he really needs the money because he's starting university at Reggio next month, he wants to do architecture but his father thinks it's a waste of time, says he'll never stick five years of it, so he knows they're going to keep him dead short of money to try and make him give it up . . .

While I've been listening to this stream of consciousness from Alberto, I have been checking through the guidebook for Locri. I knew it rang a bell: Locri Epizefiri. Founded in the seventh century BC. You're spoilt for choice, I tell him. You have an Ionic temple from the fifth century before Christ, a Graeco-Roman theatre, still standing, and a Roman necropolis to visit. And a museum too, with a collection of votive ceramics. Votive ceramics! I interrupt myself. Maybe I want to go too? There might be sign-of-the-horn hands among them, mightn't there? With explanations by them, even.

Alberto likes the sound of the necropolis more. Isn't that one of those places with tunnels full of piles of skulls?

Why? I ask. Is he really going to go there? I thought he was going to a Mafia bar to get a job? Hearing myself say this aloud, it dawns on me that it isn't really a joke. I've heard about nothing all week but people getting killed, or shot at, for no very good reason. This is probably a pretty foolish thing that Alberto's planning to do. And moreover, I suspect that he's told me about it because he wants someone to stop him. Or why would he have mentioned it?

I'm sorry, I say, but I really don't think you should go, Alberto. What if this boy isn't as clever as he thinks he is, and they realize he knows too much?

Well, says Alberto, they're hardly going to gun down five teenage boys in cold blood in the middle of the afternoon, are they? In their own bar?

No, I suppose not. I've thought of a back-up plan, though. We were planning to do some touring today, and Locri sounds good. I'll get Ciccio and Marisa to drive over, and we can all meet up there. Then we'll be nearby if anything goes wrong, and he wants to be rescued. He can text us when he gets there, tell us where to meet.

Some hours later, here we are in Locri, waiting in the main piazza for Alberto, who has texted us at last. The museum was shut; but we've had a happy

362

wander around the Graeco-Roman theatre, and have sore throats from our exhaustive testing of its acoustics. Well, actually, it was only a partly happy wander in my case. I noticed, almost as soon as Alberto had left, that I had made a serious mistake in not telling Marisa what they were planning to do. But I couldn't tell her, could I, now that he'd gone, and there was nothing to do but wait until he texted us. It might have given her a nervous breakdown. So I've been having my own private nervous breakdown in her stead ever since.

Legend has it, the *Storia della Calabria* says, that this city was founded by slaves who had run off with their owners' wives: but adds that this was probably invented *post facto*, to explain the city's unusual tradition of treating women as the equals of men. Annunziata, Carmela and Francesca have all told us another story: that the place was actually built by its women. But none of the literature mentions this, not even the Italian guidebook. A legend invented *post facto*, by the residents of other less democratic towns, Marisa says, to convince their own women that they didn't really want to be the equals of men anyway—because then they'd end up having to build whole cities all by themselves?

Alberto appears, riding Antonello's bike, at the entrance to a narrow side street, and beckons us to follow him. Down a side street off that side street, and in through a pair of plate-glass doors, we find ourselves in a long room with a bar almost cutting it in two; there are chairs and tables at this end of the room, various pool tables and table football games at the other; and at the far end, another set of doors giving on to a back street.

Vaiu e votu, says Alberto casually, in Calabrese.

363

I'll be back in a minute! And he heads off to join Antonello at the table football. *Vaiu e votu!* says his mother. Did you hear that? Alberto's speaking Calabrese!

A barmaid with lots of gold jewellery and dark hair scraped back Spanish-style into a bun is chatting to a bunch of men in early middle age, who lounge on bar-stools and chairs around her bar in the centre of the room, wearing the obligatory autumnal leather jackets. Apart from this group, all the other customers are young males somewhere between puberty and adulthood. And whatever they are doing—sitting, standing, chatting, posing, playing desultory games of pool, you can sense that their entire attention is focused on the group of older men at the bar. Hand on hip, jacket flipped back to reveal plenty of electric blue silk, one of these older ones, a man with iron grey hair and black sideburns, is holding court: telling some story to four impressionable-looking youths who are hanging upon his lips, spellbound by his every word. Next to him, another of the in-crowd, slightly balding with a long hooked nose, rests his elbows on the bar, surveying a group of young men who are chatting away brightly for the benefit of the hook-nosed observer at the bar; who now puts his hands into his trouser pockets, jingles some coins, and walks slowly over in the direction of the group. You'd think you were in a gay bar, except the body language is all wrong. Here comes Alberto, Antonello at his side, heading our way. Hook-nose makes some joke as Antonello passes by, laughs and claps him on the shoulder. Antonello does his best to respond in kind; but his answering clap belongs, it has to be said, more in the nervous-pat category.

Weird place, says Ciccio as we head for the bar and a drink. What are you boys doing in here? I thought you went roaming the countryside hunting for girls? You certainly haven't picked the right spot here, have you? Unless you're after the barmaid?

How's it going, then? I ask Alberto, as soon as I manage to get him out of earshot. I can't believe this place, I add. I've never been anywhere like it. Have you seen anyone get taken on yet? Has anyone given you a job interview?

No. Not yet. But he doesn't think it's funny. The man that just slapped Antonello on the back thinks he knows him from somewhere; and instead of saying no, you must be mistaken, he agreed that they'd met before. He's an idiot. If he gets offered a job, he'll have to do it, whatever it is, won't he? And even then, they might kill him off anyhow, when they realized they didn't really know him, for getting in under false pretences.

Alberto is not a happy bunny. They've been here nearly two hours, and the man they wanted to see, the only one Lino would recognize, hasn't turned up. Maybe he won't turn up at all? Alberto wants to go away from here. He is bored, and he is scared. Either of those is bad on its own, but in combination they are unbearable. He thinks the others would like to go, too, but nobody dares be the first to suggest leaving, in case it looks as if they are bottling out.

I have the perfect solution.

Let's all go for a pizza! I say. I'm buying!

The faces round the pool table light up. *Figura* saved, honour satisfied, the boys are out of there

365

and on their bikes in seconds.

The next hour is hard on my purse, but the relief is worth it. Alberto made it out of there in one piece: and Marisa need never know.

Some time later, well pizza'd up, we decide to follow in the footsteps of the fleeing survivors of the Saracen devastation of Locri, some time in the seventh century. Fifteen minutes' drive up a steep and tortuous road, we arrive at their refuge. They had the same good idea as the founders of Palmi: get up high, preferably on top of a cliff. At least you'll see them coming nice and early next time, and get a decent head start. This cliff, at Gerace, is even safer than Palmi's, though: ten kilometres inland, and no sea at the bottom of it, only a plain. Impressive. Just watch a Saracen try and sail up that! they must have said to themselves, as they founded their new town here. Robert Guiscard was impressed too, when he came across the place three centuries later. He stayed to strengthen its defences, and to build a beautiful Norman church within them. Ciccio and I are amazed when we walk in: it is so similar to a church in Normandy that made a great impression on us some years ago: which is saying a lot, because we are no connoisseurs of churches. It was just something to distract us from our rumbling stomachs while we waited for the only restaurant in this tiny French town to open. And we stepped into a vision of beauty and simplicity: a forest of tall slender pillars, plain and simple, monotone pale grey, soaring straight and high to graceful vaulted arches, made ethereal by the light: an extraordinary, inexplicable amount of light that seemed to come from nowhere and from everywhere, to be percolating through solid stone. Two thousand miles to the south, yet you would almost believe this was the same place; except that the abundance of choice in local building materials has gone to the architect's head —and in place of the plain grey stone of Normandy, the pillars here are of granite and marble: we count twenty columns, not one the same as the other. And by the altar, a dark grey-green marble column that changes colour according to the weather. The Norman New Age touch. I have imagined Robert Guiscard so far as an almost baroque figure, a creature of labyrinthine hypocrisy, brutal and self-seeking. But in this building you get a glimpse of how he must have imagined himself; an upright, honourable man doing the work of God, his simple, noble project blessed by the heavens above.

46

One of the stolen cars has been found on the ferry leaving for Sicily, wearing a new set of number-plates. Amazing, I say, I'm impressed! After seeing the forces of law and order spend days and days on that car accident, where there was no question of there being any crime involved, I'd have expected them to make a good year's work out of an actual theft.

Francesca looks at me reprovingly. Don't be silly, she says, you couldn't expect policemen to go getting themselves mixed up in something like that!

What does she mean? Something like what? Solving a crime? Isn't that their job, then, detecting things, catching thieves?

But I am an innocent fool. Well, not necessarily a fool. Just innocent. Simple.

Did anyone mention any thieves having been caught? asks Zia Annunziata, kindly helping with my education.

No, they didn't, contributes Gianni Versace.

They expected that car to be found on the ferry: it will have been planned, of course. Because it's not in the *malavita*'s interest to make any of the police forces look utterly incompetent.

No, because then you get all sorts of trouble, says Carmela, questions asked and State Investigators sent down making Official Enquiries . . . All sorts of inconveniences.

Or Clean Hands magistrates starting anti-corruption campaigns, joins in Gianni, and getting themselves shot—and then that causes even more trouble . . .

The *malavitosi* will naturally sacrifice one of the vehicles, just for the *figura* of the law-enforcing organizations. Improve the crimes-solved statistics, less graft for everybody all round, and the status quo is undisturbed. Everybody is undisturbed. The perpetrators get to enjoy the rest of their booty in peace: and nobody need waste their time going around trying to investigate anything, stirring up any number of hornets' nests into the bargain.

Simple. I see what Francesca means. Fancy my imagining the police would want to get mixed up in something like that.

*   *   *

Back at Graziella, we have walked up the path on

the far side of the river to see the lake—a clear, blue rock pool, mirror smooth. Beautiful!

It's lovely now, Annunziata says, but it was nothing like this when they were children, was it, Francescella? It was a linen pond: stinking stagnant water where they left the linen to rot down before they beat the thread out of it. The boys would dare one another to jump into it, and it was so hot down here in the height of summer us girls would even be jealous of them! People used to think it was the linen that gave you malaria, once upon a time, she tells us. Anyone who worked the linen was ten times as likely to get it, and the doctors hadn't worked out that it was mosquitoes that carried it then, it was all a mystery. Vincenza has a book back at the house somewhere, don't you Vincenza, with some doctor saying the malaria was caused by people keeping pigs under the stairs. Though I don't know when anybody ever did that, not in my lifetime!

Yes, says Vincenza, she'll show it to us later, if we remind her . . . it's not really a book, more of a health-warning pamphlet from the mid-1800s: it's mainly fascinating (she's gone off into her tourist-guide style of speech again) because once you know the malaria had nothing to do with pigs under the stairs, in spite of the author's *disprezzativo* tone—he disapproves intensely, of course—you can tell it was a fine system: feed the pigs on your leftovers, throw more and more straw into the sty over the winter, and by spring you have a great pile of composted manure, rich stuff to boost your vegetable gardens . . . and plenty of bacon, ham, salami and *soppressata* for the year. All done by simple folk, with a simple cupboard under

369

the stairs. And a strong stomach, naturally, to handle the stench . . .

How eccentric Vincenza is! She should definitely have stayed on at that university, in my opinion. Francesca is looking askance at her. Annunziata returns to the topic of the stinking linen pond.

A contare le pene del lino, canta il gallo e fa mattino, she quotes . . . That's an old linen-growers' saying, and believe her it's true. 'Start telling the miseries of linen-making, the cock will be crowing and dawn will be breaking.' Or something along those lines. Does Annunziata remember the tale of the woman who met a witch down by the river, kept her at bay all night by telling her the sufferings of the linen-grower? That was one her mother Serafina used to tell when they were little. The woman had come down here to do her washing, she'd got here very late, but she wanted to get her work done, and there she was, bashing away at her sheets on those big flat rocks over there, engrossed in her work: and dusk was upon her before she knew it. You should never be out by the river at dusk, of course, because that's when witches appear . . . and just as she's gathering up the clothes in a panic—she doesn't care if they're still all wet and soapy and only half-washed as long as she gets away before sunset—of course, along comes a witch, and starts chatting to her. She can't walk away, you never can once a witch has you talking, and she knows she mustn't fall asleep—if you fall asleep, that's it, the witch will have your soul for her own. So now she's desperate, three small children at home and a husband to look after, she has to stay awake, keep a hold of her soul . . . And now she remembers that saying, *a contare le pene del lino, canta il gallo e fa mattino*, and she says to herself, I just hope that's true . . . and she begins telling the witch all about the life of a linen-grower, blow by blow, from planting the seeds to harvest, from harvest to scutching, from scutching to beating, from beating to spinning, from spinning to weaving . . . and she's on the preparing of the cloth, the last cleaning with lye and vinegar, right near the end of the story, wondering will she hold out, not much more to tell . . . And, lo and behold, as she says her last word, there is the tip of the sun, a tiny curved strip of gold, just appearing over the horizon! She's made it! And it catches the witch right in the eyes! The witch lets out a horrible shriek, as witches do in the sunlight; the first cock crows—and pouff! she turns into a floating shred of grey dawn mist before the woman's very eyes!

And so on your good woman goes with her washing, just as she was before, one more lather, one more scrub, one more rinse, folds it all neatly into her basket and away she goes, back home to hang it out to dry, back to the husband and the babies, *come se niente fosse!* Just as if nothing at all had happened!

You see? says Annunziata, you look at the linen growing, the wide fields of blue flowers; beautiful, you say, lovely the way it ripples in the wind . . . but that's just your ignorance!

It certainly is in my case, I say. I've never knowingly seen a field of linen. But I am not alone. Nor has Ciccio, nor has Marisa. Where do they make it now, then?

Ah, somewhere even poorer than here, no doubt, says the Zia. There's nothing so terrible as linen, the choking dust that comes up off the fields

371

when you cut it and stook it . . . everyone has red eyes for weeks afterwards. Worse still for the ones who have to thresh the seeds out of it.

Seeds? Does it have seeds too then?

Of course it does. Where do I think *olio di lino* comes from?

Linen oil? Never heard of it. What do you do with it?

Annunziata regards me with deep concern. What do you do with *olio di lino*? she repeats incredulously. Well, you make paint out of it, just to start with. It is the only natural oil that hardens in contact with air. All wood paints used to be made from it, until they invented these new chemical paints. You seal your terracotta tiles with it. You protect anything wooden that has to be outside by rubbing it in or painting it on, depending. And artists use it too . . .

I've got there at last. Linseed oil! Oil paintings! Cricket bats! Oil of linen. Didn't know the two things were connected. Though it's obvious once you look at the name. Obvious with a bit of help from an aged aunt, that is. I decide not to mention the cricket bats. Could require a very long explanation. Tragic that I know of no other use for linseed oil without prompting—though I have actually used *olio di lino* on my floor tiles back home, without spotting the *lino*/linen/linseed connection.

Comunque! Anyhow! says the Zia, passing lightly over my astonishing ignorance, and determined to finish her list of the Pains of Linen. You'd collect the seeds up to crush to make the oil later . . . then you'd load the lot up on to your donkeys, trying not to breathe while you did it, and cart it up here.

Then, into the water with it to rot down—you would block off that whole section of the river over there, and the smell that came off it . . . ! But still, you had to get in there with it a few weeks later, beat the rotting part off, and there you'd have the bare fibres at last, that's the pure linen . . . and then you'd have to get it into the main part of the river, into the flowing water to clean it, then lay it all out to dry and bleach in the sun . . . Then, before you could get on with the spinning . . .

How long till the weaving, I wonder? I think I already hear that cock crowing.

47

He couldn't come to the month-memorial, says Zio Fantino, unlocking his *Ape*. He was sorry to miss it, but Elisabetta isn't well enough to go out and about, and he doesn't like to leave her alone at night. Anyway, they both need to conserve their strength for San Rocco's feast day next week. He has high hopes of San Rocco.

Zio! You've taken leave of your senses! says Ciccio. You don't even believe in it!

He's spent his whole life telling people off for believing in mumbo-jumbo instead of science, Ciccio says; for letting themselves be terrorized into submission by a bunch of money-grubbing priests! He was always an out-and-out atheist. What about your *figura*, Zio? Talk about letting yourself down!

But the Zio doesn't care about his *figura* any longer, he says. He's past it. And it just might help

Elisabetta. The psychological thing, you know, he says, looking a bit sheepish. He's decided to just think of it as a bit of healthy exercise. And a bit of healthy bloodletting, too. People used to do that for their health once upon a time, didn't they? Might exorcize a few of his own demons, too, he adds quietly.

But isn't San Rocco's feast day in the summer, anyway? asks Ciccio. He certainly remembers going to the San Rocco *festa* as a child, it was unforgettable, the long line of penitents all pouring sweat and blood under a baking sun, struggling up off that steep track with their eyeballs starting from their heads and those terrible thorns digging into them, stumbling on to the courtyard of the church looking as if they'd had half the flesh shredded off them. Horrifying . . .

Yes, that's the main one, says his uncle: but there's another San Rocco pilgrimage on All Saints' Eve. And if he's going to do it, he's better off doing it now than waiting for the summer one in the broiling heat . . . Same amount of thorns, but less sweat! He can't bear to see Elisabetta like this any longer, nothing else works, why not try San Rocco? And the shrine's only a few villages away, near enough to get her to it easily. Marisa, Alberto and I are all waiting agog to hear more about this horrendous-sounding event. What is it? What do they do? Why?

Zia Annunziata and *la mamma* took him there that time the whole family came down in the car, Ciccio tells us. The penitents wrap themselves in a kind of big tangle of huge fierce thorns, don't they, Zio? It covers their whole body from head to toe. And they carry the statue of San Rocco for miles

374

across rocks and crevasses . . . or something . . .

Wait, says Marisa, I must have been here too, then! I can't believe I don't remember that. It sounds like something that would scar you for life!

No, says her brother, you were too little, they just took you to the picnic afterwards, didn't let you see the scary bit.

Shut up, you two, says Alberto, gripped. Go on, Zio!

Well, says Fantino, you wear a kind of cage twisted out of thorn branches, most of the weight rests on your head, it's meant to be like the Crown of Thorns. Only more so . . . You put that on, and then you walk up from the shrine below in the valley, it's a couple of kilometres, to the chapel above. There's a path, but a lot of it goes scrambling over rocks. And the thorns rip away at you, every step you take, you can't help it.

Aargh! says Alberto. It sounds gross! We definitely have to come and see it! Can we come back in the summer?

Well . . . says Marisa.

There's a good party afterwards, too, says Ciccio. He remembers the picnic was huge, hundreds of people cooking and eating and drinking wine and singing and dancing and . . .

Ah, says Fantino, that was a good few years ago, when you came: but you got there just in time. The thing was already toned down a lot, compared to the good old days. Nowadays it's hardly worth bothering with! When Fantino was young, it was a really good, bloodthirsty show. Every family that could afford to would bring a goat, and once the penitents had done their thing—and in those days it was all the finest young lads did the walk, keen to show off how strong they were, how much pain they could take—then the goats were slaughtered on the spot, right there on the church courtyard, and the priest did his bit of consecration. Rivers of blood, what with the goats' throats cut, and the blood pouring from the human sacrifices too! A proper pagan festival. There's not a lot left of that. Not any more. We're much too civilized for that these days. Turning into a bunch of squeamish Northerners. All reasonable and good-mannered. Might as well be protestants, he adds, giving me a sly look as he opens the passenger door of the three-wheeler for me to climb in.

Damn. This means that Marisa will be getting in after me, and I'll be in the middle seat. Women always have to sit squashed up in the cab of these things with the driver, unless there are too many of them to fit. The open truck bed at the back is infinitely more comfortable, in my opinion. Look how much good it did Francesca. And the middle seat in the cab is a nightmare. These things have hardly any suspension worth mentioning, and in the middle you have nothing to hold on to as you lurch and bounce your way up whatever awful track you're bound for.

Not too bad a track, it turns out, leading down to Fantino's good acre of almost-flat land, just a couple of low terraces to it, a nice gentle balcony in the side of these harsh mountains, overlooking the broad plain down below. Shed full of chickens, fruit trees with beans growing up them just like Annunziata's—and every vegetable you can imagine planted down on the lower terrace, in the Calabrian mix-and-match style, all jumbled up together.

376

In England, I say, people usually plant just one kind of vegetable in one area, and the next in another. Not all mixed up like this.

Well, says Fantino, they must be idiots. He's seen that on the TV though—foreigners with everything all separated out. Stupid. Just encourages pests and diseases. Unless maybe it's so cold in those countries that you don't get pests and diseases?

The broad grassy area over there is pasture for Fantino's milk-sheep, he says, but the sheep's away up at his neighbours for lawn-mowing purposes till tomorrow. It's a lovely spot for summer picnics when the wee nephews and nieces, the migrant relatives return for their summer holidays . . . barbecues on bonfires of olive prunings and kilo after kilo of *rostelle* going down, not to mention litre after litre of his good black wine!

I wander off across the grass, towards the fringe of hazel trees and canes at the edge of the cultivated bit, and step in among them to pick a few nuts I've spotted in their branches.

Stop! Stay where you are! comes a terrible roar from Fantino; and he launches himself across the field towards me. There's a hole there! Watch out! he shouts.

I look down. There certainly is. Not what I would call a hole, though. A ravine, more like. A horribly impressive ravine that slices right down to the plain below, rocks and boulders protruding from its sides, as if a giant had slashed a slice out of the earth with his knife. It's nicely hidden by the fringe of canes—and I nearly walked right off into it. The mothers of those nieces and nephews must have nerves of iron, is all I can say. A huge great precipice, completely unexpected, just inches from a nice grassy flat field.

It wasn't always there, explains Fantino apologetically, once I am back on solid ground. It just appeared, so they say, after one of the big earthquakes, a couple of centuries ago. The village was more over this way in those days, and they had to rebuild the whole thing—the ground had cracked right open, not just here but in half a dozen places over on this side of the hill. There are still a lot of ruins down at the bottom, bits of the old village, whole sides of houses almost intact. If you climb right down you can still see them under the undergrowth. There are a couple of caves on the way down, too—in his youth you used to get brigands on the run using them for hiding places. Fantino and the other kids would creep down, trying to get a look without being spotted . . . he managed to catch a glimpse of one who'd been on the run for nearly ten years, people said. Villagers would come and leave him food, just there on that flat rock below the edge, whatever they could spare, on the way to Mass.

What had he done, then, to be on the run?

Ah, who knows, says Fantino. There were so many *latitanti*, fugitives from justice, in those days . . . nobody bothered asking. You just fed them anyway.

48

Marisa and I have done ourselves up to the nines, as promised, for our night out with the younger generation. We are off to hunt down a man for

Concetta the Disconsolate and her friend Laura Borgia, and have earned ourselves worried looks from Cousin Carmela on the one hand—Will you not catch cold, dressed like that? Shall I lend you something warmer?—and a stream of rude cackles from Aunt Annunziata on the other. That's the way to do it! she tells Marisa. You've hardly any time left to find yourself a nice Calabrian boy! Quick, bring one home tonight, and we'll move you both into Zia Maria's—you won't have to bother with that long trip back up North!

I think myself, although the subject seems to be taboo for now, that Marisa's got one up her sleeve already.

Concetta and Laura are taking us, they say, to a place above the town of Gioia Tauro—Joy Bull. A most peculiar name for a town: but looking it up in the tourist guide I discover that it was once a colony of Locri, up until that devastating Saracen attack that had Locri running for Gerace, and find a place for it in my heart.

We're meeting a pair of cousins of Laura's, two brothers who work at the port as electronic engineers or some such esoteric thing. These boys will be escorting us for the night. They have been drafted in, because you couldn't have just Ciccio and Alberto and four women, could you?

Evidently not.

Not only does Gioia Tauro have a cheery name, Concetta tells us as we drive the last few miles of squiggly olive-tree road, but it's a cheery place into the bargain. Just to start with, there is actually work there. Full-time work, indeed, and with decent pay. The huge container port that so annoys Zia Annunziata is working flat out, and the spin-off

379

jobs are legion. Then there are all the people from everywhere else in the world, whose work brings them there: the happy, thronging crowds of the gainfully employed folk of Gioia Tauro create just the right upbeat atmosphere for a good night out.

Dinner first, though. The electronic cousins are meeting us at the restaurant. A small restaurant in a small town just outside Gioia. Sounds promising. Ciccio feels in his bones that there will be braised goat on the menu. And he is right. We walk into a small, crowded, old-style family restaurant full of mouth-watering aromas, where Laura's cousins Claudio and Giovanni—long floppy dark hair and short spiky dark hair respectively—await us at a corner table. And, gladdening Ciccio's heart, the first thing we meet as we start to squeeze our way across the room is a pair of dishes of voluptuous-looking braised meat, piping hot, being borne head-high by a waitress who looks as if she's about nine years old.

We sit down and get introduced. Yes! The cousins share the same sinister surname. We're having dinner with the Borgias!

Great place! says Ciccio. Isn't it, though? says Claudio Borgia. He and his brother only found the place because it does workmen's lunches in the daytime: but nowadays they often eat here of an evening too. The family who run the place are sweethearts, *la mamma* is a great cook, and the customers are pleasant and down-to-earth. A lot of them are friends from work, Giovanni Borgia adds, as a bunch of new arrivals starts *ciao*'ing away to us. That lot are mostly Russians, he says: they're brilliant at repairing echo-sounders. Anyhow, says Claudio, the food is always good, and always cheap.

No pretentious *nouvelle cuisine* or Mediterranean this-that-and-the-other. Proper small-town-Italy food in a proper down-home atmosphere.

Well found, boys. We get on with the business of extricating ourselves from our jackets, untangling our handbags, settling ourselves in, and consulting the menu. Now, at last, we can begin to look around us, check out our fellow-clients for any sign of the man of Concetta's dreams. Or, indeed, Laura's.

Once you start examining the other customers closely, one by one, you are struck by the fact that every possible skin colour on the face of the earth seems to be represented here: and that the myriad tongues of the Tower of Babel are being spoken all around you. Yet all are melding together, somehow, into the down-home small-town-Italy ambience.

People from everywhere in the world . . . I say, wonderingly.

Of course, say the Borgias. It's an international container port, isn't it, in the middle of the Mediterranean? And it's at the crossroads from everywhere: you get people from North Africa and Black Africa, from Spain, Greece, Turkey. Then Eastern Europe—Bulgaria, Albania, ex-Yugoslavia, Poland; not to mention the whole of the Middle East. Plenty of Egyptians, for some reason. And the old Soviet Republics to the east— all those places like Uzbekistan and Kazakhstan and Turkmenistan, they've turned out not to be so far away as we imagined when there was an iron curtain in the way!

The very existence of this port is a sort of accident, Laura tells us; a chance spin-off from

some of the very corrupt doings in these parts—
and, not to put too fine a point on it, at the very
heart of the Italian State—in the sixties and
seventies. A success by mistake: another great
booster for the Calabrian self-image.

All this is down to an accident? asks Alberto.
How could anyone build a port by accident?

Well, says Giovanni, all right, a mistake, then.
They built the port, decided it was a mistake, and
just left it there to rot, unused. Did their best never
to mention it again. Put it this way: they certainly
didn't plan for this to happen. It began with a
project to build a huge steel plant and a massive
power station at Gioia Tauro. Contracts were
drawn up for them—and for the port that would
service them both. The port was begun; and then,
some time later, unusually for these parts, it was
finished. But the steel plant and the power station,
the entire reason for the port's existence, says
Giovanni, were never even begun.

I am momentarily distracted here by Claudio
pulling a black velvet alice-band from his pocket,
slipping it on to his forehead, and pushing it back
over the long floppy hair to keep it out of the food.
Young men in this country have been using alice-
bands for some years now—I think it all began with
Giro d'Italia cyclists—but I am still surprised when
they suddenly do it in front of me.

So the state-of-the-art port facility at Gioia
Tauro sat and languished for ten long years,
unused: thousands of pointless cubic metres of
concrete, a white elephant, an embarrassment to all
concerned, and a constant reminder of the utter
failure of government policy. Until, one day, some
man from Liguria, from a Genoese import-export

company, spotted the place by chance, thought that it might make a half-decent little container port for their Mediterranean business, and got permission to try out the notion. A container port turned out to be just what was needed, and the Genoese company has never looked back. These days Gioia Tauro is the biggest container port around the Mediterranean, with a massive volume of traffic.

A boy in the back starts playing the guitar while we eat—jazzy pieces from well-known Italian *cantautori*, singer-songwriters, to start with, and soulful popular ballads; and once the feeding frenzy is over, people begin to sing along—and our Laura and Claudio do a brilliant duet of a Mina song, 'Sei Bellissima'. They used to sing in a piano-bar in Reggio together, a good way to earn some money in the tourist season, they tell us.

We are wondering whether to bother going on somewhere else—it hardly seems worth it, we're having a great time where we are—when a man with a fiddle comes and joins the guitarist, and they start to play the *tarantella*. Right, we're definitely going nowhere! I'm hooked on this music since the night of the month-memorial, the soaring, wailing melodies, heart-rending and almost Arabic-sounding, pulsing rhythms that set your adrenalin flowing. Two boys get up from one of the tables and start to dance: no room to do much twirling in here, but they can get the mad complex footwork in all right—until a couple of tables are moved away into the kitchen to make space for them. This always happens on a Saturday night, we're used to it now, says the owner as he passes us. And now another bunch of young men joins in: much hilarity as they turn out to be Greeks, trying to fit the dance steps of their own country to this music, doing their best to copy the Calabrian boys. The music's similar enough, they say, they couldn't resist trying. Naturally, now it's turned into open season, beginners welcome, we all have a go. Concetta, who actually knows how to dance the *tarantella*—how many hidden talents these Calabrians have!—takes a turn with one of the Greeks, then sits laughing and chatting with him for some time. Back at our own table, we are all on tenterhooks. Has she found the man of her dreams?

Certainly not, says Concetta. What would my father say if I brought home a sailor? Are you mad?

49

Marisa comes into the mausoleum/bedroom while I'm hanging clothes out on the balcony. I've just used that concrete vat for the first time—been using the bathroom handbasin till now for fear of making a public display of my incompetence as a housewife. There is almost always some potential witness out there, doing some kind of laundry operation. Once I managed to catch up with the vat in a moment of solitude, alone and unattended, the laundering turned out a rather enjoyable procedure, especially the built-in scrubbing-board at the side. I may have to recommend this to people back home as a substitute for going to the gym. Throw away your washing-machine and bring in a vat! Full-body exercise! That might be a good new career: sole importer of high-style aerobic Italian scrubbing-vats.

Marisa has come, she says, to ask me whether Vincenza has ever discussed the father of her twins with me?

No, she hasn't, I say. She started to once, when we first got here, but Zio Antonio was there, he kind of shut her up, changed the subject . . . I suppose they don't want to talk about him, do they?

Well, says Marisa, they have good reason not to. Shall I tell you who he is? Vincenza told me this morning. Eddie Irvine!

What? I say. The Eddie Irvine? Or no, it must just be somebody else with the same name, is it?

Marisa looks pityingly at me. No, no, she says. The Eddie Irvine. Did you not know he was born in Sicily? And among other little-known facts about him, his mother was Calabrese? Vincenza met him while she was at university in Reggio. They miss one another a lot while he's away racing, but they decided it was better to live apart.

So she really is off her trolley? I say.

Off and on, Francesca says. Marisa's just been and had a row with Francesca about why on earth nobody bothered to mention that some of the things Vincenza tells you might occasionally be completely off the wall. It's ridiculous. Anything might have happened!

So—did she make him up to explain the absence of a father for her children?

The children appeared on her wall the year she gave up university, says Marisa. But they are not real. Eddie Irvine is a more recent development.

Funny way round to do it, kids first and father afterwards, but there you are.

What, she hasn't got any children either? I take a seat on the bed to think this one over.

Everyone knew, except for us two and Alberto! says Marisa. Ciccio knew too, *la mamma* told him ages ago, when he answered a couple of weird phone calls from her. He says he thought if he knew already, we must too. And anyway, it's obvious, according to him! I'm sure it is, too, if you know already. *La mamma* said the same: she thought everyone knew. Of course, this being Calabria, Marisa isn't even sure that anyone was intentionally concealing it from us—Francesca said that Annunziata and Carmela never mention it among themselves, not even if Vincenza does something really batty right in front of them: they just ignore it and get on with a bit of housework— so why would they have mentioned it to us? They're all as mad as Vincenza, if you ask me. Everyone that lives here, everyone in the town, knows that she goes loopy every so often—so why leave us in the dark, when you know we're going to be in her company every day we're here? Marisa is fuming.

And by the way, she adds, if you go and look closely at that photo next time you're round at her place, you'll see that her children are cut out from a photo in a women's magazine. *Bella*, I think. An illustration for a knitting pattern. She hasn't even bothered to get rid of the bit at the bottom where they tell you how much wool you'll need. Check it out.

And Marisa goes off, leaving me sitting on the bed racking my brains, trying to go over everything

Vincenza has ever told me since we got here. The Madonna? No, she was real, I saw her myself, and Zio Antonio was there with us, wasn't he, while she was telling me the bit about her appearing mysteriously waterborne from who-knows-where, down the river in the flood . . . but the bit in the scullery, then, about her growing up in there in the dark . . . ? Oh Lord. I see now. And starting to look sadder and uglier since she'd been shut up in the church . . .

No, don't go there.

Fantino's wedding photo, featuring Francesca's *mamma*, is still sitting on the bedside table. Something cheerful to do—I'll take it through to her, not much time left to get it blown up and enamelled and on to the grave before we go home to Liguria.

Francesca is overwhelmed—isn't it beautiful, her *mamma* looks so lovely in it, she'll get them to make an extra copy to take home with her, the only photos she has of her mother are ones where she's in the background. Annunziata will know where we can get it enamelled for the cemetery. And once that has been taken care of, Francesca says, she'll have no unfinished business left down here. She won't be returning. This is her last visit to Calabria.

Come on, don't say that, Francesca! I say.

Why shouldn't she? It's true. Twenty-five years since her last visit. And she's not going to live another twenty-five years, is she?

But we've got the lovely house to stay in now, I protest. We can come down a lot more often, once we've got it sorted out a bit.

You young ones can, she says. But I won't be coming. And there's an end to it! Do you know, she adds, that when I decided to come back down I had a powerful notion to get my Ciccio set up down here? It could easily happen, I said to myself, with no man down in Melipodio to act as head of the family, and all that land going to waste . . . he could take over the lot, I thought. But my brain's half-addled. Why would I want him to do that? Why would he want to? That's what I would have wanted for my son fifty years ago. Not now. Who wants land any more? Who wants to tie themselves to Calabria? The place is never going to get itself sorted out. Not in our lifetime.

But we don't need to tie ourselves to it! I say. That's the good thing about modern times, we can go up and down as much as we want, flit in and out; we don't have to choose the one or the other, do we?

But Francesca doesn't look very cheered. She's picked up the photo again now.

It's too sad. Look at all the Santa Cristina relations, so young, Fantino with all his hair! That's how she likes to remember them. Santa Cristina, though. You don't know how terrified I was, she says, going to live up there with a man I didn't really know, among the goats and rough country folk . . . A strange unknown place, she says, where she didn't know the local ways, didn't have any family of her own to take her part, or any friends for advice and company, all of them left behind in Melipodio—and who knew what a dog's life Salvatore's family might lead her, all alone and with nobody to take her part, no mother to run to for help and comfort? There were plenty of stories of outsider wives turned into miserable skivvies, treated like slaves, doing dogsbody work on the land and in the kitchen from dawn till dusk . . .

So that's how she came to think of leaving Calabria altogether—well, if she had to leave her home at all, much better go far away, to a place where Salvatore's family and neighbourhood had no power over her. Why not leave for the North, then, lots of people were doing it . . . She would miss her mother, but then she missed her already up in Santa Cristina. So she put the flea in Salvatore's ear, as you say in Italian, and soon he thought it was his own idea—and away they went, down off those wild hills at last, and up to the sunny plains of the North!

*   *   *

We set off downstairs with the photo to find Annunziata. You can hardly get across the hallway today: piles of crates and sacks have suddenly appeared in it. I stumble over something and swear to myself. What on earth is all this stuff? What is it? The gifts from Calabria for us to take home to the rest of the family in Liguria, of course! says Francesca. That's the stuff Zio Antonio brought round for us this morning. Annunziata and Carmela haven't got theirs packed up yet; we'll help them sort it out tomorrow.

Of course.

50

Ciccio might as well have come to the church of San Rocco after all: he chickened out of the trip because Marisa, Alberto and I said we were going to the Mass first. It looked too rude not to, we said, when we wanted to ask a favour from the priest. But as it turned out, Mass had already started when we got here. It was probably even ruder to Father Pierino to walk in half-way through than to blank the service, we decided. So here we are, sitting outside in the great stone-flagged courtyard next to the church in the balmy evening air, admiring the view. This must be the goat-butchering area, as described by Zio Fantino. Across the yard from it stands a set of long, low stone outbuildings that look like stables or cowsheds.

That must be where they kept all the goats on the big day, mustn't it? says Alberto, whose thoughts are obviously running along the same lines as mine.

I try to imagine the courtyard running with rivers of blood: the ecstatic worshippers. Easily done. Why, I wonder, do I always get to these sorts of places after people have stopped doing all the most interesting bits?

*   *   *

It must have been some sort of pre-Christian ritual originally, mustn't it? I say to Alberto. A midsummer solstice feast, a sacrifice of blood to the earth. That's why you'd get another one now, at

390

the winter solstice.

Alberto kicks his heels. Must have been a lot less boring in those days, he says, copying my thought processes again.

Not necessarily, I say. How do you know pagans didn't stand about in their rivers of goat-blood bored to death, moaning about the tedious modern priestesses with their new-fangled ideas, spoiling all the fun they used to have in the good old days, when they would rip the living hearts out of human sacrifices?

Alberto gives me a long, pitying look and crosses the road to the gap between two buildings where you can see the view down into the valleys: stands staring out across the mountains with his hands in his pockets.

Mass must have finished: people have started to trickle out. We nip into the church sharpish to make sure the priest doesn't leave by some other, secret route out back and escape us. Marisa goes round the side of the altar, and disappears through a side door. Reappears a minute or two later to say that Father Pierino is lovely. He says he bumped into Zio Fantino the other day, and Fantino told him we would be coming up—so he's brought the registers with him. What a nice man! He'll be with us in ten minutes, he said.

*   *   *

St Rocco's statue stands in the middle of the church, brightly painted: he wears a short tunic, and has a deep, bleeding sore on his right thigh: a statue-dog stands at his side, gazing faithfully up at him. A youngish-looking man in a raincoat is standing at the statue praying, with his forehead pressed to St Rocco's feet, holding what looks like a brown paper bag of groceries in his hand. He finishes his prayer, kisses the feet, and places the something-in-the-bag on the pedestal; then he starts to move backwards, step by step, all the way to the door of the church, keeping his eyes fixed on the saint until he is right outside.

I can't resist going to have a look in the bag. A loaf of bread, a round wholemeal loaf. Just like the one the dog is holding in his jaws. I wonder what happens to loaves left at the feet of saints?

Sore leg, loaf of bread, dog . . . What on earth can he be the patron saint of? Nothing immediately suggests itself. Alberto doesn't know, he says, and he couldn't care less. He's only interested in the pagan stuff. St Marisa knows what Rocco is good at—healing physical ailments, she says. But she knows nothing else about him. What about his wound? His dog? If I'd been brought up in a place full of interesting statues of saints doing interesting strange things, I say to Marisa reprovingly, I would certainly have made it my business to know more about them.

Would you just? says she. Do you know how many thousands of them there are? Bah! I say, doing my best imitation of her father, and I set off round the church looking for clues to St Rocco's life and works. I spot a small printed notice pinned to the first column back from the altar, and squeeze through the seating towards it, full of hope.

Do Not Gossip With Your Neighbours While The Holy Sacrament Is Being Said! it says. But look, on a table near the door lies a pile of those cigarette-card-sized Holy Images. Of St Rocco, naturally, this being his shrine; so they're bound to have something about his background, aren't they? Over I go and take one. No. No use at all. Beyond suggesting that St Rocco was himself miraculously healed, and that the cure owed a lot to a dog, the prayer on the back gives no clue. Tantalizing. I must remember to get myself a book of saints.

Father Pierino is very pleased to meet us, and knows various de Giglios well. Especially Aunt Elisabetta, who was a regular here until she became ill: he is sorry not to be able to say the same about her husband Fantino, the well-known atheist!

Just come through into the vestry now, he says, we'll be more comfortable there . . . He has had a look through the registers for us, he says—we're welcome to look at them ourselves, too, if we like, there they are over there on the table—but they're very hard to read, especially the older ones, what with the style of handwriting and the dialect. He's afraid, in any case, that they don't have a lot to tell us. The first de Giglio recorded there, he says—but Marisa stops him there, in mid-flow. With two 'g's? she says. Is that right?

Yes, says Father Pierino, looking a bit puzzled.

Alberto, over at the table, poring over one of the three leather-bound tomes lying there, gives a small cheer.

There! says Marisa. That was already worth coming all this way for! The end of idiotic conversations around the family dinner table about the spelling of the name!

So, as Father Pierino was saying, the first de

393

Giglio recorded, in 1783, a boy, christened Antonio, has no entry at all where the name of the father should be. It's marked with a sheet of paper, look, in the left-hand volume, he says to Alberto, who obediently turns to the page in question.

So he was illegitimate, then?

Exactly, says Father Pierino, and looks around the room. He hopes nobody is embarrassed by that, are they?

No, we're all perfectly fine.

Good. He has to ask, because some people find this sort of information deeply shocking and hurtful.

He takes another long look at us, but we still haven't fainted from the shock.

It's all right, says Marisa, we were already told that he might have been illegitimate, and the name just made up—but did priests really allow people to do that, instead of just using the mother's maiden name? Why would they?

Well, he says, that is the good news, you see. The giving of the name in itself, by the parish priest at the time, more or less rules out any guilt on the part of the mother . . . Down here in the feudal South, names like your own were often made up by the local parish priest, and bestowed on the illegitimate offspring of the local aristocracy as what you might call a form of protest.

An obviously made-up flower-name for her illegitimate child, preceded by the 'de' of the nobility, would show the world that—in the eyes of her own local church, at least, even if not of the Establishment—no shame or blame attached to the mother. Even more usefully, it seems, this broad hint from the priest would occasionally embarrass

394

the culprit into making some material provision for his illegitimate offspring.

A priest in those days, says Father Pierino, would have come across plenty of young women, employed in the landowners' establishments as domestics or farmhands, who found themselves with child, having certainly had no choice in the matter. The landowning classes had many weapons with which to make a young woman of the lower orders submit. Her whole family might acquiesce, even, for fear of getting no land at all when the next year's hiring came around: tantamount to being driven away destitute. He is proud, says Father Pierino, of his forerunners who found the courage to stand up to the aristocracy in this way. No doubt they had to give up any hope of furthering their career in the church, once they had crossed that line. It is good to know, he adds, that some of us have always been men of principle.

Well, there we are, that's that solved! I say to Marisa.

Solved? Of course it isn't! says she, going over to be shown the de Giglio entry. We can just have endless debates about who the aristocrat might have been, instead! Nothing's changed at all!

While she's busy over the tome, I naturally ask for some information about St Rocco. Father Pierino will get a booklet sent down to Fantino's for us, with the whole story in it, he says. But Rocco nursed many people back to health in the times of the Plague; became infected himself and took refuge far from human habitation while he waited to die. Until the dog in the statue found him, and miraculously saved him by licking his plague sores and bringing him bread.

And what is he the patron saint of, then?

St Rocco? Spies. He is the patron saint of spies.

51

I can't believe it! says Francesca. It looks just the way it used to! Not a ghost any more—a proper orange grove again!

We have all been battling away all day at the old man's beard, trying to get it cleared before we leave. We only have tomorrow left, now, and we'll be spending that up at Santa Cristina with Zio Fantino and the Finanza, trying to get at least a glimpse of the Lost Inheritance before we have to leave for the long trek North. The clearing wasn't as much of a nightmare as it first looked, at any rate, because old man's beard turns out not to cling or twine the way a lot of parasitic plants do; it just drapes itself lovingly over its host. We were ready to announce the joyful liberation of the forty-eighth orange tree when Francesca turned up with Anselmo and this friend of his, an architect, to see how it was going. Francesca's looking all cheerful and positive again, seems to have dropped the doom-laden I'm-never-coming-here-again stuff.

We won't bother with any major works till we've thought out what the long-term plan is, Ciccio tells Anselmo and friend. We'll come back down in the spring, once the olive harvest is over and done back home in Liguria, for the Easter holidays, probably, and bring a bunch of friends and relations; we can all stay here, in the usable rooms, and the quicker the guests get the other rooms sorted out, the quicker they'll get a private bedroom! Good plan, eh?

But the architect does not think it's a good plan at all. Nor does Anselmo. It's never a good plan to do things piecemeal. We should draw up a proper project, get it put through the *Comune* and approved, have the whole job done in one clean sweep. According to Anselmo, it will end up costing us more in the long run if we don't do it that way. We should decide how much we want to spend on it, what we want done, and he will organize it all for us. In a situation like this, you need local people who know their way about, local labour, local suppliers. Or you end up in a mess.

Well, I know I'm sometimes a bit slow-witted, but isn't that the exact same phrase that figured in Ciccio's tale of his short-lived attempt to start a restaurant down here? The tale that proved, according to Pino, that the Mafia and the EEC are one and the same. I wonder which Anselmo supports? Or would it be both?

But Anselmo, I say, how could it be cheaper than nothing, however local it was? We're not paying our friends. They'll just muck in with us, do a bit of mending and painting and filling, in exchange for their board and lodging.

But I'd forgotten that Anselmo doesn't care about logic when it doesn't suit him. He just repeats the same thing all over again. Francesca looks impressed; and Francesca is the official heiress. Handily, just as Anselmo's got to the bit about local suppliers, Rocco turns up with Aldo.

Look! I tell Anselmo. There you are! We've already got a local supplier! How much more local could you get than Rocco?

397

And Rocco, it seems, has no problem with us doing the work ourselves. He even offers to join in himself. As long as the hospitality's up to scratch, he adds. Right in front of Anselmo, too, who now looks utterly flummoxed, abandons the conversation, and goes off, taking Francesca and the architect with him.

I am utterly flummoxed myself, probably about the same matters as Anselmo, though from a rather different and more clueless angle. If Anselmo was offering to get us these famous local people and suppliers, surely Rocco has to be one of the suppliers he meant? Weren't we told he was the only builders' merchant about? And you couldn't really imagine he was mister squeaky-clean, could you, even if you decided to follow Francesca's example and discount the murmurings-in-the-village about his cornering the local market by getting his competitors' tyres shot at? There still seems to have been an unusually large number of violent deaths in his family. But then again, most of them were in the past . . . and look at the number of violent deaths there once used to be round here! Just take a walk with Zio Antonio.

So, back to the matter in hand. Am I supposed to believe that Anselmo was trying to hint-and-blackmail us into using a yard we were going to use anyway? It doesn't make sense. That would make Anselmo keener to look out for Rocco's interests than Rocco himself, wouldn't it, if Rocco was offering to help us for nothing? No: I suppose doing a bit of painting and decorating isn't really anything to do with Rocco's professional life. He does seem to be very keen on Marisa, too: perhaps love has reformed his character out of all

398

recognition? Just look at the way they're gleaming at one another now!

But then, if nobody was going around telling me that there was something fishy about it, I wouldn't turn a hair over the fact that Anselmo, who works for the local *Comune*, was keen to get work for locals, would I?

Oh, I give up. As usual. Whenever I decide to concentrate hard on making some sense of the corruption-and-*malavita* theme that crops up so annoyingly often here, I suffer terminal brain-collapse in no time. You'd need a degree in business studies before you could make head or tail of what anyone was up to. If, indeed, they are up to anything at all apart from a little light corruption. Thank goodness we're going home soon. This would be a perfect place for holidays, if we manage to get the house sorted out without anybody getting kneecapped or shot at, but you'd need the mind of a Machiavelli, or should I say a Borgia, to be up to actually participating in local life.

I have a little shout to myself about Anselmo and his half-built houses and his vagabond *vigili*, now he's gone, just to relieve my feelings a bit.

Rocco surprises me by taking me up on it. Not all the half-built houses you see around here are just scams, he says, not at all. You Northerners always see the negative side. Look at them as proof that people don't give up hope down here, no matter how many times we get knocked back. You're right, he says, that most of the sites inside the town are investments; but not all of them. And the ones you see standing alone in the countryside, around here at any rate, are mostly family projects that have run out of money—or out of time. There are the houses started by parents who want to believe that their émigré children will return, settle down, be needing a place to bring up their kids— then maybe they run out of money, or wait for the young ones to return to finish the place off themselves. And it never happens. Or the ones started by people who were hoping to come back, to retire to the old home *paese*, but ran out of money. Or lost their partner: or got too decrepit to move again. Or died before they made it. They are proof of the Calabrian *testa dura*. Optimism in the teeth of despair.

52

To Ciccio's horror, the piles of packages, bags and bottles are growing ever larger in the hallway and the back scullery. Annunziata's revenge has been added to Zio Antonio's: and we are going to have to pack it all, somehow, into the car tonight, for the return trip tomorrow. We are to go up to Santa Cristina to meet Zio Fantino and the Finanza this morning—and Francesca has surprised us by deciding to face up to Salvatore's home town at last. She is coming too. Marisa has surprised us even more by announcing that she will be travelling separately, with Rocco. Alberto has not surprised us at all by asking if he and Antonello can follow on behind on their Vespas. In the meantime, though, we need some breakfast. And it is unbearable in all three of the kitchens here. Francesca, Carmela and Annunziata are milling in and out with armsful of stuff, sorting out the goodies to be taken back to Liguria, the gifts for each of the daughters who couldn't make it. Featuring plenty of stuffed figs. Now Vincenza arrives to help them.

We'll go to the bar for breakfast, we decide: we'll get some peace and quiet along with our coffee and brioches there.

*   *   *

Did you not hear that story, then? asks Gianni Versace, who always takes his morning coffee here. That was a good one! Quite a few people saw Vincenza walking purposefully through the town at dusk, carrying a stepladder over her shoulder. Next thing, it seems, she'd climbed up on to the balcony at Lina's place . . . Lina got a terrible fright, seeing a strange figure standing out there, and not knowing about the ladder, you couldn't see it from inside, she had no idea how a person could have got there at all unless they'd come right up through the house, which made it all the more terrifying . . . Lina stood peeping through the slats of the shutters trying to get a look at them, couldn't see who it was, but there was enough moonlight on the scene for her to work out that it was a woman—so she opened the shutter and there was Vincenza looking like some kind of ghost, all wrapped up in a huge black curtain, draped around her like some kind of shawl! Seemed to be just standing there staring at the moon. Imagine Lina's amazement. And the ladder there, too. So she asked her what on earth she was doing on her balcony, and Vincenza just acted as if it was completely normal to be standing about on other people's balconies in the middle of

401

the night, stood there chatting away about how her husband was about to buy the place back for her— it used to be Vincenza's grandfather's, she and her mother lived there for a while, but it was sold up a good twenty years ago—and she'd come round to think over a few ideas about colour schemes and curtains and how she'd like the kitchen re-done . . . ! Asking Lina what she thought about whether pale green was better than pink for bedroom curtains, which was more soothing or seductive or something, and was it better to go for a pattern because it would show the dirt less!

It may sound terrible, but I can't help giggling inwardly to myself. I can just imagine the scene, Vincenza's cool ironic look, not turning a hair as she chatted away about curtain materials in her best homes-and-gardens housewifely manner to a woman who was about to faint from shock.

Where is it, then, this house? The grandfather's, I mean Lina's? I ask.

No surprise there. Of course, it's the one on the piazza with the lovely pale green-painted wrought-iron balcony—the one where, according to Vincenza, an unknown woman lives a hermit's life, her food sent up in baskets, never to be seen by the light of day.

What will become of Vincenza when Annunziata and Carmela are gone? It must be a worry to the family, says Aldo. She acts so independent, but it's hard to imagine she would really look after herself properly without them to look after her, isn't it?

Well, says Gianni, there's always the other side of the family.

Other side of the family? says Marisa. Ciccio and I look at him, mystified.

Annunziata's brother's family. They're a lot younger than Carmela, and there's their son, too. Maurizio. He'd be your cousin . . .

Annunziata's brother? We have never heard of Annunziata having a brother, never mind there being any other cousins. He's never been mentioned to any of us, we say. Only a sister in Rome.

Aldo gives Gianni Versace a look. Well, says Gianni defensively, they couldn't have stayed here much longer without finding out, anyway. No point in keeping secrets from you, he adds. You would have heard soon enough . . .

Heard what, though?

Annunziata's brother only got out of prison last year—did thirty years in Regina Cieli jail. He's paid the price now, hasn't he, and there's no point in his family going on shunning him, not as far as Gianni can see. Water under the bridge, what's done is done.

But what did he do? asks Marisa. What was he in for?

Killed his father, didn't he? says Gianni. His and Annunziata's father. With a shotgun, at point-blank range. Nobody knows why. He just picked up a shotgun when they were out working the olive groves one afternoon, and shot his father in the face. Stone dead. He went on the run, then. But it was no life on the run, not with his family against him and nobody prepared to help him out . . . so he gave himself up after a year or two. And that was that. Thirty years. Annunziata and her mother never mentioned his name again, never spoke about him at all, all that time. Wouldn't acknowledge his wife and his son, either . . .

The three of us sit there trying to digest this startling piece of news, under the interested gaze of its bearers. A murderer in the family! Related to a killer, even if only by marriage: as well as to a madwoman! No wonder Francesca doesn't talk too much about Calabria. This place gets odder and odder. How many things can people manage to not mention, even though they all know about them? We decide, upon reflection, to follow their example, and not mention it to Francesca. If it's stayed in the closet all this time, we may as well let her think she's got away with it. I'm impressed by the name of the prison, anyway. *Regina Cieli*: Queen of Heaven. Even the jails here are called after the Virgin Mary.

53

Leaning on a very disreputable-looking *Ape* parked outside the appointed bar in Santa Cristina, its truckbed full of old sacking and twigs, an equally disreputable-looking wall-eyed dog sitting in a corner of it, we find Rosario and Carmelo, the Finanza. From across the road we get a strong hint of the glassy-eyed about them as they stand chatting to Fantino: have they been at the Amaro del Capo already? Close up, they are positively fearsome, armed to the teeth. Rosario is testing one of a pair of machetes lying in the *Ape* with a black, calloused thumb; while Carmelo is waving a large rusty sickle for emphasis as he talks, its gleaming silver blade-edge razor-sharp, belying its decrepit looks.

Fantino has just picked up the other machete when he spots us crossing the road towards them. Francescella!! he cries, dropping the weapon back on to the truckbed with a clang, and opening his arms wide. She looks startled, freezes for a second—I'm not surprised, Fantino looks so much like Salvatore—and now she's in his arms, squeezing tight, holding back the tears. Tears of what, though? Everything, I should think—good memories, bad memories, chances lost, certainties found, things that might have been . . .

Alberto and Antonello are enjoying the prospect of this tour in the mountains a lot more now they've seen the state of our guides. Who knows where we'll end up! This is going to be a real mystery tour! They start winding up the long-suffering Uncle Ciccio. Are these doddering ancients the only people who still bother to remember where this precious place is, then? Is he sure he really wants to find it?

The Finanza, meanwhile, stand looking dubiously at Francesca, now arm in arm with Fantino. Is the *signora* coming along too? There's a long bit on foot, you know, they say. Could be a couple of kilometres . . . ?

Signora? What *signora* is that? says Francesca. Don't you know me, then?

Through the fog of Amaro the realization slowly dawns.

No! It can't be!—Francescella? says Rosario.

Francescella! says Carmelo.

She has repented! says Rosario. This woman who stole the pride of the de Gilios, their oldest son!

Inveigled him into abandoning home and family,

says Rosario, keeping up the double act. And here she is at last, the shameless one! You and Salvatore have finally admitted, then, that there's no place like Santa Cristina?

Yes, of course, Carmelo! says Francesca. That's why you see Salvatore standing here by my side! As soon as we've found this bit of old pastureland we're looking for, he'll be straight back up the mountain to his old trade. He can't wait!

*   *   *

Seriously, though, Fantino wants to know, how bad is the road really, up there? Are we going to ruin our suspensions?

But the Finanza aren't sure. They haven't been near the place for years. There was a road bulldozed through, not long before the place ended up abandoned for good. It was never asphalted . . . who knows if it's still passable? It depends whether the hunters have been using it. Nobody else has, that's for sure. Could have ten-foot trees grownup in the middle of it, for all they know. That's why they've come tooled up for the occasion. We might be able to clear it easily—but then we might end up doing the whole lot on foot, says Rosario.

Still, says Carmelo, Francescella can just wait in the car, wherever we have to give up. And the other ladies, he adds politely.

Don't you worry about me, Carmelo! says Francesca, laughing. Just look at the state of you two! Who are you to be talking?

Now don't go crossing Francescella, says Fantino affectionately, you know what a temper the girl has once you get her going.

406

Antonello has got bored and started the circling-and-revving that Vespa-riding Italian youth engage in to get rid of their excess nervous energy, where the youth of other less favoured nations would just be sitting quietly chewing gum or biting their nails. Alberto lets out an experimental roar, flicks his handlebar clutch into gear, making to follow suit.

Now then, enough of that, stop where you are, boys, says Rosario, fingering his machete.

We don't appreciate it at all, says Carmelo. Not in Santa Cristina.

Alberto's eyes widen as he recalls the salutary tale of the orange Vespa: and he scoots quietly off, not a roar to be heard, to get alongside Antonello. Peace falls. The mating cry of the internal combustion engine is stilled to a mere hum.

Our cavalcade sets off up a lot of heavily forested hairpin bends; now along a track that rises above the treeline, and turns for a short way into living rock with a sheer drop to one side of it. The rocks and shrubbery get too much for the car: then too much for the *Ape*. Eventually only the Vespa boys are still motorized. The rest of us trudge on foot, first through half-abandoned olive land, then across overgrown ditching and into marshy land where wild cane sprouts head-high—the Vespas fall by the wayside too, now—and into trees again: wild scrubby woodland this time. We round the brow of a hill and find a deep narrow river-bed barring our way, almost a ravine, half-choked with fallen tree trunks and rocks, its banks steep and muddy. You used to be able to cross over here, once upon a time, say our guides, looking a bit dubious. Maybe we should try a bit higher up?

But where is Francesca? And Fantino? They

have vanished off into the woodland. Yes. Of course. They've detected food there. Hazelnuts, they shout to us, as if we had nothing more important to be getting on with.

There should be a path this side of the river, heading uphill, say the Finanza, starting to look a bit less sure of themselves.

There's no sign of one, though. It doesn't look as if anybody's cleared the land round here for decades. Or put any animals to graze on it, rather—I suppose that's how it was kept clear once upon a time. We cast about uphill a bit, but the terrain's just getting worse. Carmelo fights through brambles and thorns to get to where he thinks the crossing once was. Impassable.

Nature has taken her own back with a vengeance. From this side of the mini-ravine, it looks as though the walnut trees have run wild. With nobody to carry away the nuts, a couple of decades of them have taken root and sprouted into what is now an impassable walnut forest. Thick undergrowth fills the gaps between the slender trunks of this new generation of trees; the liana-like vines of the ubiquitous old man's beard run wild from above, wrist-thick after being left to their own devices all this time; they trail down, tangling with some kind of viciously thorny creeper with heart-shaped leaves, to meet and meld with the undergrowth.

But Carmelo and Rosario are convinced there'll be a gap in there somewhere. In the centre, they say, there were flat rocks lying right close to the surface, just a thin layer of grassy turf over them— no tree could have taken root there, for certain.

The home team—the Finanza and Rocco,

followed by the bikeless Vespa Kids—go on casting around for a way in uphill.

*   *   *

Look at that, says Marisa. It's done Alberto a world of good being down here. She has, on more than one occasion in this last couple of weeks, seen her son engaged in an activity that does not involve either TV screens or computer games. And he hasn't made a fuss at all about riding around on an old Vespa. Imagine that! Back home he wouldn't be seen dead on such unmodish transport.

Activities? says Ciccio. What, shelling beans? Playing table football?

Well, look at him now, scrambling through a wilderness with Antonello, full of enthusiasm! Her brother may laugh, says Marisa, but even shelling beans and playing table football make a difference. Has he noticed that Alberto has even been coming out with bits of Calabrian dialect? He's learning something, voluntarily, at last. She thinks she should go for it: move down here, to a place where young people have other interests in life than being first with the new mobile phone ring-tone. She and Rocco have been talking in depth about all this: and she might really do it. She wants to get the house in the grove sorted as quickly as possible, just in case.

Fantino and Francesca the nut-gatherers scramble round the brow of the hill to join us now, breathless and pink-cheeked, their pockets bulging.

And Rocco says, Marisa adds nervously, treading on delicate ground here . . . Rocco says that if we put the thing in his hands, he could get it all done

409

in no time. She could get herself down here with Alberto before the spring school term starts, if she wanted.

What? says Francesca, wrinkling up her eyes and compressing her lips into the well-known puzzled expression.

We might as well, mightn't we? Marisa goes on, ignoring her mother. We'd get it done quicker, and not look like we were stealing bread out of the mouths of locals . . . because, Marisa adds, gaining conviction as she speaks, do we really want to get a *figura* of cheapskate scrimpers who'd rather save a few *lire* by doing it themselves than pay a decent wage to a few Melipodio boys to do the work properly? What are we, a bunch of Ligurian penny-pinchers?

Francesca is looking most perturbed. She's just decided that her plan to set up her only son down here was a foolish mistake, a snare and a delusion. Is she going to end up sacrificing a daughter to the Old Country in his place?

I, on the other hand, am wondering about two-pronged attacks. And about the newly suspicious mind I've developed since I've been down here. Does it really just take a few dubious scraps of gossip, a bit of murmuring-in-the-village, to make me doubt the good faith of Rocco, when all my instincts tell me he's a good bloke? Why suspect him of being in cahoots with Anselmo, when the pair of them seem to hate the sight of one another? What difference does it make anyhow? No time to worry about that now, though. Shouts from up ahead. Have the boys found a way through?

Yes! More shouting, an outbreak of machete-wielding, and they're through.

We head up towards them, thorns ripping at our clothing—all of us except Fantino, that is, who has lost sight of the aims and objectives of this expedition again.

Porcini! he shouts out excitedly, and heads off downhill towards a small clump of trees. Francesca, hearing this clarion call, takes off after him: all fears for the future of her brood, or joys at the final reclaiming of the lost inheritance, forgotten in the food-collecting frenzy.

And here we are at last. A clearing in the middle of a wild wood of walnut trees: fine turf beneath our feet, stony outcrops poking through it here and there. Are they lost fragments of antiquity, or just part of the mountain's rocky backbone? No way of telling just now. Carmelo and Rosario are casting about for the freshwater well that was up here somewhere. No, it must be over there, where the new saplings are growing thick. Alberto and Antonello, who have somehow gained control of the machetes, start slashing away haphazardly, to the consternation of the Finanza. Not like that! they say.

There! You see! says Marisa, as her son takes with a will to his first lesson in the art of machete-wielding. He's a different boy down here!

Ahead of us the land falls away, an ocean of treetops rolling on as far as the eye can see. To our left, the Straits of Messina and the pale coastline of Sicily beyond, blurry in the heat. To our right, the Aeolian Islands, tiny specks in a violet sea.

Yes! says Ciccio. This is it! Just how he imagined it would be! Well, even if nobody else wants to camp up here, this is the place for him! Bring on the tents!

411

Alberto and Antonello are now improvising a victorious machete-swinging *tarantella* with Carmelo and Rosario. Rocco has taken Marisa's arm. Francesca and Fantino come into sight, battling their way through the prickles. Ah! says Francesca. She was away back in her youth for a moment there, the autumn mushroom-hunts up here with Salvatore! How she loved that: the high woodland in autumn, the excitement of the chase! Then back home with the booty, slicing the *porcini* as fine as you could, laying them out to dry on the racks, stringing up the *gambe secche* with needle-and-thread to hang from the beams, the rest to be pickled and potted, under olive oil or under vinegar. Salvatore was a good hunting companion.

In fact, she can't wait to get back home. We should finish the packing as soon as we get back. Did we manage to get all that stuff into the bags this morning? She thinks there is another half-a-sack of beans from Giuseppa down by the scullery door . . . did we notice that? Poor Salvatore! He must be dying to eat a decent meal, cooked in his own kitchen. Who knows what his daughters will have been feeding him on, with their strange new-fangled notions. Raw stuffed peppers, no doubt. And how he will enjoy the figs-and-walnuts of his youth! The fresh *pappaluni*! The black wine of Calabria, the flavour of the olive oil of home! The real *'nduia* that he hasn't tasted for years! And there's a whole carrier of fresh chilli peppers somewhere—did anyone remember to pack them?

We should leave at dawn tomorrow. No, before dawn. This time, there must be no mistakes. We have to make the journey back in time to cook dinner.

412

And, says Francesca, she hopes this stay has taught us something. Take no notice of maps: ignore signposts. This time, whatever else we do, we must not take the Castellace road!